Congressional Quarterly's
AMERICAN
CONGRESSIONAL
DICTIONARY

Congressional Quarterly's

AMERICAN CONGRESSIONAL DICTIONARY

Walter Kravitz

Congressional Quarterly Inc.
Washington, D.C.

Book design: Kaelin Chappell
Cover design: Carol Crosby Black

Library of Congress Cataloging-in-Publication Data

Kravitz, Walter.
    Congressional Quarterly's American congressional dictio-
nary / Walter Kravitz
        p.   cm.
    ISBN 0-87187-861-5 — ISBN 0-87187-864-X (pbk.)
    1. United States.   Congress—Dictionaries.   2. Legisla-
tion—United States—Dictionaries.   3. United States—Politics and government—Dictionaries.   I. Title.   II. Title:
American congressional dictionary.
JK9.K73   1993
328.73'003—dc20   93-13258
                                                   CIP

Preface

The *American Congressional Dictionary* provides a quick reference source of definitions and relatively brief explanations of many terms and expressions in current use in the U.S. Congress. Most of the entries focus on the legislative process and particularly on congressional procedures, but a few deal with other subjects, such as organization, staff, and officers of Congress.

Two types of cross-references appear under most of the entries. *See* refers to terms directly or indirectly mentioned in the entry. *See also* refers to related terms or terms that provide supplementary information about the entry.

Wherever appropriate, the explanations point out differences in procedure, practice, and terminology between the House of Representatives and the Senate and, when such information is available, between the political parties in each house.

I am greatly indebted to Fred Pauls and Judy Schneider who provided me with many useful materials from the files of the Congressional Research Service in the Library of Congress, to Larry Filson who enlightened me about terms that are applied to certain types of provisions in bills, and to Senate Parliamentarian Alan Frumin and

House Parliamentarian Bill Brown and their assistants for many clarifications on procedural matters. I also thank Stanley Bach and Paul Rundquist whose invaluable comments on the first draft saved me from errors of fact and grammar, Sherry and Norman Friedman who tried their best to make the text more intelligible, and finally, but not least, my wife, Adele Soffer Kravitz, who did the same and also read and reread and proofed and reproofed the entire text.

I would like to blame all of these people for any errors, ambiguities, and infelicities of language that remain, but convention rightly requires me to take full responsibility for them.

Walter Kravitz

A

AA (*See* Administrative Assistant.)

Absence of a Quorum Absence of the required number of members to conduct business in a house or a committee. When a quorum call or roll-call vote in a house establishes that a quorum is not present, no debate or other business is permitted except a motion to adjourn or motions to request or compel the attendance of absent members, if necessary by arresting them. When a committee lacks a quorum, it may adjourn or wait for a quorum to arrive. (*See* Adjourn, Arrest of Absent Members, Business, Quorum, Quorum Call, Roll Call. *See also* Counting a Quorum.)

Absolute Majority A vote requiring approval by a majority of all members of a house rather than a majority of members present and voting. (*See* Constitutional Votes. *See also* Super Majority, Voting.)

Act (1) A bill passed in identical form by both houses of Congress and signed into law by the president or enacted over his veto. A bill also becomes an act without the president's signature if he does not return it to Congress within ten days (Sundays excepted) and if Congress has not adjourned within that period. (*See* Adjournment Sine Die, Veto. *See also* Pocket Veto.)

(2) Also, the technical term for a bill passed by at least one house and engrossed. (*See* Engrossed Bill.)

Ad Hoc Select Committee A temporary committee formed for a special purpose or to deal with a specific subject. Conference committees are ad hoc joint committees. A House rule adopted in 1975 authorizes the Speaker to refer measures to special ad hoc committees, appointed by him, with the approval of the House. These committees are supposed to consider measures that overlap the jurisdictions of several standing committees. (*See* Bills

1

and Resolutions Referred, Committee Jurisdiction, Select *or* Special Committee.)

Additional Committee Meeting (*See* Special Committee Meeting.)

Additional Views (*See* Supplemental, Minority, and Additional Views.)

Adhere A motion by a house to reiterate its previous position during the process of amendments between the houses. The motion is permitted if both houses have insisted on their previous positions. Adherence, unlike insistence, represents an uncompromising position and may not be accompanied by a request for a conference; but a house may recede from its adherence and agree to a conference requested by the other. If both houses adhere to disagreement over amendments, the measure fails. (*See* Amendments Between the Houses, Concur, Conference, Disagree, Insist, Recede. *See also* Stage of Disagreement.)

Adjourn A formal motion to end a day's session or meeting of a house or a committee. A motion to adjourn usually has no conditions attached to it, but it may specify the day or time for reconvening or make reconvening subject to the call of the chamber's presiding officer or the committee's chairman. In both houses, a motion to adjourn is of the highest privilege, takes precedence over all other motions, is not debatable, and must be put to an immediate decision. Adjournment of a house ends its legislative day.

Despite its high privilege, the House does not permit a motion to adjourn after it has agreed to go into Committee of the Whole, is in Committee of the Whole, or when the previous question has been ordered on a measure to final passage without an intervening motion. (*See* Committee of the Whole, Legislative Day, Precedence of Motions (House), Precedence of Motions (Senate), Previous Question, Privilege. *See also* Rule.)

Adjourn for More Than Three Days Under Article I, Section 5 of the Constitution, neither house may adjourn for more than three days without the approval of the other. The necessary approval is given in a concurrent resolution and agreed to by both houses, which may permit one or both to take such an adjournment. (*See* Adjourn, Concurrent Resolution. *See also* Adjournment Prohibited, August Adjournment, Conditional Adjournment, Precedence of Motions (House), Precedence of Motions (Senate), Pro Forma Session.)

Adjournment by July 31 The Legislative Reorganization Act of 1946 requires Congress to adjourn sine die no later than July 31 of each year unless Congress provides otherwise. Except in 1952 and 1956, Congress has provided otherwise. (*See* Adjourn, Adjournment Sine Die. *See also* August Adjournment.)

Adjournment Prohibited The Congressional Budget Act of 1974 prohibits the House of Representatives from adjourning for more than three calendar days during the month of July unless it has completed action on reconciliation legislation if a budget resolution requires the reporting of such legislation for an upcoming fiscal year. (*See* Adjourn, Adjourn for More Than Three Days, Budget Resolution, Fiscal Year, Reconciliation.)

Adjournment Sine Die Final adjournment of an annual or two-year session of Congress; literally, adjournment without a day. The two houses must agree to a privileged concurrent resolution for such an adjournment. A sine die adjournment precludes Congress from meeting again until the next constitutionally fixed date of a session (January 3 of the following year) unless Congress determines otherwise by law or the president calls it into special session.

Article II, Section 3 of the Constitution authorizes the president to adjourn both houses until such time as he thinks proper when the two houses cannot agree to a time of adjournment, but no president has ever exercised this authority. (*See* Adjourn, Concurrent Resolution, Privilege, Session, Special Session. *See also* Adjournment by July 31, Conditional Adjournment.)

Adjournment to a Day (and Time) Certain An adjournment that fixes the next date and time of meeting for one or both houses. It does not end an annual session of Congress. In the House, the motion is of equal privilege with the motion to adjourn if the Speaker, at his discretion, recognizes a member to propose it. (*See* Adjourn. *See also* Conditional Adjournment, Precedence of Motions (House), Precedence of Motions (Senate), Privilege.)

Administration Bill A bill drafted in the executive office of the president or in an executive department or agency to implement part of the president's program. An administration bill is introduced in Congress by a member who supports it or as a courtesy to the administration. (*See* By Request.)

Administrative Assistant (AA) The title usually given to a member's chief aide, political advisor, and head of office staff. The administrative assistant often represents the member at meetings with visitors or officials when the member is unable (or unwilling) to attend.

Adoption The usual parliamentary term for approval of a conference report. It is also commonly applied to amendments. (*See* Amendment, Conference Report. *See also* Approval Terminology.)

Advance Appropriation In an appropriation act for a particular fiscal year, an appropriation that does not become available for spending or obligation until a subsequent fiscal year. The amount of the advance appropriation is counted as part of the budget for the fiscal year in which it becomes available for obligation. (*See* Appropriation, Budget, Fiscal Year, Obligation. *See also* Forward Funding.)

Adverse Report A committee report recommending against approval of a measure or some other matter. Committees usually pigeonhole measures they oppose instead of reporting them adversely, but they may be required to report them by a statutory rule or an instruction from their parent body.

The Senate places adversely reported measures on its calendars. In the House, they are automatically laid on the table, but they may be referred to a calendar by unanimous consent at the request of the reporting committee, or at any member's request made within three days of the date of the report. (*See* Calendar, Committee Report on a Measure, Instructions, Lay on the Table, Pigeonhole, Statutory Rules, Unanimous Consent.)

Advice and Consent The Senate's constitutional role in consenting to or rejecting the president's nominations to executive branch and judicial offices and the treaties he submits. Confirmation of nominees requires a simple majority vote of the full Senate. Treaties must be approved by a two-thirds majority of senators present and voting. (*See* Nomination, Treaty. *See also* Courtesy of the Senate, *Executive Calendar.*)

Agency Generic term for a governmental organization, such as a department, bureau, office, commission, board, administration, advisory council, and so forth.

Agency Debt Federal debt incurred by an agency authorized to borrow money from the public or from other government funds or accounts. (*See* Borrowing Authority, Public Debt.)

Agreed to The usual parliamentary term for approval of motions, amendments, and simple and concurrent resolutions. It is also sometimes applied to approval of amendments of the other house. (*See* Approval Terminology, Concurrent Resolution, Resolution. *See also* Amendments Between the Houses, Concur.)

Aisle The center aisle of each chamber. When facing the presiding officer, Republicans usually sit to the right of the aisle, Democrats to the left. When a member speaks of "my side of the aisle" or "this side," he means his party. (*See* Chamber. *See also* Floor, Well.)

Allocation (*See* Budget Allocation.)

Allowances Amounts in the budget to cover possible additional expenses for statutory pay increases, contingencies, and other requirements. In congressional budget resolutions, allowances are a special functional classification. In the president's budget, they also include amounts for possible additional proposals and for contingencies related to relatively uncontrollable programs. (*See* Budget, Budget Resolution, Function *or* Functional Category, Uncontrollable Expenditures. *See also* Members' Allowances.)

Amendment A formal proposal to alter the text of a bill, resolution, amendment, motion, treaty, or some other text. Technically, it is a motion. An amendment may strike out (eliminate) part of a text, insert new text, or strike out and insert—that is, replace all or part of the text with new text. Under some circumstances, an amendment to strike out and insert is called a substitute amendment or an amendment in the nature of a substitute.

Amendments are voted on in the same manner as a bill or other motions. When an amendment contains two or more substantive provisions, each may be voted on separately, except in the case of an amendment to strike out and insert. Conference reports and certain motions are not amendable. The texts of amendments considered on the floor are printed in full in the *Congressional Record*. (*See* Amendment in the Nature of a Substitute, Conference Report, *Congressional Record,* Division of a Question for Voting, Floor, Strike Out, Strike Out and Insert, Substitute. *See also* Bigger Bite Amendment, Committee Amendment, Degrees of Amendment, En Bloc, En Gros, Five-Minute Rule, Floor Amendment, Germane, Markup, Numbered Amendments, Page and Line Identification, Perfecting Amendment, Previously Noticed Amendment, Printed Amendment, Pro Forma Amendment, Reading for Amendment, Reading of Amendments, Rider, Voting Order on Amendments.)

Amendment in the Nature of a Substitute Usually, an amendment to replace the entire text of a measure. It strikes out everything after the enacting clause and inserts a version that may be somewhat, substantially, or entirely different. When a committee adopts extensive amendments to a measure, it often incorporates them into such an amendment. Occasionally, the term is applied to an amendment that replaces a major portion of a measure's text.

Ordinarily, an amendment in the nature of a substitute is a first degree amendment and therefore amendable only to one further degree. The Senate, however, permits two degrees of amendment to an amendment in the nature of a substitute reported by a committee or if the substitute is offered by a senator when no other amendment is pending to the measure.

In the House, an amendment in the nature of a substitute is treated as a first degree amendment even when reported by a committee, but the Rules Committee frequently reports special rules requiring that it be "considered as an original bill for purposes of amendment," which makes it amendable in two degrees. Both houses usually permit perfecting amendments directly to the measure while an amendment in the nature of a substitute is pending, but in practice this is rarely possible in the House.

Conference committees often must resolve the differences between a measure passed by one house and an amendment in the nature of a substitute adopted by the other. Under the rules of both houses, the conferees may agree to one measure or the other, or they may devise a third version that is a germane modification of one or the other. (*See* Amendment, Committee Amendment, Conferees, Conference Committee, Degrees of Amendment, Enacting Clause, Germane, Perfecting Amendment, Rule, Strike Out and Insert. *See also* Bigger Bite Amendment, Reading for Amendment.)

Amendment Tree A diagram showing the number and types of amendments that the rules and practices of a house permit to be offered to a measure before any amendment is voted on. It shows the relationship of one amendment to another, and it may also indicate the degree of each amendment, whether it is a perfecting or substitute amendment, the order in which amendments may be offered, and the order in which they are put to a vote. The same type of diagram can be used to display an actual amendment situation. (*See* Degrees of Amendment, Perfecting Amendment, Substitute, Voting Order on Amendments.)

Amendments Between the Houses The basic method for reconciling House and Senate differences on a measure is passing it back and forth between them until both have agreed to identical language by means of amendments. The method is used routinely for relatively noncontroversial measures and sometimes for major legislation that must be passed quickly.

It begins when house B amends, passes, and returns a measure passed by house A. If house A agrees to house B's amendments, the houses have reached exact agreement and the measure is enrolled and sent to the president. If house A disagrees, it may return the measure with its rejections or with amendments to house B's amendments. House B may do the same with house A's amendments. Although in theory third degree amendments are not permitted, house A's amendments count as the first degree; it is therefore possible, for example, to have a Senate amendment to a House amendment to a Senate amendment to a House bill.

At any stage of this process a house may (1) insist on its most recent position, or (2) after insisting or disagreeing with the position of the other house, request a conference to resolve the remaining differences, or (3) refuse to take further action, holding the measure in limbo indefinitely or letting it die.

The houses usually send major and controversial measures to conference immediately after one house amends the other's version. (*See* Degrees of Amendment, Disagree, Enrolled Bill, Insist, Request a Conference. *See also* Adhere, Amendment in the Nature of a Substitute, Amendments in Disagreement, Concur, Conference, Recede, Stage of Disagreement.)

Amendments in Disagreement Amendments in dispute between the houses. A conference committee is required to deal only with these amendments, and its conference report may contain recommendations concerning only those amendments on which it has reached agreement. Amendments on which the conference committee is unable to agree are presented to the houses as still in disagreement. After a house agrees to the conference report, the majority manager offers motions to dispose of the amendments in disagreement, either one at a time or en bloc. Most often, the manager moves to insist on disagreement, to recede from disagreement and concur with the amendment, or to recede and concur with a further amendment.

Frequently, the conferees report an amendment in technical disagreement. This signifies that they have reached an agreement on an amendment that violates the rules of one or both houses concerning the permissible content of conference reports. Excluding the proposed amendment from the report protects it from such points of order. After a house agrees to the report, it may decide whether it wishes to accept the conferees' recommendations on each amendment in technical disagreement as they are called up. (*See* Amendments Between the Houses, Amendments in Technical Disagreement, Concur, Conference, Conference Report, Disagree, En Bloc, Insist, Managers, Point of Order, Recede. *See also* Scope of Differences.)

Amendments in Technical Disagreement Amendments agreed to in a conference but not included in a conference report. These amendments are excluded because they violate the rules of one or both houses concerning the permissible content of conference reports and would therefore open the report to points of order on the floor. After a house agrees to the partial report, it decides whether to accept the conferees' recommendations on each amendment in technical disagreement as they are called up.

These amendments frequently involve senate proposals for appropriations that are regarded as unauthorized under House rules or that change existing law in general appropriation bills. If House conferees submit a conference report containing such provisions without the prior permission of the House, a valid point of order kills the entire report. But if the House conferees bring such Senate amendments to the floor separately, "in technical disagreement," the conferees' proposals for disposing of them are not subject to points of order. (*See* Amendments Between the Houses, Conferees, Conference, Conference Report, General Appropriation Bill, Point of Order, Unauthorized

Appropriation. *See also* Authorization-Appropriation Process, Scope of Differences.)

Amendments Submitted A section of the Senate's proceedings in the *Congressional Record* that lists printed Senate amendments. (*See* Printed Amendment.)

Annual Authorization Legislation that authorizes appropriations for a single fiscal year and usually for a specific amount. Under the rules of the authorization-appropriation process, an annually authorized agency or program must be reauthorized each year if it is to receive appropriations for that year. Sometimes Congress fails to enact the reauthorization but nevertheless provides appropriations to continue the program, circumventing the rules by one means or another. (*See* Appropriation, Authorization, Authorization-Appropriation Process, Fiscal Year.)

Anthony Rule A Senate rule that permits consideration of measures on the legislative calendar during the morning hour, if no senator objects to them. The rule limits each senator to one speech of no more than five minutes on the measure and on any amendment to it.

Named after its author, Sen. Henry B. Anthony (R-R.I.), it is one of the few Senate rules that limit debate. The Senate first adopted it in 1870 and made it a standing rule in 1880, but is has been rarely used in recent decades. (*See* Call of the Calendar, Morning Hour.)

Appeal A member's formal challenge of a ruling or decision by the presiding officer. On appeal, a house or a committee may overturn the ruling by majority vote. The right of appeal ensures the body against arbitrary control by the chair. In the House, appeals are not permitted against certain decisions of the chair; for example, on recognition of a member or on his count of a quorum. In both houses, appeals are often killed by successful motions to table them.

The majority party in the House usually votes overwhelmingly to uphold a ruling, viewing an appeal as an attack on the Speaker or his surrogates and, through them, on its control over the proceedings. Consequently, appeals are rarely made in the House and are even more rarely successful. Rulings are more frequently appealed in the Senate and occasionally overturned, in part because its presiding officer is not the majority party's leader, as in the House. (*See* Counting a Quorum, Lay on the Table, Recognition. *See also* President of the Senate, President Pro Tempore; Presiding Officer.)

Apportionment The action, after each decennial census, of allocating the number of members in the House of Representatives to each state. By law, the total number of House members (not counting delegates and a resident commissioner) is fixed at 435. The number allotted to each state is based approximately on its proportion of the nation's total population. Since the Constitution guarantees each state one representative no matter how small its population, exact proportional distribution is virtually impossible. The mathematical formula currently used to determine the apportionment is called the Method of Equal Proportions. (*See* Method of Equal Proportions.)

Appropriated Entitlement An entitlement program, such as food stamps or veterans' pensions, that is funded through annual appropriations rather than by a permanent appropriation. Because such an entitlement law requires the government to provide eligible recipients the benefits to which they are entitled, whatever the cost, Congress must appropriate the necessary funds. If the amount Congress provides in the annual appropriations act is not enough, it must make up the difference in a supplemental appropriation. (*See* Entitlement Program, General Appropriation Bill, Permanent Appropriation, Supplemental Appropriation Bill.)

In the House, the sergeant at arms may be instructed to compel or arrest absentees in two situations: (1) under the rule that provides for an automatic vote by the yeas and nays, and (2) under a rule that, in the absence of a quorum, authorizes fifteen members (including the Speaker, if there is one) to order such arrests by majority vote. (*See* Automatic Roll Call, Leave of Absence, Quorum, Sergeant at Arms, Yeas and Nays.)

Assignments The committees and subcommittees on which a member serves. (*See* Committee Assignments, Subcommittee Assignments. *See also* Committee on Committees.)

At-Large Elected by and representing an entire state instead of a district within a state. The term usually refers to a representative rather than to a senator. Through 1966, states that did not complete a required redistricting before the first general election after a reapportionment elected all their representatives at-large, but states gaining seats in the reapportionment sometimes elected only their new representatives at-large. In 1967, Congress enacted a law prohibiting at-large elections in states with more than one representative. (*See* Apportionment, Congressional District, Redistricting.)

August Adjournment A congressional adjournment during the month of August in odd-numbered years, required by the Legislative Reorganization Act of 1970. The law instructs the two houses to adjourn for a period of at least thirty days before the second day after Labor Day, unless Congress provides otherwise or if, on July 31, a state of war exists by congressional declaration. The adjournment requires a concurrent resolution agreed to in each house on a roll-call vote. (*See* Adjourn, Adjourn for More Than Three Days, Concurrent Resolution, Roll Call. *See also* Adjournment by July 31.)

Authorization (1) A statutory provision that establishes or continues a federal agency, activity, or program for a fixed or indefinite period of time. It may also establish policies and restrictions and deal with organizational and administrative matters.

(2) A statutory provision that authorizes appropriations for an agency, activity, or program. The appropriations may be authorized for one year, several years, or an indefinite period of time, and the authorization may be for a specific amount of money or an indefinite amount ("such sums as may be necessary"). Authorizations of specific amounts are construed as ceilings on the amounts that subsequently may be appropriated in an appropriation bill, but not as minimums; either house may appropriate lesser amounts or nothing at all. (*See* Multiyear Authorization, Permanent Authorization. *See also* Authorization-Appropriation Process, Backdoor Spending Authority.)

Authorization-Appropriation Process The two-stage procedural system that the rules of each house require for establishing and funding federal agencies and programs: first, enactment of authorizing legislation that creates or continues an agency or program; second, enactment of appropriations legislation that provides funds for the authorized agency or program.

The rules and precedents of the House establish four basic prohibitions: (1) no appropriation without an authorization in law, (2) no authorizing language in a general appropriation bill, (3) no appropriation in an authorizing measure, and (4) no appropriation larger than the amount, if any, specified in the authorization.

The Senate's rules differ from those of the House in several ways. They permit appropriations for authorizations the Senate has previously passed in the same session of Congress, not only for those enacted into law as the House requires. Furthermore, the

Senate permits appropriations for unauthorized purposes if proposed by its Appropriations Committee, by any committee with jurisdiction over that purpose, or by any senator if the appropriation appears in the president's budget estimates. The Senate also allows appropriations in authorizing measures. In all other respects, the Senate's prohibitions are the same as those in the House. And both houses agree that Congress may appropriate less than the authorized amount or no amount at all.

To protect itself from the Senate's more liberal interpretation of the process, the House prohibits its conference managers from agreeing to (1) Senate amendments that violate the House's interpretation of authorized appropriations, or (2) appropriations in measures other than general appropriation bills. Although the conferees may agree to such provisions with the prior permission of the House, they ordinarily circumvent the rule by reporting the provisions as amendments in technical disagreement.

The rules of this process are enforced only when members raise points of order against potential violations. Moreover, one or more of the prohibitions may be waived, and often are, by unanimous consent, suspension of the rules, or, in the House, by a special rule.

The historical rationale for the process has been to prevent the delay of appropriation bills caused by disputes over substantive policy. However, such disputes still arise because the houses often circumvent the rules of the process. (*See* Amendments in Technical Disagreement, Appropriation, Authorization, Budget Estimate Pursuant to Law, Conferees, General Appropriation Bill, Managers, Point of Order, Rule, Suspension of the Rules (House), Suspension of the Rules (Senate), Unanimous Consent. *See also* Non-Selfenforcing Rules.)

Automatic Roll Call Under a House rule, the automatic ordering of the yeas and nays when a quorum is not present on a voice or division vote and a member objects to the vote on that ground. It is not permitted in the Committee of the Whole.

A member invokes the procedure by declaring, "Mr. Speaker, I object to the vote on the ground that a quorum is not present, and I make a point of order that a quorum is not present." The yeas and nays are automatically ordered only if the Speaker determines that a quorum is indeed not present. Members frequently try for an automatic roll call when their request for a recorded vote is not supported by the required number of members. On certain matters, the Speaker may postpone the automatic roll call to a designated time on the same legislative day or within two legislative days. (*See* Committee of the Whole, Division Vote, Point of No Quorum, Point of Order, Quorum, Recorded Vote, Voice Vote, Yeas and Nays. *See* also Cluster Voting, Counting a Quorum.)

B

BA (*See* Budget Authority.)

Backdoor Spending Authority Authority to incur obligations that evades the normal congressional appropriations process because it is provided in legislation other than appropriation acts. The most common forms are borrowing authority, contract authority, and entitlement authority. From the perspective of the appropriations committees, funding by these forms of spending authority slips away from their control through legislative back doors. However, the Congressional Budget Act of 1974 gave those committees some control over new borrowing and contract authority. (*See* Authorization-Appropriation Process, Borrowing Authority, Congressional Budget and Impoundment Control Act of 1974, Contract Authority, Entitlement Program, Obligation. *See also* Permanent Appropriation, Spending Authority.)

Balanced Budget Loosely, a budget with a surplus rather than a deficit. In governmental accounting terms, a budget in which anticipated or actual total revenues equal anticipated or actual total expenditures. Conversely, an unbalanced budget is one in which expenditures exceed revenues, or vice versa.

The president's budget and the one Congress agrees to each year are anticipatory budgets, consisting of estimates and assumptions—some might call them guesses—about future economic conditions, demographic developments, and workload. Even using the most sophisticated and rigorously objective techniques, those estimates and assumptions are subject to error. A one percent mistake in the assumption about the number of unemployed in an upcoming fiscal year, for instance, may change expected revenues and expenditures by tens of billions of dollars. Moreover, the estimates and assumptions made by both the president and Congress are often influenced by political considerations and therefore subject to further error. Consequently, a nominally "balanced" budget on paper may turn out to be unbalanced when government auditors add up actual expenditures and revenue collections after a fiscal year has ended. (*See* Budget, Budget Resolution, Cost Estimates, Deficit, Expenditures, Fiscal Year, Surplus. *See also* Balanced Budget Amendment, Budget Receipts, Obligation, Offsetting Receipts, Outlays.)

Balanced Budget Amendment A proposal for a constitutional amendment mandating that federal expenditures not exceed federal revenues in any fiscal year.

Several versions have been offered. Most permit exceptions when both houses of Congress agree by votes larger than a simple majority; most also require the president to submit balanced budgets each year. (*See* Balanced Budget, Budget.)

Balanced Budget and Emergency Deficit Control Act of 1985 (*See* Gramm-Rudman-Hollings Act of 1985.)

Balanced Budget and Emergency Deficit Control Reaffirmation Act of 1987 A law that amended the Gramm-Rudman-Hollings Act of 1985 by extending the goal of a balanced budget until fiscal year 1993, revising the sequestration process, and requiring the director of the Office of Management and Budget to determine whether a sequester is necessary. (*See* Gramm-Rudman-Hollings Act of 1985, Sequestration. *See also* Budget and Accounting Act of 1921.)

Baseline A projection of the levels of federal spending, revenues, and the resulting budgetary surpluses or deficits for the upcoming and subsequent fiscal years, taking into account laws enacted to date and assuming no new policy decisions. It provides a benchmark for measuring the budgetary effects of proposed changes in federal revenues or spending, assuming certain economic conditions. Baseline projections are prepared by the Congressional Budget Office and used by the budget committees to develop the annual budget resolution and reconciliation instructions. (*See* Budget Resolution, Congressional Budget Office, Deficit, Fiscal Year, Reconciliation, Surplus. *See also* Budget Process, Current Services Estimates, Reestimates.)

Bicameral Consisting of two houses or chambers. Congress is a bicameral legislature whose two houses have an equal role in enacting legislation. In most other national bicameral legislatures, one house is significantly more powerful than the other. (*See* Equality of the Houses.)

Bigger Bite Amendment An amendment that substantively changes a portion of a text, which includes language that was previously amended. Normally, language previously amended may not be amended again. However, a part of a sentence that has been changed by amendment, for example, may be changed again by an amendment that amends a "bigger bite" of the text—that is, by an amendment that also substantively changes the unamended parts of the sentence or the entire section or title in which the previously amended language appears. Because a bigger bite amendment is permitted only if it also changes previously unamended text, the biggest possible bite is an amendment in the nature of a substitute that amends the entire text of a measure. Once adopted, therefore, such an amendment ends the amending process.

Bigger bite amendments are permitted on the theory that their changes of unamended language make it reasonable to change related amended language. For example, an amount of money that has been increased by an amendment may reasonably be reduced by an amendment that also narrows the purpose for which the money may be expended. (*See* Amendment, Amendment in the Nature of a Substitute, Section, Title. *See also* Budget Resolution.)

Bill The term for the chief vehicle Congress uses for enacting laws. Bills that originate in the House of Representatives are designated as H.R., those in the Senate as S., followed by a number assigned in the order in which they are introduced during a two-year Congress. A bill becomes a law if passed in identical language by both houses and signed by the president, or passed over his veto, or if the president fails to sign it within ten days after he has received it while Congress is in session. (*See also* Administration Bill, Bills and Resolutions Introduced, Clean Bill, Companion Bills, Enacting Clause, Engrossed Bill, Enrolled Bill,

Joint Resolution, Measure, Omnibus Bill, Original Bill, Private Bill, Public Bill.)

Bill of Attainder An act of a legislature finding a person guilty of treason or a felony. The Constitution prohibits the passage of such a bill by Congress or any state legislature.

Bill Time Time for debate usually controlled by the majority and minority floor managers of a measure under a Senate unanimous consent agreement. (*See* Debate, Floor Manager, Manager, Unanimous Consent Agreement.)

Bills and Resolutions Introduced Members formally present measures to their respective houses by delivering them to a clerk in the chamber when their house is in session. Both houses permit any number of members to join in introducing a bill or resolution. The first member listed on the measure is the sponsor; the other members listed are its cosponsors.

Many bills are first written in committee and then introduced by the chairman of the committee or one of its subcommittees and are often cosponsored by other committee members. (*See also* By Request, Clean Bill, Hopper, Original Bill, Report at Any Time.)

Bills and Resolutions Referred After a bill or resolution is introduced, it is normally sent to one or more committees that have jurisdiction over its subject, as defined by House and Senate rules and precedents. Officially, the Speaker refers measures in the House; the president of the Senate or president pro tempore refers measures in the Senate. In practice, those officers delegate the function to their parliamentarians, intervening only to deal with disputed referrals.

A Senate measure is usually referred to the committee with jurisdiction over the predominant subject of its text, but it may be sent to two or more committees by unanimous consent or on a motion offered jointly by the majority and minority leaders.

In the House, a rule requires the Speaker to refer a measure to the committees that have jurisdiction over any part of it "to the maximum extent feasible." The Speaker is also authorized to refer measures to special ad hoc committees that the Speaker has appointed, subject to approval by the House.

Measures are usually referred on the same day they are introduced. On the opening day of a session, however, the number of introduced measures is so large that many of them are not referred until several days later. (*See* Ad Hoc Select Committee, Committee Jurisdiction, Multiple and Sequential Referrals, Parliamentarian, Precedent, Rule.)

Bipartisan Committee A committee with an equal number of members from each political party. The House Committee on Standards of Official Conduct and the Senate Select Committee on Ethics are the only bipartisan permanent full committees. On April 9, 1992, however, the House agreed to a rule creating a bipartisan Subcommittee on Administrative Oversight under the Committee on House Administration. Its mandate is to provide oversight of the clerk, sergeant at arms, doorkeeper, director of non-legislative and financial services, and the inspector general. Under the rule, whenever a tie vote on any matter occurs in the subcommittee, members must notify the Speaker, the House majority and minority leaders, and the chairman and ranking minority members of the House Administration Committee. (*See* Clerk of the House, Director of Non-Legislative and Financial Services, Doorkeeper of the House, Full Committee, Majority Leader, Minority Leader, Ranking Minority Member, Sergeant at Arms, Tie Vote.)

Bipartisan Measure A measure introduced or supported by members of both political parties, sometimes by both party leaders. When those leaders, sometimes joined by the president, agree that an issue is of such importance that they are willing to set aside normal considerations of partisan advantage, majorities in both houses usually vote for such a measure.

Blue Slip Resolution A House resolution ordering the return of a Senate bill or amendment that allegedly violates the constitutional prerogative of the House to originate revenue legislation. The "blue slip" characterization is derived from the practice of printing all House messages, measures, and other documents sent to the Senate on blue paper. The resolution raises a question of the privileges of the House and the House therefore must immediately consider it. (*See* Message, Origination Clause, Questions of Privilege, Revenue Legislation. *See also* Engrossed Bill.)

Body A term members in both the House and Senate use when referring to the other house, as in "the other body," or when referring to their own house, as in "this body." The Senate is often called the "upper body," the House the "lower body," terms disliked by many senior representatives and rarely heard on the floor of either chamber. (*See also* Comity, Other Body.)

Borrowing Authority Statutory authority permitting a federal agency, such as the Export-Import Bank, to borrow money from the public or the Treasury to finance its operations. It is a form of backdoor spending. To bring such spending under the control of the congressional appropriation process, the Congressional Budget Act requires that new borrowing authority shall be effective only to the extent and in such amounts as are provided in appropriations acts. (*See* Backdoor Spending Authority, Congressional Budget and Impoundment Control Act of 1974. *See also* Federal Debt.)

Breach The amount above the limits set by the Budget Enforcement Act of 1990 on a discretionary category's spending and new budget authority for a fiscal year. The act requires that the breach be eliminated by sequestering budgetary resources in that category. (*See* Budget Enforcement Act of 1990, Budgetary Resources, Discretionary Appropriations, Sequestration. *See also* Firewall.)

Budget A detailed statement of actual or anticipated revenues and expenditures during an accounting period. For the national government, the period is the federal fiscal year (October 1-September 30). The budget usually refers to the president's budget submission to Congress early each calendar year. The president's budget estimates federal government income and spending for the upcoming fiscal year and contains detailed recommendations for appropriation, revenue, and other legislation. Congress is not required to accept or even vote directly on the president's proposals, and it often revises the president's budget extensively. (*See* Fiscal Year.)

Budget Act Common name for the Congressional Budget and Impoundment Control Act of 1974, which established the basic procedures of the current congressional budget process; created the House and Senate budget committees; and enacted procedures for reconciliation, deferrals, and rescissions. (*See* Budget Process, Deferral, Impoundment, Reconciliation, Rescission. *See also* Budget Enforcement Act of 1990, Gramm-Rudman-Hollings Act of 1985.)

Budget Allocation (1) In congressional budgeting usage, the portion of budget authority, outlays, and other resources from a budget resolution that is assigned to a committee that has jurisdiction over such resources.

The Congressional Budget Act of 1974 requires the distribution of allocations to all appropriate committees in each house, and it also directs each committee to subdivide its allocation among its programs or subcommittees. The allocations appear in the statement of the managers that accompanies the conference report on a budget resolution. (*See* Budget Authority, Budget Resolution, Conference Report, Congressional Budget and Impoundment Control Act of 1974, Explanatory Statement, Outlays. *See also* Budget Crosswalk, Subdivisions.)

(2) In executive branch budgeting parlance, the budget authority and other resources transferred from one agency's account to another agency to carry out the purposes of the parent account. (*See* Agency, Budget Authority.)

Budget Amendment A formal revision of the president's annual budget submitted to Congress before it has completed action on appropriations. (*See* Budget.)

Budget and Accounting Act of 1921 The law that, for the first time, authorized the president to submit to Congress an annual budget for the entire federal government. Prior to the act, most federal agencies sent their budget requests to the appropriate congressional committees without review by the president. The act also established a Bureau of the Budget (renamed the Office of Management and Budget [OMB] in 1970) to assist the president in preparing a budget and the General Accounting Office (GAO), headed by the comptroller general of the United States, to act as the principal auditing agency of the federal government. (*See* Budget, General Accounting Office.)

Budget Authority Generally, the amount of money that may be spent or obligated by a government agency or for a government program or activity. Technically, it is statutory authority to enter into obligations that normally result in outlays. The main forms of budget authority are appropriations, borrowing authority, and contract authority. It also includes authority to obligate and expend the proceeds of offsetting receipts and collections. Congress may make budget authority available for only one year, several years, or an indefinite period, and it may specify definite or indefinite amounts. (*See* Appropriation, Borrowing Authority, Contract Authority, Multiyear Appropriation, No-Year Appropriation, Obligation, Offsetting Receipts, One-Year Appropriation, Outlays, Permanent Appropriation.)

Budget Authority Balances The amount of budget authority provided in previous fiscal years that had not been spent by the start of the current fiscal year.

Obligated balances are amounts that were obligated but not paid before that date; usually these amounts remain available in succeeding fiscal years until they are used to pay for the obligation.

Unobligated balances of budget authority that Congress made available for only one fiscal year lapse at the end of that year; the agency to which the budget authority was granted loses it. The balances of multiyear or no-year budget authority may be obligated, respectively, during the years for which they have been made available or for an indefinite period. (*See* Borrowing Authority, Budget Authority, Contract Authority, Fiscal Year, Multiyear Appropriation, No-Year Appropriation, Obligation, One-Year Appropriation, Permanent Appropriation, Unobligated Balance.)

Budget Crosswalk Another term for the allocation of budget authority and outlay amounts in a budget resolution to congressional committees according to their jurisdictions and the committees' subdivision of those amounts among their programs or subcommittees. (*See* Budget Allocation.)

Budget Enforcement Act of 1990 An act that revised the sequestration process of the Gramm-Rudman-Hollings Act of 1985, replaced its fixed deficit targets with adjustable ones, established discretionary spending limits for fiscal years 1991 through 1995, instituted pay-as-you-go rules to enforce deficit neutrality on revenue and mandatory spending legislation, and re-formed the budget and accounting rules for federal credit activities. Unlike Gramm-Rudman-Hollings, the 1990 act emphasized restraints on legislated changes in taxes and spending instead of fixed deficit limits. (*See* Deficit Neutrality, Direct Spending, Discretionary Appropriations, Federal Credit Reform Act of 1990, Gramm-Rudman-Hollings Act of 1985, Maximum Deficit Amounts, Pay-As-You-Go, Revenue Legislation.)

Budget Estimate Pursuant to Law A dollar amount requested in the president's budget or in his revision of it. Although a Senate rule bans amendments that increase an appropriation in a general appropriation bill or that adds unauthorized appropriations to it, an exception is made for amendments "proposed in pursuance of an estimate submitted in accordance with law." This is interpreted to mean that an amendment to appropriate funds for an unauthorized purpose is allowed if the president's estimate does not mention the need for an authorization and if the amount in the amendment does not exceed the estimate. (*See* Authorization-Appropriation Process, Budget, Budget Amendment, General Appropriation Bill, Unauthorized Appropriation.)

Budget Process (1) In Congress, the procedural system it uses (a) to approve an annual concurrent resolution on the budget that sets goals for aggregate and functional categories of federal expenditures, revenues, and the surplus or deficit for an upcoming fiscal year; and (b) to implement those goals in spending, revenue, and, if necessary, reconciliation and debt-limit legislation.

(2) In the executive branch, the process of formulating the president's annual budget, submitting it to

Congress, defending it before congressional committees, implementing subsequent budget-related legislation, impounding or sequestering expenditures as permitted by law, auditing and evaluating programs, and compiling final budget data.

The Budget and Accounting Act of 1921 and the Congressional Budget and Impoundment Control Act of 1974 established the basic elements of the current budget process. Major revisions were enacted in the Gramm-Rudman-Hollings Act of 1985 and the Budget Enforcement Act of 1990.

In Congress, the budget committee of each house prepares and reports a budget resolution after reviewing the president's budget, the views of other committees, and analyses and baseline data prepared by the Congressional Budget Office. The two houses are supposed to approve their respective versions of the resolution and settle the differences between them by April 15. Each budget committee then allocates spending amounts set in the resolution among the appropriate committees in its house. Congress implements the budget resolution through its annual appropriation bills and, if necessary, revenue and other legislation, including reconciliation bills. All of this is supposed to occur before October 1, the beginning of the new federal fiscal year.

The laws provide a variety of points of order to enforce compliance with the process and with the provisions of the budget resolution. One bars consideration of any revenue, spending, entitlement, or debt-limit measure for a fiscal year before Congress has agreed to the resolution for that year. Other points of order can be raised against consideration of legislation or amendments that (1) violate the aggregate spending ceiling or revenue floor in a budget resolution, (2) exceed a committee's allocations or subdivisions, (3) breach the discretionary spending limits established in law for certain specified years, (4) increase the deficit target for a fiscal year set forth in the Gramm-Rudman-Hollings Act, if such a target is invoked by a presidential action, (5) violate the deficit neutrality rules that apply to reconciliation bills and legislation increasing entitlement spending or reducing revenues, or (6) add extraneous matters to a reconciliation bill. However, points of order may be waived in each house by various means.

Because the houses often miss the April 15 deadline, the regular annual appropriation bills are allowed to come before the House beginning May 15 even if the budget resolution has not yet been approved. In any event, the House Appropriations Committee is required to report all annual appropriation bills no later than June 10 of each year. (*See* Baseline, Budget Allocation, Budget Resolution, Congressional Budget Office, Debt Limit, Deficit Neutrality, Discretionary Appropriations, Entitlement Program, Fiscal Year, Function *or* Functional Category, General Appropriation Bill, Impoundment, Maximum Deficit Amounts, Point of Order, Reconciliation, Sequestration, Views and Estimates Report. *See also* Authorization-Appropriation Process, Budget Crosswalk, Byrd Rule, Current Services Estimates, Emergency Appropriation, Firewall, Non-Selfenforcing Rules, Pay-As-You-Go, Scorekeeping.)

Budget Receipts Monies collected by the government from the public generally and from premium payments by participants in certain social insurance programs. Collections from the general public consist primarily of taxes, but they also include court fines, certain license fees, deposits of earnings by the Federal Reserve System, and gifts. Budget receipts do not include various offsetting receipts; under federal government accounting practices, these are deducted from outlays. The budget surplus or deficit is calculated by comparing total budget receipts with total outlays. (*See* Deficit,

Offsetting Receipts, Outlays, Surplus. *See also* Balanced
Budget.)

Budget Resolution A concurrent resolution in which Congress establishes or revises its version of the federal
budget's broad financial features for the upcoming
fiscal year and several additional fiscal years. Like
other concurrent resolutions, it does not have the force
of law, but it provides the framework within which
Congress subsequently considers revenue, spending,
and other budget-implementing legislation.

The framework consists of two basic elements: (1)
aggregate budget amounts (total revenues, new budget
authority, outlays, loan obligations and loan guarantee
commitments, deficit or surplus, and debt limit); and
(2) subdivisions of the relevant aggregate amounts
among the functional categories of the budget. The
resolution also may contain reconciliation instructions
to various committees. Although it does not allocate
funds to specific programs or accounts, the budget
committees' reports accompanying the resolution often
discuss the major program assumptions underlying its
functional amounts. Unlike those amounts, however,
the assumptions are not binding on Congress.

The Congressional Budget Act requires only one
budget resolution each year but permits additional
ones as necessary. Congress should complete action on
the first resolution by April 15 of each year. For fiscal
years 1992 through 1995, the resolution must cover five
fiscal years. Thereafter it will revert to three fiscal
years unless Congress extends the five-year
requirement.

In both houses, budget resolutions are privileged
and debate time on them is limited. One budget act
rule permits amendments that change numbers in the
resolution to achieve internal mathematical consistency, even when the amendment alters numbers
previously amended. (*See* Budget Authority, Budget

Process, Concurrent Resolution, Congressional Budget and Impoundment Control Act of 1974, Debt Limit, Deficit, Direct Loan, Fiscal Year, Function *or* Functional Category, Loan Guarantee, Outlays, Privilege, Reconciliation, Revenue Legislation, Spending Authority, Surplus. *See also* Appropriation Account, Bigger Bite Amendment, Credit Budget.)

Budgetary Resources (1) In general budgeting parlance, amounts available for obligation in a fiscal year, including new budget authority, unobligated balances of budget authority, direct spending authority, and obligation limitations.

(2) Resources that are subject to sequestration under the terms of the Gramm-Rudman-Hollings-Act. (*See* Budget Authority, Direct Spending, Gramm-Rudman-Hollings Act of 1985, Sequestration, Unobligated Balance.)

Bullets (*See Congressional Record.*)

Business The Constitution permits a house to "do business" only if a quorum is present, but it does not define "business." Consequently, each house, through its rules and precedents, has developed some implicit concepts of business that are similar and some that are not.

Both generally agree that business signifies a measure or matter that may be considered or is being considered, as in business on a calendar, legislative business, pending business, and unfinished business. With some differences, both agree that business also includes certain actions, such as approval of the *Journal*, offering of motions, referral of measures and communications, receipt of messages, and presentation of committee reports.

The House and Senate differ radically, however, on what constitutes the business that must be transacted between the time a quorum has been established and the time that a member may make a point of order that a quorum is no longer present. Under the Senate's precedents, almost any action is considered intervening business for that purpose. Under rules the House adopted during the 1970s, a member's right to make a point of no quorum is limited almost entirely to situations in which the chair has put a question to a vote. Implicitly, these House rules reduce its concept of intervening business to nearly the barest minimum. (*See also* Continuing Business, Legislative Business, Morning Business, Order of Business, Pending Business, Quorum Call, Unfinished Business.)

Business Meeting A committee meeting for the transaction of business, as distinguished from a hearing. Among other matters, business includes the consideration of measures (markups) and internal administrative matters such as organization of its subcommittees and decisions concerning its budget and staff. (*See* Hearing, Markup, Subcommittee. *See also* Closed Hearing, Leave to Sit, Regular Meeting Day, Special Committee Meeting.)

By Reference (*See* Reference.)

By Request A designation indicating that a member has introduced a measure on behalf of the president, an executive agency, or a private individual or organization. Members often introduce such measures as a courtesy because neither the president nor any person other than a member of Congress can do so. The term, which appears next to the sponsor's name, implies that the member who introduced the measure does not necessarily endorse it. A House rule dealing with by-request introductions dates from 1888, but the practice goes back to the earliest history of Congress. (*See* Bills and Resolutions Introduced.)

Byrd Rule Popular name of an amendment to the Congressional Budget Act that bars the inclusion of extraneous matter in any reconciliation legislation considered in the Senate. Enforcement of the ban requires a point of order sustained by the chair. The provision defines different categories of extraneous matter, but it also permits certain exceptions. Its chief sponsor was Sen. Robert C. Byrd (D-W.Va.). (*See* Point of Order, Reconciliation, Sustained.)

C

Calendar A list of measures or other matters (most of them favorably reported by committees) that are eligible for floor consideration. The House has five calendars; the Senate has two. A place on a calendar does not guarantee consideration. Each house decides which measures and matters it will take up, when, and in what order, in accordance with its rules and practices. (For the House, see Consent Calendar, Discharge Calendar, House Calendar, Private Calendar, Union Calendar. For the Senate, *see* Calendar of General Orders, *Executive Calendar. See also* Adverse Report, Committee Calendar.)

(2) The familiar name for the daily publications of each house that contain their calendars and other pertinent information. (For the House, *see Calendars of the United States House of Representatives.* For the Senate, *see Calendar of Business, Executive Calendar.)*

Calendar Monday A Senate rule that requires measures on the legislative calendar be called up for possible consideration on Mondays after morning business is completed at the beginning of a new legislative day. The rule is usually waived by unanimous consent. (*See* Call of the Calendar, Legislative Day, Morning Business, Unanimous Consent.)

Calendar Number The number assigned to a measure when it is placed on a calendar to await consideration. The numbers merely indicate the chronological order in which measures were put on the calendar, not necessarily the order in which the body may choose to consider them. On a call of the calendar, however, measures are called in numerical order. (*See* Call of the Calendar. *See also* Calendar Monday.)

Calendar of Business A Senate publication appearing each day that the Senate meets. Among other items, it contains the calendar of general orders (sometimes called the legislative calendar); a cross-index of general orders, resolutions and motions "over under the rule"; motions entered for reconsideration; bills in conference; status of appropriation bills; and, on the front and following pages as necessary, unanimous consent agreements not yet fully executed. (*See* Calendar of General Orders, Over Under the Rule, Reconsider a Vote, Unanimous Consent Agreement.)

Calendar of General Orders The Senate's legislative calendar. It lists measures (but not treaties or nominations) reported by committees and also those placed directly on the calendar by the Senate. (*See* Calendar, Call of the Calendar, *Executive Calendar.*)

Calendar of Special Orders A calendar that is evidently obsolete although still mentioned in a Senate rule. (*See* Special Order.)

Calendar Wednesday A House procedure that on Wednesdays permits its committees to bring up for floor consideration nonprivileged measures they have reported. It is primarily a method for circumventing the Rules Committee's refusal to report special rules granting privilege to those measures. The procedure is so cumbersome and susceptible to dilatory tactics, however, that committees rarely use it, and the call is normally dispensed with by unanimous consent. If unanimous consent is denied, it may be dispensed with by a two-thirds vote.

The Calendar Wednesday rule requires that committees be called in alphabetical order. When called, a committee may pass or call up one of its measures from the Union or House calendar, but any member may demand a vote on whether to consider it. Union calendar measures must be considered in Committee of the Whole. General debate is limited to two hours and is equally divided between proponents and opponents.

If the House does not finish with a measure on the legislative day it is called up, that measure is set aside until all other committees have been called unless the House, by a two-thirds vote, permits continued consideration of that measure on the next Wednesday. Failing that, the measure may wait for weeks or months if all twenty-two legislative committees choose to call up their measures. A committee near the end of the alphabetical list may have to wait almost that long for its first call.

Calendar Wednesday is not in order during the last two weeks of a session, and the Rules Committee may not report a rule setting aside the two-thirds vote required to dispense with it. (*See* Committee of the Whole, Consider, Dilatory Tactics, General Debate, House Calendar, Legislative Day, Privileged Business, Rule, Session, Unanimous Consent, Union Calendar.)

Calendars of the United States House of Representatives A publication that contains all the House calendars and other useful information about pending measures. It is published each day the House is in session. (*See* Consent Calendar, Discharge Calendar, House Calendar, Private Calendar, Union Calendar.)

Call of Committees (*See* Calendar Wednesday, Order of Business (House).)

Call of the Calendar (1) A procedure in which the measures on a calendar are called up for possible floor consideration in the order of their calendar numbers. The House consent and private calendars are called on days set aside for them in the rules. A Senate rule requires a call of its legislative calendar each legislative day after it concludes morning business. When called, a measure is considered if no one objects, and no senator may speak more than once and for no more than five minutes on the measure or on any amendment to it.

(2) An informal Senate practice, analogous to House consent calendar procedure, in which non-controversial measures on the calendar are called up and passed without objection and with little or no debate. Party leaders and their aides check with senators beforehand to make certain that no one objects to the measures, a system referred to as the "clearance process." The leaders then arrange for a call of the calendar at some convenient time by unanimous consent. (*See* Calendar Number, Consent Calendar, Floor, Legislative Calendar, Legislative Day, Morning Business, Private Calendar, Unanimous Consent. *See also* Special Order of Business.)

Call of the House Another term for a quorum call in the House of Representatives. A member may move for a call of the House only when the Speaker recognizes the member for that purpose. (*See* Quorum, Quorum Call, Recognition.)

Call of the Roll A clerk's reading of the roster of members' names. (*See* Roll Call.)

Call to Order A request or admonition by the presiding officer, at his or her initiative or by the demand of a member, that members observe the rules of appropriate parliamentary behavior during a meeting. Ordinarily, a presiding officer opens a meeting by banging his gavel and announcing, "The House (or Senate, or committee) will be in order." (*See also* Decorum, Taking Down the Words.)

Call Up To bring a measure or report to the floor for immediate consideration. Technically, only privileged business or business made in order by a special rule may be called up in the House and, if reported by a committee, only by an authorized member of the committee. The term is seldom used in the Senate, where immediate consideration of any business usually requires agreement to a motion to consider or to a unanimous consent request. (*See* Privileged Business, Rule, Unanimous Consent.)

Cannon's Procedure in the House of Representatives A digest of leading House precedents and procedural terminology compiled by Clarence A. Cannon, a former unofficial House parliamentarian and later a House member and chairman of the Appropriations Committee. It is still a useful guide to House procedures and terminology, although it was last published in 1963 and is therefore outdated in some areas. (*See* Precedent, Procedures.)

Cap The legal limit on new spending and budget authority in a discretionary appropriations category of the budget during a particular fiscal year. The Budget Enforcement Act of 1990 requires a sequester in a category if its cap is exceeded. (*See* Budget Authority, Discretionary Appropriations, Sequestration. *See also* Breach.)

Caption (*See* Title.)

Casework Assistance to constituents who seek assistance in dealing with federal and local government agencies. Constituent service is a high priority in most members' offices. Caseworkers on members' staffs advise constituents about agency regulations and procedures, determine whether any complaints are justified, and try to persuade agencies to rectify errors or injustices. If an agency remains adamant or uncooperative, the member may take up the case himself. Occasionally, case investigations reveal shortcomings in the administrative process or in the law that prompt the member to push for remedial legislation. Most cases involve problems with Social Security benefits, veterans' benefits, and immigration.

Casting Vote The vice president's vote while presiding over the Senate. It may be cast only to break a tie vote, but the vice president is not required to vote. (*See* President of the Senate, Tie Vote.)

Caucus (1) A common term for the official organization of each party in each house. (*See* Party Caucus.)

(2) The official title of the organization of House Democrats. House and Senate Republicans and Senate Democrats call their organizations "conferences."

(3) A term for an informal group of members who share legislative interests; some groups are referred to as legislative service organizations. Several of these use the term in their titles, such as the Arts Caucus, Black Caucus, Hispanic Caucus, Mushroom Caucus, Children's Caucus, and Crime Caucus. (*See* Legislative Service Organizations.)

CBO (*See* Congressional Budget Office.)

Censure The strongest formal condemnation of a member for misconduct short of expulsion. A house usually adopts a resolution of censure to express its condemnation, after which the presiding officer reads its rebuke aloud to the member in the presence of his colleagues. Under a rule of the House Democratic Caucus, a censured Democratic representative loses his committee and subcommittee chairmanships for the remainder of that Congress.

The authority of Congress to censure stems from the constitutional provision permitting it to "punish its members for disorderly behavior." Most House censures have been applied in cases of unparliamentary language, assaults on other members, or insults to the House by introducing offensive resolutions. Others have dealt with corrupt acts of one kind or another, taking kickbacks from staff, and sexual misconduct. The House has sometimes ended the proceedings when members have apologized after censure procedures were initiated against them.

Senators have been censured for disloyalty during the Civil War, fist fights on the floor, insulting remarks to colleagues, and accepting stock for legislative favors. Most experts regard the Senate's 1954 condemnation of Sen. Joseph R. McCarthy (R-Wis.) as equivalent to censure. (*See* Expulsion, Unparliamentary. *See also* Code of Official Conduct, Decorum, Denounce, Ethics Rules, Fining a Member, Reprimand, Seniority Loss.)

Chair (1) The person presiding over a meeting, as in "the decision of the chair."

(2) The seat occupied by that person. To "take the chair" is to preside. (*See also* Presiding Officer.)

Chairman The presiding officer of a committee (including Committee of the Whole), a subcommittee, or a task force. At meetings, the chairman preserves order, enforces the rules, recognizes members to speak or offer motions, and puts questions to a vote. The chairman of a committee or subcommittee usually appoints its staff and sets its agenda, subject to the panel's veto. A committee chairman is required to report measures approved by the committee, usually manages measures during floor consideration, and recommends members for appointment to conference committees.

Senate committee chairmen are invariably selected on the basis of seniority on the committee, but they may not chair more than one standing committee.

House chairmen are chosen by their party's caucus or conference, usually on the basis of seniority, and they, too, may chair only one standing committee. Although chairmen are formally elected by their houses, they are always the nominees of the majority party.

The Speaker always appoints majority party members as chairmen of the Committee of the Whole. In the past, the Speaker often appointed the same member to preside over the committee each year when it took up a regularly recurring measure, such as an annual appropriation bill, but this practice has recently declined. (*See* Committee of the Whole, Conference Committee, Floor Manager, Presiding Officer, Report, Seniority System, Task Force. *See also* Subcommittee Assignments.)

Chairman's Mark The written recommendations of a chairman to his committee or subcommittee concerning a measure it is about to consider. The chairman's mark often takes the form of a draft of a bill (or of a budget resolution in a budget committee) that the panel uses as the basis for consideration. (*See* Budget Resolution, Legislative Committee.)

Chamber (1) The Capitol room in which a house of Congress normally holds its sessions. The chamber of the House of Representatives, officially called the Hall of the House, is considerably larger than that of the Senate because it must accommodate 435 representatives, 4 delegates, and 1 resident commissioner. Unlike the Senate chamber, members have no desks or assigned seats.

In both chambers, the floor slopes downward to the well in front of the presiding officer's raised desk. A chamber is often referred to as "the floor," as when members are said to be on or going to the floor. Those expressions usually imply that the member's house is in session.

For nearly fifty years until 1857, the House met in what is now Statuary Hall. The Senate moved to its present chamber in 1859, after meeting for about forty years in what is now called the Old Supreme Court Chamber.

(2) By extension, one of the houses of Congress, as in "a chamber agreed to a conference." (*See* Delegate, Floor, Presiding Officer, Resident Commissioner from Puerto Rico, Well. *See also* Aisle, Party Tables.)

Changing Existing Law In House terminology, a reference to language changing existing substantive or authorizing law that appears in, or is offered as an amendment to, a general appropriation bill. A House rule prohibits such changes except to retrench expenditures or rescind appropriations. (*See* Authorization, General Appropriation Bill, Rescission, Retrenchment, Substantive Law. *See also* Authorization-Appropriation Process, General Legislation, Legislation on an Appropriation Bill, Limitation on an Appropriation Bill.)

Christmas Tree Bill Jargon for a bill adorned with amendments, many of them unrelated to the bill's subject, that provide benefits for interest groups, specific states, congressional districts, companies, and individuals. Such amendments are usually attached in the Senate where, unlike in the House, nongermane amendments are normally permitted, but both houses tend to add them to must-pass bills, such as debt ceiling increases and continuing resolutions, especially toward the end of an annual session of Congress. (*See* Congressional District, Continuing Resolution, Germane, Must-Pass Bill, Session. *See also* Pork *or* Pork Barrel Legislation.)

Claims Legislation (*See* Private Bill.)

Class A Committees Common designation of a group of twelve Senate standing committees: Agriculture, Nutrition, and Forestry; Appropriations; Armed Services;

Banking, Housing, and Urban Affairs; Commerce, Science, and Transportation; Energy and Natural Resources; Environment and Public Works; Finance; Foreign Relations; Governmental Affairs; Judiciary; and Labor and Human Resources. The Senate's rules require each senator to serve on two of these major committees, but no more than two. (*See also* Committee Assignments, Exclusive Committee.)

Class B Committees Common designation of a group of seven Senate committees. Four are standing committees: Budget, Rules and Administration, Small Business, and Veterans' Affairs; two, Aging and Intelligence, are permanent select or special committees; and the seventh is the Joint Economic Committee. The Senate's rules permit each senator to serve on no more than one of these committees. (*See also* Committee Assignments.)

Class C Committees Common designation of a group of five Senate committees: Indian Affairs, Permanent Select Ethics, Joint Taxation, Joint Library, and Joint Printing. The Senate's rules permit each senator to serve on any number of them. However, senators may not serve on Joint Taxation unless they sit on the Finance Committee, nor may senators serve on Joint Library or Joint Printing unless they sit on the Rules and Administration Committee. (*See also* Committee Assignments.)

Classes of Senators A class consists of the thirty-three or thirty-four senators elected to a six-year term in the same general election. Since the terms of approximately one-third of the senators expire every two years, there are three classes. When a new state is admitted to the union, the Senate assigns each of its two senators to a different class, usually by lot, keeping the sizes of the classes as equal as possible. Consequently, the first term of at least one of the senators from a newly admitted state will end in two or four years. (*See* Congressional Terms of Office.)

Clause (1) A special and separate provision in a measure or law, such as an enacting clause or resolving clause. (*See* Enacting Clause, Resolving Clause.)

(2) In the House, the first subdivision of a standing rule: for example, Rule I, clause 1. (*See also* Rule Citations.)

(3) A second subdivision of the Constitution.

Clean Bill After a House committee extensively amends a bill, it often assembles its amendments and what is left of the bill into a new measure that one or more of its members introduces as a "clean bill." The revised measure is assigned a new number and referred back to the committee, which promptly reports it back to the House. Reporting a clean bill avoids separate floor votes on the committee's amendments and protects amendments that might be subject to points of order concerning germaneness. (*See* Amendment, Bills and Resolutions Introduced, Bills and Resolutions Referred, Germane, Report. *See also* Original Bill.)

Clearance Process (*See* Call of the Calendar.)

Cleaves' Manual Short title for "Cleaves' Manual of the Law and Practices in Regard to Conferences and Conference Reports," usually published as a section of the *Senate Manual*. Although compiled in about 1900, most of the procedures it describes are still applicable today. (*See* Conferees, Conference, Conference Committee, Conference Report, *Senate Manual*.)

Clerk of the House An officer of the House of Representatives responsible principally for administrative support of the legislative process in the House. The clerk's former functions as chief administrative and budgetary officer were assigned to a director of non-legislative and financial services by a resolution agreed to on

April 9, 1992. Invariably the candidate of the majority party, the clerk is elected by resolution at the beginning of each Congress and continues in office until a successor is chosen. Among other duties, the clerk presides over the House pending election of a Speaker, and supervises the maintenance of the *Journal* and the calendars, processing of legislative documents, reading of bills and amendments to the chamber, recording and certification of votes, and engrossment of measures. (*See* Calendar, Director of Non-Legislative and Financial Services, Engrossed Bill, *Journal*, Officers of Congress, Reading for Amendment, Reading of Amendments, Readings of Bills and Resolutions. *See also* Secretary of the Senate.)

Clerk-Hire The personal staff to which a member is entitled. The clerk-hire allowance is the maximum amount of money available to a member to compensate his or her staff.

In the House, both the number of staff a member may hire and the allowance amount are established by law or resolution. A senator's personal staff allowance is included in an official personnel and expense account. The Senate sets no limit on the number of personal staff a senator may hire within the limits of the allowance (technically called the administrative, clerical, and legislative assistance allowance), but senators from the more populous states are authorized larger sums. (*See also* Administrative Assistant, Legislative Assistant, Members' Allowances.)

Cloakrooms Two rooms with access to the rear of each chamber's floor, one for each party's members, where members may confer privately, sit quietly, or have a snack. The presiding officer sometimes urges members who are conversing too loudly on the floor to retire to their cloakrooms. (*See also* Decorum.)

Closed Business Meeting (*See* Business Meeting.)

Closed Door Session (*See* Secret *or* Closed Session.)

Closed Hearing A hearing closed to the public and the press. A House committee may close its hearing only if it determines that disclosure of the testimony to be taken would endanger national security, violate any law, or tend to defame, degrade, or incriminate any person. The Senate has a similar rule. Both houses require roll-call votes in open session to close a hearing. (*See* Hearing, Roll Call. *See also* Executive Session, Sunshine Rules.)

Closed Rule A special rule reported from the House Rules Committee that prohibits amendments to a measure or that only permits amendments offered by the reporting committee.

Under a House Democratic Caucus rule, when a committee chairman intends to request a special rule prohibiting the offering of any germane amendment to a measure reported by the committee, the chairman must first give notice of his or her intention in the *Congressional Record* and then wait four legislative days. If, within those four days, fifty or more Democratic members notify the chairman and the Rules Committee that they wish to offer a particular germane amendment, Democratic members of the Rules Committee are prohibited from supporting any rule that prohibits that amendment until the caucus has met and decided whether it should be allowed. (*See* Amendment, Germane, Legislative Day, Rule. *See also* Party Caucus, Self-Executing Rule.)

Cloture A Senate procedure that limits further consideration of a pending proposal to thirty hours in order to end a filibuster.

Sixteen senators must first sign and submit a cloture motion to the presiding officer. One hour after the Senate meets on the second calendar day thereafter, the chair puts the motion to a yea-and-nay vote following a live quorum call. If three-fifths of all senators (sixty if there are no vacancies) vote for the motion, the Senate must take final action on the clotured proposal by the end of the thirty hours of consideration and may consider no other business until it takes that action. Cloture on a proposal to amend the Senate's standing rules requires approval by two-thirds of the senators present and voting. The vote on cloture occurs after the presiding officer asks the question: "Is it the sense of the Senate that the debate shall be brought to a close?"

Once cloture is invoked, each senator may speak for a total of no more than one hour. Senators may yield all or part of their hour to one of the floor managers or floor leaders who may in turn yield that time to other senators, but each manager and leader may be yielded no more than two hours.

No dilatory amendments or motions are allowed, and all debate and amendments must be germane. Only amendments filed before the cloture vote may be considered, but no senator may call up more than two amendments until every other senator has had an opportunity to do so. Printed amendments that have been available for at least twenty-four hours are not read when called up.

The time for votes, quorum calls, and all other actions is charged against the thirty-hour limit. That time limit may be extended by a three-fifths vote of all senators on a nondebatable motion. Any extended time is equally divided and controlled by the majority and minority leaders. When the limit is reached, senators who have used less than ten minutes of their hour are guaranteed up to ten minutes, but only for debate. When all time expires, no further amendments may be called up, and the Senate immediately votes on any pending amendments and then on the underlying proposal. (*See* Dilatory Tactics, Filibuster, Floor Leader, Floor Manager, Germane, Live Quorum, Nondebatable

Motions, Printed Amendment, Put the Question, Quorum Call, Reading of Amendments, Standing Rules, Yeas and Nays, Yielding Time. *See also* Continuing Body, Rule Twenty-Two, Unlimited Debate.)

Cluster Voting House jargon for sequential recorded votes on a series of measures that the House finished debating at an earlier time or on a previous day. The rule on cluster voting may be applied to votes on passing bills, adopting resolutions, ordering the previous question on special rules from the Rules Committee, agreeing to conference reports and motions to suspend the rules, and agreeing to motions to instruct conferees.

The Speaker, at his discretion, may postpone such votes to a designated time on the same legislative day or within two legislative days. The Speaker may also reduce the minimum time for the second and subsequent votes in the series to five minutes each. Cluster voting was adopted to avoid frequent interruptions of committee meetings and members' other business.

The Senate occasionally uses an analogous process under which it "stacks" a series of votes, but this requires unanimous consent. (*See* Conference Report, Instruct Conferees, Legislative Day, Previous Question, Recorded Vote, Rule, Stacked Votes, Suspension of the Rules (House), Unanimous Consent. *See also* Electronic Voting, Time Limits for Voting.)

Code of Official Conduct A House rule that bans certain actions by House members, officers, and employees; requires them to conduct themselves in ways that "reflect creditably" on the House; and orders them to adhere to the spirit and the letter of House rules and those of its committees.

The code's provisions govern the receipt of outside compensation, gifts, and honoraria, and the use of campaign funds; prohibit members from using their clerk-hire allowance to pay anyone who does not perform duties commensurate with that pay; forbids discrimination in members' hiring or treatment of employees on the grounds of race, color, religion, sex, handicap, age, or national origin; orders members convicted of a crime who might be punished by imprisonment of two or more years not to participate in committee business or vote on the floor until exonerated or reelected; and restricts employees' contact with federal agencies on matters in which they have a significant financial interest. The Senate's rules contain some similar prohibitions. (*See* Clerk-Hire. *See* also Censure, Decorum, Denounce, Ethics Rules, Expulsion, Fining a Member, Reprimand, Seniority Loss.)

College of Cardinals A popular term for the subcommittee chairmen of the appropriations committees, reflecting their influence over appropriation measures. The chairmen of the full appropriations committees are sometimes referred to as popes.

Colloquy A formal conversational exchange between members during floor proceedings. The device is often used to obtain information or to put mutual understandings about the intent of a measure, a provision, or an amendment into the *Congressional Record*, thereby establishing legislative history for the guidance of executive officials and the courts.

Legislative history colloquies are usually prepared and agreed to in advance by the members involved. Typically, a colloquy consists of questions posed by one member and answered by another. Toward the end of a week, the majority and minority leaders usually engage in a more extemporaneous colloquy for announcements about the floor agenda for the upcoming week. (*See Congressional Record*, Legislative History.)

Comity The practice of maintaining mutual courtesy and civility between the two houses in their dealings with each other and in members' speeches on the floor. Although the practice is largely governed by long-established customs, a House rule explicitly cautions its members not to characterize any Senate action or inaction, refer to individual senators except under certain circumstances, or quote from Senate proceedings except to make legislative history on a measure. The Senate has no rule on the subject, but references to the House have been held out of order on several occasions. Generally, the houses do not interfere with each other's appropriations, although minor conflicts sometimes occur. A refusal to receive a message from the other house has also been held to violate the practice of comity.

According to *Jefferson's Manual*, the ban on comments about the other house is based on the argument that "the opinion of each House should be left to its own independency, not to be influenced by the proceedings of the other; and the [sic] quoting them might beget reflections leading to a misunderstanding between the two Houses." (*See also* Body, Decorum, *Jefferson's Manual*, Taking Down the Words.)

Commit To send or return to a committee. As a practical matter, the terms "commit," "recommit," and "refer" are essentially synonymous. (*See* Recommit, Recommit with Instructions, Referral. *See also* Precedence of Motions (House), Precedence of Motions (Senate).)

Committee A panel of members elected or appointed to perform some service or function for its parent body. Congress has four types of committees: standing, special or select, joint, and, in the House, a Committee of the Whole.

Except for the Committee of the Whole, committees conduct investigations, make studies, issue reports and recommendations, and, in the case of standing committees, review and prepare measures on their assigned subjects for action by their respective houses. Most committees divide their work among several subcommittees or, in some cases, task forces, but only the full committee may submit reports or measures to its house or to Congress. With rare exceptions, the majority party in a house holds a majority of the seats on its committees, and their chairmen are also from that party.

Modern committees vary in size from about twelve to almost seventy members in the House and from six to about thirty members in the Senate. The Appropriations Committee is always the largest standing committee in each house. Every committee is entitled to staff, offices, office equipment and supplies, and funds for other expenses.

During its first several decades, Congress relied entirely on temporary select committees. Standing committees began to replace them early in the nineteenth century and are now more numerous than any other type. (*See* Committee Jurisdiction, Committee of the Whole, Committee Ratios, Investigative Power, Joint Committee, Select *or* Special Committee, Standing Committee, Subcommittee, Task Force. *See also* Ad Hoc Select Committee, Bipartisan Committee, Committee on Committees, Conference Committee, Legislative Committee, Major Committees, Policy Committees, Steering and Policy Committee (House).)

Committee Amendment An amendment recommended by a committee to a measure it has reported. Committees may not amend measures referred to them; they may only propose amendments. During floor consideration in each house, committee amendments must be acted on before others may be offered. Like other amendments, they can be amended and are subject to points of order if they violate any rules, unless protected by a rule from the Committee on Rules in the House or by a unanimous consent agreement in the Senate. (*See* Amendment, Committee Report on a Measure, Point of Order, Rule, Unanimous Consent Agreement. *See also*

Amendment in the Nature of a Substitute, Degrees of Amendment.)

Committee Assignments   The committees on which a member serves. Although each house formally makes the assignments to its committees, it invariably ratifies the recommendations of the party organizations.

Both parties consider a number of factors in making assignments, including seniority, experience, background, ideology, and the special interests of a member's district or state. In addition, the rules of the party organizations and the houses attempt to ensure an equitable number of assignments for each member and an equitable distribution of assignments to important committees. With rare exceptions, each representative is assigned to at least one standing committee; most representatives sit on two standing committees, and a few serve on three. Senators must serve on at least two standing committees but many sit on three and several senators sit on four. In addition, many members in both houses are assigned to select and joint committees.

The rules of the House Democratic Caucus divide committees into three classes: exclusive, major, and nonmajor. A Democrat who sits on an exclusive committee—Appropriations, Ways and Means, or Rules—may not serve on any other standing committee except Budget or House Administration. No Democrat may serve on more than one of the eight major committees, on more than two of the ten nonmajor committees, or on more than one major plus one nonmajor committee. In practice, however, the caucus often grants waivers from one or more of these limitations.

House Republicans follow the same general categorization. However, their rankings of committees differ by largely depending on committee vacancies and the relative interest of Republican members in serving on each particular committee.

Both Senate party conferences also designate a few committees as exclusive, but only in the sense that no senator may serve on more than one of them. In addition, the standing rules divide all committees into three classes for assignment purposes. The first, often called class A, consists of twelve standing committees, and each senator *must* serve on two of them, but no more than two. Despite the limitation, the Senate often grants waivers for many senators; in the 102d Congress, twenty-three senators were assigned to three class A committees. Class B committees consist of four standing committees, two select committees, and one joint committee. A senator *may* sit on one of them, but no more than one. Class C committees consist of two select committees and three joint committees. With certain exceptions, a senator may sit on any number of them. (*See* Class A Committees, Class B Committees, Class C Committees, Exclusive Committee, Joint Committee, Major Committees, Nonmajor Committees, Party Caucus, Select *or* Special Committee, Standing Committee, Standing Rules. *See also* Committee on Committees, Johnson Rule, Subcommittee Assignments.)

Committee Business Meeting (*See* Business Meeting.)

Committee Calendar A list of all measures referred to a particular committee during a Congress, its actions on them, and chamber action on those it has reported. It also usually includes the committee's rules and miscellaneous other information. Most standing committees publish their calendars periodically. (*See also* Bills and Resolutions Referred.)

Committee Hearing (*See* Hearing.)

Committee Jurisdiction The legislative subjects and other functions assigned to a committee by rule, precedent, resolution, or statute. A committee's title usually indicates the general scope of its jurisdiction but often fails to mention other significant subjects assigned to it.

The measures introduced in each Congress cover a vast number of subjects. Because each house has a relatively small number of standing committees, many of them consequently have immense jurisdictions, which was one reason for the creation of numerous subcommittees. The Legislative Reorganization Act of 1946 established the basis for this system in order to consolidate decision making on broad public policy areas in single committees. Despite these consolidations, committee jurisdictions overlap on a number of complex subject areas. In 1992, for example, a comprehensive energy bill was referred to eight House committees.

The 1946 act also attempted to establish parallel jurisdictions between House and Senate committees—that is, to assign the same subjects to a single committee in each house. Parallel jurisdictions avoid conference problems that arise when a bill's provisions are all within the jurisdiction of a single committee in one house but overlap the jurisdictions of two or more committees in the other house. For a variety of reasons, the houses have since eroded some of the parallelism established by the 1946 act. (*See* Conference, Precedent, Resolution, Rule, Standing Committee, Subcommittee. *See* also Bills and Resolutions Referred, Multiple and Sequential Referrals, Oversight.)

Committee Meeting A term in the rules of both houses that refers to holding committee meetings for the transaction of business rather than for the conduct of hearings. (*See* Business Meeting, Hearing. *See also* Regular Meeting Day, Special Committee Meeting.)

Committee of the Whole Common name of the Committee of the Whole House on the State of the Union, a committee consisting of all members of the House of Representatives. Measures from the union calendar must be considered in the Committee of the Whole before the House officially completes action on them; the committee often considers other major bills as well. A quorum of the committee is 100, and it meets in the House chamber under a chairman appointed by the Speaker.

The committee's proceedings begin with general debate on the measure for a period of time previously ordered by the House, usually from one hour to several hours. That time is controlled by, and equally divided between, the majority and minority floor managers, but when more than one committee reports on the measure the time is distributed among them. The committee then considers amendments under the five-minute rule. Debate on amendments may be closed or limited by majority vote on a nondebatable motion. If the committee does not complete its deliberations on a measure in one day, it can meet again on subsequent days.

The committee operates partly under House rules explicitly governing its procedures and partly under practices of the House that implicitly apply to the committee, but both are often modified by special rules from the Rules Committee. In any case, the Committee of the Whole does not allow the yeas and nays or motions to adjourn, lay on the table, recess, recommit, reconsider, or for the previous question.

When the committee finishes with a measure, it rises and reports back to the House by recommending that the bill be passed with whatever amendments the committee has approved. The special rule on the measure bans additional floor amendments at this stage and prohibits debate on the measure, on the committee's amendments to it, and on all the necessary steps to passage. However, any member may demand a separate vote on any amendment reported by the Committee of the Whole.

The Senate no longer uses a Committee of the Whole. It abolished such proceedings on bills and joint resolutions in 1930 and stopped its use for the consideration of treaties in 1986.

Procedures in the Committee of the Whole expedite consideration of legislation because of its smaller quorum requirement, its ban on certain motions, and its five-minute rule for debate on amendments. Those procedures usually permit more members to offer amendments and participate in the debate on a measure than is normally possible when the measure is considered in the House, where the hour rule, the previous question motion, and the ban on dilatory motions can be far more restrictive. (*See* Adjourn, Chairman, Debate-Ending Motion, Dilatory Tactics, Five-Minute Rule, Floor Manager, General Debate, Hour Rule, Lay on the Table, Previous Question, Quorum, Recess, Recommit, Reconsider a Vote, Union Calendar, Yeas and Nays. *See also* En Gros, House as in Committee of the Whole.)

Committee of the Whole House A moribund Committee of the Whole that formerly considered business on the private calendar of the House of Representatives. Since 1935, the House has considered private measures under a procedure called "the House as in committee of the whole." (*See* House as in Committee of the Whole, Private Calendar.)

Committee on Committees A political party committee that assigns party members to positions on standing committees and most select committees in its house, subject to approval by the party organization and pro forma election by the chamber. Ordinarily, the committee only fills vacant positions, adhering to the custom that members should not be removed from their assignments without their consent.

Only the Republicans in both houses give their panels the formal name of "Committee on Committees." House Democrats assign the function to their Steering and Policy Committee, Senate Democrats to their Steering Committee. (*See* Caucus, Committee Assignments, Select *or* Special Committee, Standing Committee, Steering and Policy Committee. *See also* Party Caucus.)

Committee Print A document printed either for the use of a committee or for other informational purposes. Most committees publish their rules in committee prints. Preliminary reports and revised versions of bills are often published in this form as well.

Committee Ratios The ratios of majority to minority party members on committees. By custom, the ratios of most committees reflect party strength in their respective houses as closely as possible. In the House, however, the Appropriations, Budget, Rules, and Ways and Means committees often have disproportionate ratios to ensure firm majority party control. Leaders of the two parties in each house negotiate the ratios at the beginning of each Congress.

A rule of the House Democratic Caucus requires a Democratic Speaker to provide for a minimum of three Democrats for each two Republicans on standing committees. When the Democratic Party's majority in the House falls below 60 percent, enforcement of the rule forecloses committee ratios that accurately reflect the relative party strengths in the chamber. (*See* Party Caucus. *See also* Committee Assignments.)

Committee Report on a Measure A document submitted by a committee to report a measure to its parent chamber. Customarily, the report explains the measure's purpose, describes provisions and any amendments recommended by the committee, and presents arguments for its approval. The text of the committee's amendments appears at the beginning of the document. By rule, reports must also provide certain other information, and they may also contain the dissenting, additional, or supplementary views of some committee members. The House requires such reports; the Senate does not, but its committees usually provide them. Reports are designated S. Rpt. in the Senate, H. Rpt. in the House; both are numbered sequentially in the order of filing during a Congress. Thus, the tenth House report in the 102d Congress was designated H. Rpt. 102-10.

Both houses require that reports include a detailed description of the changes the measure makes in existing law, certain cost estimates, any relevant oversight findings, and the vote totals if the committee held a roll-call vote on reporting the measure. Senate reports must provide a regulatory impact statement; the House requires an inflationary impact statement. All of a report's contents must appear in a single volume. In the House, however, when a measure is referred to two or more committees, their reports are published as separate parts of the same report, such as H. Rpt. 102-10, Part 1, H Rpt. 102-10, Part 2. (*See* Committee Amendments, Cordon Rule, Cost Estimates, Inflationary Impact Statement, Minority Views, Multiple and Sequential Referrals, Oversight, Ramseyer Rule, Regulatory Impact Statement, Report, Roll Call. *See also* Adverse Report, Conference Report, Filed, Layover Rules, Privileged Reports.)

Committee Staff (*See* Investigative Staff, Minority Staff, Permanent Staff, Staff Director. *See also* Clerk-Hire.)

Committee Stage The stage in the legislative process when a measure is considered in one or more standing committees. (*See also* Floor.)

Committee Tables (*See* Party Tables.)

Committee Veto A procedure that requires an executive department or agency to submit certain proposed policies, programs, or action to designated committees for review before implementing them. Before 1983, when the Supreme Court declared that a legislative veto is

unconstitutional, these provisions permitted committees to veto the proposals. They no longer do so, and
the term is now something of a misnomer. Nevertheless, agencies usually take the pragmatic approach of
trying to reach a consensus with the committees before
carrying out their proposals, especially when an appropriations committee is involved. Thus, when agencies
wish to transfer appropriated funds from one purpose
to another within the same account, they almost invariably seek the prior approval of one or both appropriations committees. (*See* Agency, Appropriation. *See also*
Iron Triangle, Legislative Veto.)

Companion Bills Identical or similar bills introduced in
both houses. Like-minded representatives and senators
often introduce companion bills on the theory that this
will spur action on them in their respective houses.

Compelling Attendance of Members (*See* Arrest of Absent
Members.)

Comptroller General of the United States The head of the
General Accounting Office. The comptroller general is
appointed to a fifteen-year term by the president, but
only Congress can remove him from office before the
end of his appointed term. (*See* General Accounting
Office.)

Concur Agree to an amendment of the other house, either
by adopting a motion to concur in that amendment or
by a motion to concur with an amendment to that
amendment. After both houses have agreed to the
same version of an amendment, neither house may
amend it further, nor may any subsequent conference
change or delete it from the measure. Concurrence by
one house in all amendments of the other house
completes action on the measure; no vote is then
necessary on the measure as a whole because both
houses previously passed it. (*See* Adhere, Amendments

Between the Houses, Disagree, Insist, Recede. *See also* Approval Terminology.)

Concurrent Resolution A resolution that requires approval by both houses but is not sent to the president for his signature and therefore cannot have the force of law.

Concurrent resolutions deal with the prerogatives or internal affairs of Congress as a whole. For example, they serve as the vehicles for coordinating congressional budget decisions, fixing the time of congressional adjournments, agreeing to a joint session, expressing the sense of Congress on domestic and foreign issues, correcting errors in enrolled bills, authorizing the printing of documents of interest to both houses, and creating temporary joint committees. Designated H. Con. Res. in the House and S. Con. Res. in the Senate, they are numbered consecutively in each house in their order of introduction during a two-year Congress. (*See* Adjournment for More Than Three Days, Adjournment Sine Die, Budget Resolution, Enrolled Bill, Joint Committee. *See also* Reading of Bills and Resolutions.)

Conditional Adjournment An adjournment of Congress for a specified period of more than three days with the proviso that the Speaker of the House and the Senate's president pro tempore (or sometimes its majority leader) may reconvene Congress at an earlier date. The concurrent resolution providing for the adjournment usually requires those officers to give all members adequate notice of the reconvening. Conditional adjournments have been adopted on various occasions to provide for the possibility of an emergency or critical circumstances that might require some action by Congress. (*See* Adjourn for More Than Three Days, Concurrent Resolution, President Pro Tempore, Speaker.)

Conferees A common title for managers, the members from each house appointed to a conference committee.

The Senate usually authorizes its presiding officer to appoint its conferees. The Speaker appoints House conferees, and under a rule adopted in 1993, can remove conferees "at any time after an original appointment" and also appoint additional conferees at any time. Conferees are expected to support the positions of their houses despite their personal views, but in practice this is not always the case. The party ratios of conferees generally reflect the ratios in their houses.

Invariably, most conferees—often all of them—are members of the committee that reported the measure; the appointing officers usually accept the recommendations of the committee's chairman and ranking minority member. Some House committees require that members of the subcommittees that handled the measure must be named to the conference. When several committees have dealt with the measure, members from all of them may be appointed.

House rules direct the Speaker to appoint "no less than a majority of members who generally supported the House position," members "who are primarily responsible for the legislation," and, when feasible, the principal proponents of the bill's major provisions as it passed the House. On occasion, the Speaker has appointed conferees to deal only with specific portions of the measure, and the presiding officer of the Senate has also sometimes done so.

Each house may appoint as many conferees as it pleases. House conferees often outnumber their Senate colleagues; however, each house has only one vote in a conference, so the size of its delegation is immaterial. On rare occasions, more than 250 conferees from both houses have been appointed, usually to deal with massive omnibus reconciliation bills. (*See* Conference Committee, Managers, Omnibus Bill, Presiding Officer, Reconciliation. *See also* Discharge of Conferees, Instruct Conferees.)

Conference (1) A formal meeting or series of meetings between members representing each house to reconcile House and Senate differences on a measure (occasionally several measures). Also, a common reference to a conference committee.

A conference is permitted to deal only with matters in disagreement between the houses. It may not change language that both have previously approved, nor may it insert a subject not dealt with in either the House or the Senate version of the measure. In addition, House conferees may not formally agree to a Senate amendment that violates the authorization-appropriation rules of the House unless previously authorized to do so, but they may report such an amendment in technical disagreement. A point of order upheld against a conference report on the ground that it violates any of these conditions kills the report.

Since one house cannot require the other to agree to its proposals, the conference usually reaches agreement by compromise. This may involve crafting a provision that contains parts of the two versions or a trade in which the conferees agree to a provision offered by one house in return for agreement to one offered by the other.

When a conference completes action on a measure, or as much action as appears possible, it sends its recommendations to both houses in the form of a conference report, accompanied by an explanatory statement. (*See* Conferees, Conference Committee, Conference Report, Explanatory Statement. *See also* Amendment in the Nature of a Substitute, Amendments in Disagreement, Amendments in Technical Disagreement, Discharge of Conferees, Instruct Conferees, Request a Conference, Scope of Differences, Stage of Disagreement.)

(2) The official title of the organization of all Democrats or Republicans in the Senate and of all

Republicans in the House of Representatives. (*See* Party Caucus.)

Conference Committee A temporary joint committee formed for the purpose of resolving differences between the houses on a measure or, occasionally, several measures. Major and controversial legislation usually require conference committee action. Voting in a conference committee is by house as determined by a majority vote of its conferees, not by individuals. Consequently, a committee decision must be affirmed by a majority of the conferees from each house.

Both houses require that conference committees open their meetings to the public. The Senate's rule permits the committee to close its meetings if a majority of conferees in each delegation agree by a roll-call vote. The House rule permits closed meetings only if the House authorizes them on a roll-call vote. Such a vote is not binding on Senate conferees because each house has an equal vote in the committee.

Otherwise, there are no congressional rules governing the organization of, or procedure in, a conference committee. The committee chooses its chairman, but on measures that go to conference annually, such as general appropriation bills, the chairmanship traditionally rotates between the houses. (*See* Conferees, Joint Committee, Roll Call. *See also Cleaves' Manual*, Conference.)

Conference Report A document submitted to both houses that contains a conference committee's agreements for resolving their differences on a measure. It must be signed by a majority of the conferees from each house and must be accompanied by an explanatory statement.

Both houses prohibit amendments to a conference report and require it to be accepted or rejected in its entirety. If both houses agree to a report that resolves all their differences, that action passes the measure; they do not vote on the measure as amended by the report. If the first house to vote on the report rejects it, the measure can be recommitted to the conference committee for another attempt. This is not possible if the first house approves the report but the second house rejects it because the favorable vote of the first house automatically dissolves the committee. Under these circumstances, the houses may resort to further amendments between them, agree to a new conference, or let the measure die.

In the Senate, a motion to consider a conference report is privileged and not debatable, but the report itself is debatable and therefore subject to a filibuster. If the Senate, by unanimous consent, limits debate time on the report, the time is equally divided between the parties. In the House, conference reports are called up as privileged business and debated under the hour rule. The time is equally divided between the parties except when both party managers support a report, in which case a member who opposes it is entitled to one-third of the hour. A Senate rule requires that a conference report be read to the Senate before it is considered, but the reading is usually set aside by unanimous consent.

A conference report is supposed to be printed as a document in each house, but at the beginning of each Congress the Senate normally agrees to an order waiving its printing if the House has printed the report unless a senator requests otherwise. The House requires that the report and its explanatory statement be printed in the *Congressional Record* at least three calendar days before floor consideration. Both houses may waive these requirements by unanimous consent or, in the House, by a special rule. (*See* Amendments Between the Houses, Conferees, Conference, Conference Committee, *Congressional Record*, Debate, Desk, Explanatory Statement, Hour Rule, Privilege, Privileged Business, Recommit a Conference Report, Rule,

Unanimous Consent. *See also* Amendments in Disagreement, Amendments in Technical Disagreement, Custody of the Papers.)

Confirmation A Senate action approving a nomination submitted by the president. (*See* Nominations.)

Congress (1) The national legislature of the United States, consisting of the House of Representatives and the Senate.

(2) The national legislature in office during a two-year period. Congresses are numbered sequentially; thus, the 1st Congress of 1789-1791 and the 102d Congress of 1991-1993. Before 1935, the two-year period began on the first Monday in December of odd-numbered years. Since then it has extended from January of an odd-numbered year through noon on January 3 of the next odd-numbered year. A Congress usually holds two annual sessions, but some have had three sessions and the 67th Congress had four. When a Congress expires, measures die if they have not yet been enacted. (*See* Session. *See also* Special Session.)

Congressional Budget and Impoundment Control Act of 1974 The law that established the basic elements of the congressional budget process, the House and Senate budget committees, the Congressional Budget Office, and the procedures for congressional review of impoundments in the form of rescissions and deferrals proposed by the president. The budget process consists of procedures for coordinating congressional revenue and spending decisions made in separate tax, appropriations, and legislative measures. The impoundment provisions were intended to give Congress greater control over executive branch actions that delay or prevent the spending of funds provided by Congress. (*See* Budget Process, Congressional Budget Office, Deferral, Impoundment, Rescission. *See also* Budget Enforcement Act of 1990, Gramm-Rudman-Hollings Act of 1985.)

Congressional Budget Office (CBO) A congressional support agency created by the Congressional Budget and Impoundment Control Act of 1974 to provide nonpartisan budgetary information and analysis to Congress and its committees. The statute requires CBO to give priority for its services to the budget committees, to the appropriations and revenue committees in each house, and to all other committees, in that order.

The office produces five-year economic projections, budget baseline projections, spending and revenue options for reducing the budget deficit, and analyses of the president's budget. It also provides budget scorekeeping reports, cost estimates on pending legislation, and a variety of special studies.

Under the original version of the Gramm-Rudman-Hollings Act, CBO played an equal role with the Office of Management and Budget in calculating sequestration data. After the Supreme Court struck down a related part of that act as unconstitutional in 1986, CBO's role was limited to providing advisory sequestration reports. (*See* Baseline, Scorekeeping, Sequestration. *See also* Congressional Support Agencies.)

Congressional Directory The official who's who of Congress, usually published during the first session of a two-year Congress. Among other features, it contains brief biographies of all members; their committee assignments, office locations and telephone numbers; seniority in their chambers; membership and staff of all committees, subcommittees, joint committees, and congressional commissions and boards; names of all congressional officials and many of their staff; names of all federal judges, top officials in the executive agencies and the District of Columbia government;

diplomatic representatives in the United States; and members of the congressional media galleries. The *Directory* has been published by Congress continuously since 1821.

Congressional Disapproval (*See* Legislative Veto. *See also* Committee Veto.)

Congressional District The geographical area represented by a single member of the House of Representatives. For states with only one representative, the entire state is a congressional district. As of 1993, seven states had only one representative each: Alaska, Delaware, Montana, North Dakota, South Dakota, Vermont, and Wyoming. (*See also* Apportionment, At-Large, Locality Rule, Redistricting.)

Congressional Record The daily, printed, and substantially verbatim account of proceedings in both the House and Senate chambers. Extraneous materials submitted by members appear in a section titled "Extensions of Remarks." A "Daily Digest" appendix contains highlights of the day's floor and committee action plus a list of committee meetings and floor agendas for the next day's session.

Although the official reporters of each house take down every word spoken during the proceedings, members are permitted to edit and "revise and extend" their remarks before they are printed. In the Senate section, all speeches, articles, and other material submitted by senators but not actually spoken or read on the floor are set off by large black dots, called bullets. However, bullets do not appear when a senator reads part of a speech and inserts the rest. In the House section, undelivered speeches and materials are printed in a distinctive typeface. The term "permanent *Record*" refers to the bound volumes of the daily *Records* of an entire session of Congress. (*See* Daily Digest, Extensions of Remarks, Revise and Extend

One's Remarks, Session. *See also* Correction of Remarks, Strike from the *Record*.)

Congressional Research Service (CRS) A department of the Library of Congress whose staff provide nonpartisan, objective analyses and information on virtually any subject to committees, members, and staff of Congress. Established in 1917 as the Legislative Reference Service, it is the oldest congressional support agency. The Legislative Reorganization Act of 1970 gave it additional research functions and its current name. (*See* Congressional Support Agencies.)

Congressional Response to Subpoenas A House rule permits its members, officers, and employees to comply with subpoenas served on them in connection with their official functions without receiving permission from the House. However, the individual served must notify the Speaker, who must then inform the House. Before the House adopted this automatic compliance system in 1977, it had to adopt a resolution in each case granting the subpoenaed individual authority to respond. This is still the situation in the Senate. (*See also* Subpoena Power.)

Congressional Support Agencies A term often applied to four agencies in the legislative branch that provide nonpartisan information and analysis to committees and members of Congress: the Congressional Budget Office, the Congressional Research Service of the Library of Congress, the General Accounting Office, and the Office of Technology Assessment. (*See* individual agencies by name.)

Congressional Terms of Office A term normally begins on January 3 of the year following a general election and runs two years for representatives and six years for senators.

A representative chosen in a special election to fill a vacancy is sworn in for the remainder of his predecessor's term. An individual appointed to fill a Senate vacancy usually serves until the next general election or until the end of the predecessor's term, whichever comes first. Some states, however, require their governors to call a special election to fill a Senate vacancy shortly after an appointment has been made.

Congressional Veto (*See* Legislative Veto.)

Consent Calendar A House calendar, and the procedures associated with it, used to expedite passage of non-controversial legislation. Any member can have a measure on the House or union calendar placed on the consent calendar. Measures on the calendar for at least three legislative days are called for consideration on the first and third Mondays of each month at the beginning of the day's floor session.

The first time a measure is called, a single objection blocks its consideration. If three members object when the measure is called again on a subsequent consent calendar day, it is stricken from that calendar but remains available for action on its original calendar. If no member objects to a measure on its first call or fewer than three object on its second call, it is immediately considered and usually passed with little or no debate. Technically, measures called up from the consent calendar are supposed to be considered in the House as in Committee of the Whole. But any measure may be removed from the calendar by unanimous consent and returned to its original calendar.

Official objectors from both parties screen the calendar to forestall consideration of legislation on which there is any controversy or that does not meet certain other criteria. Often a member asks unanimous consent to pass over a calendar measure without prejudice. This prevents its immediate consideration but does not change the measure's status on the calendar since no objection was made. (*See* House as in Committee of the Whole, House Calendar, Objection, Official

Objectors, Unanimous Consent, Union Calendar. *See also* Special Order of Business.)

Consider To take up a measure, motion, or matter for the purpose of acting on it. In most cases, the Senate uses a debatable motion to proceed to consider a bill or resolution and a nondebatable motion to proceed to the consideration of executive business.

The House regards the term as a question rather than as a motion. When a measure or motion is brought up in the House, a member may usually demand that the question of consideration be put and decided by majority vote. That question has the negative purpose of preventing rather than furthering consideration; it is a method by which the House may protect itself from business it does not want to consider. However, it may not be used against motions relating to the order of business or against the consideration of a special rule from the Committee on Rules. In practice, the question of consideration is rarely raised. (*See* Executive Business, Motion, Nondebatable Motions, Order of Business (House), Put the Question, Rule.)

Constitutional Privilege (*See* Immunity, Privilege.)

Constitutional Rules Constitutional provisions that prescribe procedures for Congress. In addition to certain types of votes required in particular situations, they include: (1) the House chooses its Speaker, the Senate its president pro tempore, and both houses their officers; (2) each house requires a majority quorum to conduct business; (3) less than a majority may adjourn from day to day and compel the attendance of absent members; (4) neither house may adjourn for more than three days without the consent of the other; (5) each house must keep a journal; (6) the yeas and nays are ordered when supported by one-fifth of the members present; (7) all revenue-raising bills must originate in the House, but the Senate may propose amendments to them; (8) the procedure in the House for electing a president; (9) the procedure in the Senate for electing a vice president; (10) the procedure for filling a vacancy in the office of vice president; (11) the procedure for overriding a presidential veto. (*See* Adjourn, Constitutional Votes, *Journal*, Officers of Congress, Override a Veto, Quorum, Yeas and Nays. *See also* Arrest of Absent Members.)

Constitutional Votes Constitutional provisions that require certain votes or voting methods in specific situations. They include: (1) the yeas and nays at the desire of one-fifth of the members present; (2) a two-thirds vote by the yeas and nays to override a veto; (3) a two-thirds vote by one house to expel one of its members and by both houses to propose a constitutional amendment; (4) a two-thirds vote of senators present to convict one of its members of impeachment charges and to consent to ratification of treaties; (5) a two-thirds vote in each house to remove political disabilities from persons who have engaged in insurrection or rebellion or given aid or comfort to the enemies of the United States; (6) a majority vote in each house to fill a vacancy in the office of vice president; (7) a majority vote of all states to elect a president in the House of Representatives when no candidate receives a majority of the electoral votes; (8) a majority vote of all senators when the Senate elects a vice president under the same circumstances; (9) the casting vote of the vice president in case of tie votes in the Senate. (*See* Casting Vote, Expulsion, Impeachment, Override a Veto, Treaty, Yeas and Nays.)

Constitutionality The presiding officer in either house does not rule on questions or points of order concerning the constitutionality of a measure, amendment, or other matter. In the House, the Speaker declines to answer such questions. Under the Senate's precedents, its presiding officer must submit such questions to the Senate for its decision.

Contempt of Congress Willful obstruction of the proper functions of Congress. Most frequently, it is a refusal to obey a subpoena to appear and testify before a committee or to produce documents demanded by it. Such obstruction is a misdemeanor and persons cited for contempt are subject to prosecution in federal courts. A house cites an individual for contempt by agreeing to a privileged resolution to that effect reported by a committee. The presiding officer then refers the matter to a U.S. attorney for prosecution. (*See also* Executive Privilege, Investigative Power, Privilege, Subpoena Power.)

Contingency Appropriation An appropriation that becomes available only if some specified future action occurs. Such an action might be submission of a report by a federal official, settlement of litigation, enactment of an authorization, or enactment of some other specified law. Contingency appropriations in general appropriation bills are not in order in either house if points of order are raised against them, although their frequency has increased in recent years in contentious policy areas. (*See* Appropriation, General Appropriation Bill, Point of Order. *See also* Authorization-Appropriation Process, Legislation on an Appropriation Bill.)

Contingent Fund A sum of money appropriated annually to each house for expenditures that are not separately authorized and appropriated. Each house uses its fund for a variety of miscellaneous purposes, including payment of certain allowances, housekeeping actions, and the expenses of select and special committees. The fund also pays the expenses of standing committees for investigations, for all or some of their staff salaries, and for other necessary expenditures.

Monies in the fund are made available for spending by the adoption of resolutions reported by the

Rules and Administration Committee in the Senate and the House Administration Committee in the House. (*See* Appropriation, Authorization, Members' Allowances, Resolution, Select *or* Special Committee, Standing Committee, Temporary Staff. *See also* Investigative Power, Reprogramming.)

Contingent Liability A conditional commitment by the government, such as a loan guarantee, price guarantee, or bank deposit insurance, that may become an actual liability in the future and require the expenditure of federal monies because of an event beyond the government's control, such as a bank failure. (*See* Loan Guarantee.)

Continuing Appropriations (*See* Continuing Resolution.)

Continuing Body A characterization of the Senate on the theory that it continues from Congress to Congress and has existed continuously since it first convened in 1789. The rationale for the theory is that under the system of staggered six-year terms for senators, the terms of only about one-third of them expire after each Congress and, therefore, a quorum of the Senate is always in office. Consequently, the Senate, unlike the House, does not have to adopt its rules at the beginning of each Congress because those rules continue from one Congress to the next. This makes it extremely difficult for the Senate to change its rules against the opposition of a determined minority because those rules require a two-thirds vote of the senators present and voting to invoke cloture on a proposed rules change. (*See* Cloture, Quorum, Rule. *See also* Filibuster, Unlimited Debate.)

Continuing Business By rule or practice, all measures introduced in a two-year Congress and still awaiting final action at the end of an annual or special session of that Congress continue to be available for action during any subsequent session of that Congress. Measures that have not been passed by the end of a Congress die but may be reintroduced in the next Congress.

The Senate rule defines it as "legislative business ... which remained undetermined at the close of the next preceding session of that Congress." The House rule once contained approximately the same language, but it was inadvertently deleted in 1890. Although the rule's title is still "Unfinished Business of the Session," its text only requires the resumption of "business before committees." Nevertheless, the House continues the practice as if it is a rule, a not infrequent congressional eccentricity. (*See* Business, Congress, Session. *See also* Adjournment Sine Die.)

Continuing Resolution (CR) A joint resolution that provides funds to continue the operation of federal agencies and programs at the beginning of a new fiscal year if their annual appropriation bills have not yet been enacted; also called continuing appropriations. Enacted shortly before or after the new fiscal year begins, the first continuing resolution usually makes funds available for a specified period; additional resolutions are often needed after the first expires.

Some CRs have provided appropriations for an entire fiscal year. Continuing resolutions for specific periods customarily fix a rate at which agencies may incur obligations based either on the prior year's appropriations, the president's budget request, or the amount in the agency's regular annual appropriation bill that has already been passed by one or both houses. In the House, CRs are privileged after September 15. (*See* Appropriation, Fiscal Year, General Appropriation Bill, Joint Resolution, Obligation, Privilege. *See* also Funding Gap.)

Contract Authority Statutory authority permitting an agency to enter into contracts or incur other obligations even though it has not received an appropriation to pay for them. Congress must eventually fund them because the government is legally liable for such payments. The Congressional Budget Act of 1974 requires that new contract authority may not be used unless provided for in advance by an appropriation act, but it permits a few exceptions. (*See* Backdoor Spending Authority, Obligation.)

Controllable Expenditures Federal spending that is permitted but not mandated by existing authorization law and therefore may be adjusted by congressional action in appropriation bills. (*See* Appropriation. *See also* Authorization-Appropriation Process, Discretionary Appropriations, Uncontrollable Expenditures.)

Cordon Rule A Senate rule requiring that a committee report on a bill or joint resolution contain the text of any statutory provision it proposes to repeal and also a comparative print showing the changes in existing law that would be made by the language proposed by the committee, using typographical devices such as stricken-through type or italics. The rule may be waived by a statement in the report that such a waiver is necessary to expedite the business of the Senate. Named after its sponsor, Sen. Guy Cordon (R-Ore.) the rule is analogous to the Ramseyer Rule in the House. (*See* Committee Report on a Measure, Ramseyer Rule.)

Correction of Remarks Members are permitted to correct the transcripts of their remarks spoken on the floor or during committee meetings before they are printed. Once floor remarks have been published in the daily edition of the *Congressional Record,* they may be corrected in the permanent *Record* by unanimous consent.

If a senator cannot obtain such consent, he may offer a debatable motion to make the correction. In the House, a member denied unanimous consent to correct an allegedly inaccurate portion of the printed debate may offer a resolution making that assertion and directing that it be corrected. The resolution presents a question of the privileges of the House and therefore must be considered. (*See Congressional Record*, Questions of Privilege, Unanimous Consent.)

Correcting Recorded Votes The rules of both houses prohibit members from changing their votes after a vote result has been announced. Nevertheless, the Senate permits its members to withdraw or change their votes, by unanimous consent, immediately after the announcement. In rare instances, senators have been granted unanimous consent to change their votes several days or weeks after the announcement.

Votes tallied by the electronic voting system in the House may not be changed. But when a vote actually given is not recorded during an oral call of the roll, a member may demand a correction as a matter of right. On all other alleged errors in a recorded vote, the Speaker determines whether the circumstances justify a change. Occasionally, members merely announce that they were incorrectly recorded; announcements can occur hours, days, or even months after the vote and appear in the *Congressional Record*. (*See* Call of the Roll, Electronic Voting.)

Cosponsor A member who has joined one or more other members to sponsor a measure. (*See* Bills and Resolutions Introduced.)

Cost Estimates Estimates that provide data used in determining whether the budget resolution's requirements, the caps on discretionary spending categories, the rules on deficit neutrality, or the statutory limits on annual deficits have been violated. In both houses, a committee's report on a measure must include an estimate of its cost "in the fiscal year in which it is reported and in each of the five fiscal years following" or for the authorized duration of any program in the measure, if less than five years. These estimates are usually provided by the Congressional Budget Office. If appropriate, the report must also present five-year estimates of revenue changes, prepared by the Joint Committee on Taxation.

Both houses permit points of order to prevent floor consideration of measures if the committee reports on them do not contain such estimates. However, the Senate rule waives the point of order if the report declares that compliance is impracticable. In addition, the Office of Management and Budget must provide cost estimates of budgetary legislation within five days of its enactment to assist Congress in complying with discretionary spending limits and PAYGO requirements. (*See* Budget Resolution, Congressional Budget Office, Deficit Neutrality, Discretionary Appropriations, Fiscal Year, Maximum Deficit Amounts, Pay-As-You-Go, Point of Order, Report. *See also* Budget Process.)

Counting a Quorum In the House, the Speaker and the chairman of the Committee of the Whole are authorized to count members to determine whether a quorum is present. They count all members in sight in the chamber and in the cloakrooms, and their count may not be appealed. Normally, the Senate does not permit a count to determine whether a quorum is present. Under cloture, however, the presiding officer may count senators to reaffirm that a quorum is still present so that he may rule out a dilatory request for a quorum call. (*See* Appeal, Cloakrooms, Cloture, Dilatory Tactics, Presiding Officer, Quorum.)

Courtesy Calls The custom under which a president's nominee for an office visits individual senators to let them become personally acquainted with the nominee before the Senate takes up the nomination. The nominee usually visits about a dozen senators, most of them members of the committee that will consider the nomination, but some appointees call upon many more. It is estimated that Justice Clarence Thomas established a new record in 1991 when he met with fifty-nine senators. Some 2,500 appointees initiate senatorial visits during a president's four-year term. (*See* Nominations.)

Courtesy of the Senate (*See* Senatorial Courtesy.)

CR (*See* Continuing Resolution.)

Credit Authority Authority granted to an agency to incur direct loan obligations or to make loan guarantee commitments. The Congressional Budget Act of 1974 bans congressional consideration of credit authority legislation unless the extent of that authority is made subject to provisions in appropriation acts. (*See* Direct Loan, Loan Guarantee, Obligation. *See also* Credit Budget, Federal Credit Reform Act of 1990.)

Credit Budget The levels of new federal direct loan obligations and new loan guarantee commitments that appear in a budget resolution. They are the basis for limitations on direct and guaranteed loans in appropriations acts. Procedures established in the Federal Credit Reform Act of 1990 have largely superseded the credit budget. (*See* Budget Resolution, Direct Loan, Federal Credit Reform Act of 1990, Loan Guarantee.)

Credit Subsidy Cost The estimated long-term cost of a direct loan or loan guarantee to the federal government. The cost is calculated on the basis of the net present value of the cash flows of the loan or guarantee, excluding administrative costs and any incidental effects on governmental receipts or outlays. (*See* Budget Receipts, Direct Loan, Loan Guarantee, Outlays. *See also* Federal Credit Reform Act of 1990.)

Crosswalk (*See* Budget Crosswalk.)

CRS (*See* Congressional Research Service.)

C-SPAN Cable-Satellite Public Affairs Network, which provides live, gavel-to-gavel coverage of Senate floor proceedings on one cable television channel and coverage of House floor proceedings on another channel. C-SPAN also televises important committee hearings in both Houses. Each house also transmits its televised proceedings directly to congressional offices. (*See also* Televised Proceedings.)

Current Services Estimates Executive branch estimates of the anticipated costs of federal programs and operations for the next and future fiscal years at existing levels of service and assuming no new initiatives or changes in existing law. The president submits these estimates to Congress with his annual budget and includes an explanation of the underlying economic and policy assumptions on which they are based, such as anticipated rates of inflation, real economic growth, and unemployment, plus program caseloads and pay increases. (*See* Budget.)

Custody of the Papers Possession of an engrossed measure and certain related basic documents that the two houses produce as they try to resolve their differences over the measure. Neither house may amend the measure, act on amendments of the other house, request a conference, or reply to such a request unless it has custody of those papers. When a chamber agrees to the other's request for a conference, for example, it returns the papers to the other house with its reply.

Consequently, the house that requested the conference brings the papers to the conference table. By custom, the house that agreed to the request for a conference carries the papers out of it and therefore votes first on the conference report. Since that transfer is not required by any rule, the conferees sometimes let the requesting house take the papers in the hope that its vote may influence the other chamber's action on the report. (*See* Conferees, Conference, Conference Report, Engrossed Bill, Papers, Request a Conference.)

D

Daily Digest A section of the *Congressional Record* summarizing the day's floor and committee actions in each house, with page references to the verbatim accounts of floor actions. It also lists the measures scheduled for action during each house's next meeting and the announcements of upcoming committee meetings. The Digest appears at the back of each daily *Record*. Its pages are separately numbered and preceded by the letter *D*. In the first bound *Congressional Record*, all the Daily Digests for a session are printed in a separate volume rather than with each day's floor proceedings. (*See Congressional Record.*)

Dance of the Swans and the Ducks A whimsical description of the gestures some members use in connection with a request for a recorded vote, especially in the House. When a member wants his colleagues to stand in support of the request, he moves his hands and arms in a "gentle upward motion resembling the beginning flight of a graceful swan." When he wants his colleagues to remain seated in order to avoid such a vote, he moves his hands and arms "in a vigorous downward motion resembling a diving duck." The term was coined and described by Hyde Murray, former counsel to the House Republican leader. (*See* Recorded Vote.)

Day (*See* Legislative Day.)

Dead Pair Synonym for a specific pair. (*See* Pairing, Specific Pair.)

Dead Quorum (*See* Suggest the Absence of a Quorum.)

Dean Within a state's delegation in the House of Representatives, the member with the longest continuous service.

Dean of the House (*See* Father of the House.)

Dear Colleague Letter A letter signed by one or several members of a house urging their colleagues to support, cosponsor, or oppose a bill or some other matter. It begins "Dear Colleague," "Dear Democratic Colleague," or "Dear Republican Colleague" and is often mass produced and sent to every member of that chamber.

Debate In congressional parlance, speeches delivered during consideration of a measure, motion, or other matter, as distinguished from speeches in other parliamentary situations, such as one-minute and special order speeches when no business is pending.

Virtually all debate in the House of Representatives is under some kind of time limitation. In theory, there are no limitations for debate on points of order and during a reservation of an objection, but the Speaker can cut off the former at any time and any member may cut off the latter by demanding the regular order. Most debate in the Senate is unlimited; that is, a senator, once recognized, may speak for as long as he chooses, unless the Senate invokes cloture. (*See* Business, Cloture, One-Minute Speeches, Point of Order, Regular Order, Reserving the Right to Object, Special Order Speech, Time Limits on Debate, Unlimited Debate. *See also* Anthony Rule, Equally Divided, Five-Minute Rule, Forty-Minute Debate, General Debate, Germane, Hour Rule, Nondebatable Motions, Ten-Minute Debate, Twenty-Minute Debate, Two-Hour Debate, Unanimous Consent Agreements.)

Debate-Ending Motion A motion whose adoption normally ends discussion on a pending matter immediately. Such a motion is not debatable and is adopted by majority vote because its purpose is to expedite the proceedings.

The House has two debate-ending motions: the previous question, permitted when the House is sitting in its legislative capacity as the House of Representatives; and a motion to close debate in the Committee of the Whole. The previous question immediately shuts off debate only if some debate has already occurred; if not, forty minutes of debate are permitted. Another exception is allowed after the Committee of the Whole has voted to close debate; amendments printed in the *Congressional Record* may be debated for ten minutes each.

A third debate-ending motion—to lay on the table—is available in both houses, but not in Committee of the Whole. However, it ends debate by killing the proposal to which it is applied and, in the House, the underlying measure.

Except for the motion to lay on the table, the Senate, strictly speaking, permits no debate-ending motions; cloture sets a time limit on further consideration rather than ending debate immediately. (*See* Cloture, Committee of the Whole, *Congressional Record*, House Sitting as the House, Lay on the Table, Motion, Previous Question, Printed Amendment.)

Debt Limit The maximum amount of outstanding federal public debt permitted by law. The limit (or ceiling) covers virtually all debt incurred by the government except agency debt. Each congressional budget resolution sets forth the new debt limit that may be required under its provisions. (*See* Agency Debt, Budget Resolution, Federal Debt. *See also* Deficit, Gephardt Rule.)

Decorum Orderly and courteous behavior and speech in a parliamentary body. As enforced in the U.S. Congress, orderly procedure requires that only one member may speak at a time, the member may speak only when recognized, and that the member may not be interrupted without his consent unless a rule or practice of the chamber has been violated.

Both houses of Congress frown on loud conversations, hissing, jeering, and similar disruptive behavior while a member is speaking. Both houses permit points of order against such behavior and authorize their presiding officers to call their chambers and individual members to order. In addition, a House rule prohibits members from passing between the chair and a member who is speaking, and it is also considered impolite to walk near the member who is speaking.

Both houses also attempt to enforce civility in debate. Inevitably, Congress often deals with controversial and emotional issues that strain members' tempers and inflame their passions. To minimize personal confrontations that might disrupt their proceedings, both houses require members to address the chair, and only the chair, when they are recognized. They may not speak directly to other members; may refer to them only in the third person; and are prohibited from engaging in personalities or imputing unworthy motives or conduct to other members, the other house, or its members. Additionally, a Senate rule forbids offensive remarks about any state.

Smoking is not permitted on the floor of either house. On occasion, the Speaker has asked members to leave the floor and return only when properly dressed. Members may not wear hats in their chambers. (*See* Body, Call to Order, Chair, Debate, Point of Order, Recognition. *See also* Comity, Regular Order, Taking Down the Words.)

Defense Discretionary Appropriations Appropriations that are not mandated by law, and therefore are made available in appropriation bills in such amounts as

Congress chooses, primarily for the military activities of the Defense Department. They also include the discretionary appropriations for defense-related functions of other agencies, especially the Energy Department's nuclear weapons programs. The Budget Enforcement Act of 1990 established dollar limits on this category of appropriations for fiscal years 1991, 1992, and 1993. If Congress breaches the limit, the excess amounts are subject to presidential sequestration. (*See* Appropriation, Discretionary Appropriations, Sequestration. *See also* Breach, Cap, Firewall.)

Deferral An impoundment of funds for a specific period of time that may not extend beyond the fiscal year in which it is proposed. Under the Impoundment Control Act of 1974, the president must notify Congress that he is deferring the spending or obligation of funds provided by law for a project or activity. Congress can disapprove the deferral by legislation.

The president may defer funds to provide for contingencies when savings have been made through greater operational efficiency or for similar reasons, but not because of opposition to a program, or to reduce federal spending, or for any other policy reason. The comptroller general of the United States reviews all deferrals and advises Congress about their legality and possible effects. (*See* Congressional Budget and Impoundment Control Act of 1974, Fiscal Year, Impoundment. *See also* General Accounting Office, Recission.)

Deficit The amount by which the government's outlays exceed its budget receipts for a given fiscal year. Both the president's budget and the annual congressional budget resolution provide estimates of the deficit or surplus for the upcoming and several future fiscal years. (*See* Budget, Budget Receipts, Budget Resolution, Fiscal Year, Outlays, Surplus. *See also* Balanced Budget, Debt Limit, Maximum Deficit Amounts.)

Deficit Neutrality A requirement that certain proposals to increase spending or reduce revenues be offset by at least equivalent reductions in other spending or increases in other revenue sources so that they do not increase the deficit. The Congressional Budget Act of 1974 applies the requirement to amendments offered to a reconciliation bill. Under the Pay-As-You-Go procedures of the Budget Enforcement Act of 1990, legislation that increases entitlement spending or reduces revenues must be offset by reductions in other entitlements or increases in other revenue sources. (*See* Entitlement Program, Pay-As-You-Go, Reconciliation.)

Deficit Targets (*See* Maximum Deficit Amounts.)

Degrees of Amendment Designations that indicate the relationships of amendments to the text of a measure and to each other. In general, an amendment offered directly to the text of a measure is an amendment in the first degree, and an amendment to that amendment is an amendment in the second degree. Both houses normally prohibit amendments in the third degree—that is, an amendment to an amendment to an amendment.

The two houses differ, however, on the degree of a substitute offered for a pending first degree amendment. In the Senate, it is a second degree amendment; the House treats it as equivalent to a first degree amendment and therefore amendable to another degree. (*See* Amendment, Pending Amendment(s), Substitute. *See also* Amendment in the Nature of a Substitute, Amendment Tree, Amendments Between the Houses, Voting Order on Amendments.)

Delegate A nonvoting member of the House of Representatives elected to a two-year term from the District of Columbia, the territory of Guam, the territory of the Virgin Islands, or the territory of American Samoa. By law, delegates may not vote in the full House, but they may participate in debate, offer motions (except to reconsider), and serve and vote on standing and select committees. Under a rule adopted in 1993, they may also vote in Committee of the Whole. However, whenever a recorded vote in Committee of the Whole "has been decided by a margin within which [the delegates' votes] have been decisive," the committee must automatically rise and the House must immediately vote on that issue without the delegates' votes. The House then resolves itself back into the Committee of the Whole.

By rule, the District of Columbia delegate must be elected to the District of Columbia Committee but may also serve on other committees. On their committees, delegates possess the same powers and privileges as other members, and the Speaker may appoint them to appropriate conference committees and select committees. Under other 1993 rules changes, the Speaker may appoint them to any conference committee and to serve as chairman of the Committee of the Whole. (*See* Committee of the Whole, Conference Committee, Reconsider a Vote, Recorded Vote, Select *or* Special Committee. *See also* Committee Assignments, Resident Commissioner from Puerto Rico.)

Denounce A formal action that condemns a member for misbehavior; considered by some experts to be equivalent to censure. The Senate used it against Sen. Herman Talmadge (D-Ga.) in 1979 and against Sen. David Durenberger (R-Minn.) in 1990. (*See* Censure. *See also* Ethics Rules, Expulsion, Fining a Member, Reprimand, Seniority Loss.)

Deputy President Pro Tempore A position established in 1977 for a sitting senator who is a former president or vice president of the United States. It was originally created for former vice president Hubert H. Humphrey. Ten years later the Senate approved a resolution permitting it to designate any other senator to that position. (*See* President Pro Tempore.)

Deschler's Precedents Short title for *Deschler's Precedents of the U.S. House of Representatives,* a multivolume compilation and explanation of House precedents and practices since 1936. Begun under the direction of Lewis Deschler, parliamentarian of the House from 1928 to 1974, the first volume was published in 1976. Subsequent volumes have been prepared under the supervision of Deschler's successor, Wm. Holmes Brown. As of 1993, ten volumes had been published. (*See* Precedent. *See also Hinds' and Cannon's Precedents of the House of Representatives, Riddick's Senate Procedure.*)

Desk (1) The presiding officer's desk in each chamber. In parliamentary parlance, a member may send an amendment or a written motion to "the desk," or a measure may be "held at the desk."

(2) A senator's assigned desk and seat on the Senate floor. Traditionally, the leaders of each party sit in the first row at the first desk on their party's side of the center aisle. Many desks have been assigned to senators from the same state since the early Congresses. (*See also* Aisle, Chamber, Well.)

Dilatory Tactics Procedural actions intended to delay or prevent action by a house or a committee. They include, among others, offering numerous motions, demanding quorum calls and recorded votes at every opportunity, making numerous points of order and parliamentary inquiries, and speaking as long as the applicable rules permit.

The Senate's rules permit a battery of dilatory tactics, especially lengthy speeches, except under cloture. In the House, possible dilatory tactics are more limited. Speeches are always subject to time limits and debate-ending motions. Moreover, a House rule instructs the Speaker not to entertain dilatory motions and lets the Speaker decide whether a motion is dilatory. However, the Speaker may not override the constitutional right of a member to demand the yeas and nays, and in practice usually waits for a point of order before exercising that authority. (*See* Cloture, Debate-Ending Motion, Motion, Parliamentary Inquiry, Point of Order, Quorum Call, Recorded Vote, Unlimited Debate, Yeas and Nays. *See also* Counting a Quorum, Filibuster.)

Dire Emergency Appropriation A title sometimes given to a supplemental appropriation bill. The title has no legal, parliamentary, or procedural significance. (*See* Emergency Appropriation, Supplemental Appropriation Bill.)

Direct Loan Defined by the Budget Enforcement Act of 1990 as a disbursement of funds by the government to a nonfederal borrower under a contract that requires the repayment of such funds with or without interest. It may also be a loan made by another lender in which the government participates or that it purchases. The definition excludes federally guaranteed loans acquired in satisfaction of default claims and the price support loans of the Commodity Credit Corporation. (*See also* Credit Authority, Federal Credit Reform Act of 1990.)

Direct Spending Under the Budget Enforcement Act of 1990, direct spending consists of budget authority and resulting outlays provided in laws other than appropriation acts; entitlement authority including appropriated entitlements; and the Food Stamp Program. (*See* Appropriated Entitlement, Budget Authority, Entitlement Program, Outlays. *See also* Discretionary Appropriations.)

Director of Non-Legislative and Financial Services A position created in 1992 to manage most of the financial and general administrative functions of the House of Representatives formerly under the jurisdiction of the clerk, doorkeeper, sergeant at arms, and postmaster of the House. The director is appointed jointly by the

Speaker, majority leader, and minority leader and is required to have extensive managerial and financial experience. The director is subject to the policy direction and oversight of the House Administration Committee, receives the same basic pay as the elected officers of the House, and may be removed by the House or the Speaker. (*See* Clerk of the House, Doorkeeper of the House, Officers of Congress, Sergeant at Arms.)

Disagree To reject an amendment of the other house. When a house disagrees, it may also request a conference. (*See* Amendments Between the Houses, Conference. *See also* Adhere, Concur, Insist, Recede, Stage of Disagreement.)

Discharge a Committee Remove a measure from a committee to which it has been referred in order to make it available for floor consideration. Noncontroversial measures are often discharged by unanimous consent. However, because congressional committees have no obligation to report measures referred to them, each house has procedures to extract controversial measures from recalcitrant committees. In addition, some statutes provide special discharge procedures for specific measures, such as legislative veto resolutions and rescission bills.

Six discharge procedures are available in the House of Representatives: (1) the discharge rule when used to remove a measure directly from the committee of jurisdiction; (2) a special rule reported by the Rules Committee; (3) the discharge rule applied to a special rule from the Rules Committee; (4) suspension of the rules; (5) a reporting deadline mandated by the Speaker on a measure referred to more than one committee; and (6) privileged motions to discharge vetoed bills and resolutions of inquiry.

The Senate uses a motion to discharge, which is usually converted into a discharge resolution. If any senator objects to a resolution's immediate consideration, it goes through a procedure called "over under the rule" before it may be considered. Also, a motion for a multiple or sequential referral of a measure may include reporting deadlines for the committees involved and provisions that discharge the committees if they do not meet the deadlines. (*See* Bills and Resolutions Referred, Discharge Rule, Extraction Power, Floor, Legislative Veto, Multiple and Sequential Referrals, Objection, Over Under the Rule, Privilege, Rescission, Resolution of Inquiry, Statutory Rules, Suspension of the Rules (House), Suspension of the Rules (Senate), Unanimous Consent, Veto.)

Discharge Calendar In the House of Representatives, short title for its Calendar of Motions to Discharge Committees. (*See* Discharge Rule.)

Discharge Motion (*See* Discharge a Committee, Discharge Rule.)

Discharge of Conferees A House rule permits a motion to void the appointment of its conferees and thereby dissolve a conference committee. If House conferees have not reported within twenty calendar days after their appointment, a motion to discharge them is of the highest privilege. However, under a rule adopted in 1993, that motion must lay over one calendar day before it is considered.

A motion to discharge conferees is also privileged during the last six days of a congressional session if the conferees have not reported within thirty-six hours after their appointment. The dissolution of a conference does not necessarily kill the measure because other steps to resolve differences between the houses are still available. In any case, the House rarely discharges its conferees unless they request it. (*See* Conferees, Conference, Privilege. *See also* Amendments Between the Houses.)

Discharge Petition (*See* Discharge Rule.)

Discharge Resolution In the Senate, a resolution to discharge a measure from a committee. (*See* Discharge a Committee.)

Discharge Rule A House rule that provides a lengthy, multistage procedure for removing a measure from a committee. Thirty days after a public bill or resolution has been referred to a committee, any member may file a discharge motion on the measure. A clerk then prepares a discharge petition for members' signatures. If 218 members sign the petition, the motion is placed on the Calendar of Motions to Discharge Committees. After the motion has been on the calendar at least seven days, any member may call it up on the second or fourth Monday of a month. Debate on the discharge motion is limited to twenty minutes, equally divided between proponents and opponents. If the House agrees to the motion, any member who signed the petition may offer a privileged nondebatable motion to consider the discharged measure. Finally, if the House agrees to that motion, it takes up the measure under its general rules.

For various reasons, it is usually easier to deal with a discharged measure under the provisions of a special rule than under the general rules of the House. Therefore, if a committee has not reported a measure within thirty days after receiving it, a member may introduce a rule that discharges the measure and establishes conditions for its consideration. If the Rules Committee has not reported the rule within seven days, a member may file a discharge motion against it. By the same method, members also may discharge a special rule on a measure reported by the committee of jurisdiction but not yet reported by the Rules Committee. (*See* Privilege, Public Bill, Rule. *See also* Discharge a Committee, Extraction Power.)

Discretionary Appropriations Appropriations not mandated by existing law and therefore made available annually in appropriation bills in such amounts as Congress chooses. The Budget Enforcement Act of 1990 defines discretionary appropriations as budget authority provided in annual appropriation acts, and the outlays derived from that authority, but it excludes appropriations for entitlements.

For fiscal years 1991, 1992, and 1993, the act divides discretionary programs among three categories—defense, international affairs, and domestic—and sets dollar spending limits (also called caps) on each. For fiscal years 1994 and 1995, the act sets limits on total discretionary spending. Excess amounts are subject to presidential sequestration if Congress fails to enforce the limits. (*See* Appropriation, Budget Authority, Defense Discretionary Appropriations, Domestic Discretionary Appropriations, Entitlement Program, International Discretionary Appropriations, Outlays, Sequestration. *See also* Firewall, General Appropriation Bill.)

Discretionary Recognition The authority of a presiding officer to deny a member's request to speak. In the House of Representatives, the presiding officer has wide discretion in recognition. In the Senate, there is very little discretion. (*See* Recognition.)

Discretionary Spending Categories (*See* Discretionary Appropriations.)

Disorderly Words Words or expressions that violate the rules or practices of a house. A member who utters such words during floor proceedings may be called to order and required to sit down. (*See* Call to Order. *See also* Comity, Decorum, Taking Down the Words.)

District (*See* Congressional District. *See also* District Day.)

District Day In the House, one of two days in each month—the second and fourth Mondays—on which business reported and called up by the District of Columbia Committee is privileged for floor consideration.

By unanimous consent, District measures are usually considered under a procedure called "the House as in Committee of the Whole." However, a motion may be offered to consider a District measure on the union calendar in the Committee of the Whole.

If the House does not complete action on a District measure on its privileged day, it may not be considered again until the next District Day unless the previous question has been ordered on it.

Although the District Committee's claim to recognition is privileged on District Day, other business of a higher privilege, such as conference reports, may displace it. (*See* Committee of the Whole, House as in Committee of the Whole, Privilege, Privileged Business, Unanimous Consent. *See also* Special Order of Business.)

District Office Representatives maintain one or more offices in their districts for the purpose of assisting constituents. The costs of maintaining these offices are paid from members' allowances. A senator can use the official expense allowance to rent offices in the home state subject to a funding formula based on the state's population, among other factors. (*See* Congressional District, Members' Allowances.)

District Work Period The House term for a scheduled congressional recess during which members may visit their districts and conduct constituency business. (*See* also Nonlegislative Period, Recess.)

Division of a Question for Voting The division of an amendment or other motion into two or more parts so that each may be voted on separately. A question must be divided at the demand of any member, but only if each part presents a separate proposition, grammatically and substantively, so that if any part is rejected, the other parts can logically stand alone. An amendment to strike out and insert is not divisible, but several motions on amendments between the houses are. (*See* Amendment, Amendments Between the Houses, Motion, Strike Out and Insert.)

Division of Bills for Referral A 1975 House rule permits the Speaker to divide any measure or matter into two or more parts and refer each to a different committee if those parts deal with different subjects that come under the jurisdictions of those committees. Also called a split referral. (*See* Bills and Resolutions Referred. *See also* Multiple and Sequential Referrals.)

Division Vote A vote in which the chair first counts those in favor of a proposition and then those opposed to it, with no record made of how each member votes. In the Senate, the chair may count raised hands or ask senators to stand, whereas the House requires members to stand; hence, often called a standing vote. Committees in both houses ordinarily use a show of hands.

A division usually occurs after a voice vote and may be demanded by any member or ordered by the chair if there is any doubt about the outcome of the voice vote. The demand for a division can also come before a voice vote. In the Senate, the demand must come before the result of a voice vote is announced. It may be made after a voice vote announcement in the House, but only if no intervening business has transpired and only if the member was standing and seeking recognition at the time of the announcement. A demand for the yeas and nays or, in the House, for a recorded vote, takes precedence over a division vote. (*See* Precedence, Recorded Vote, Voice Vote, Yeas and Nays. *See also* Automatic Roll Call, Voting.)

Domestic Discretionary Appropriations Appropriations for domestic programs that are not mandated in entitlement laws and that are therefore made available in such amounts as Congress chooses. Among others, these programs include most government activities in science and space, transportation, medical research, environmental protection, and law enforcement. They are funded in ten of the thirteen annual appropriation bills.

For fiscal years 1991, 1992, and 1993, the Budget Enforcement Act of 1990 established dollar limits for this category of appropriations, and any excess over those limits is subject to presidential sequestration. (*See* Appropriation, Discretionary Appropriations, Entitlement Program, General Appropriation Bill, Sequestration.)

Doorkeeper of the House An officer of the House of Representatives responsible chiefly for enforcing the rules prohibiting unauthorized persons from entering the chamber when the House is in session. The doorkeeper and doorkeeper's staff clear the chamber of all persons, except those privileged to remain, fifteen minutes before the House convenes, assist the sergeant at arms in enforcing the rules relating to the behavior of members on the floor, and supervise the galleries of the House. Elected by resolution at the beginning of each Congress, the doorkeeper is usually the candidate of the majority party. (*See* Officers of Congress, Sergeant at Arms. *See also* Privilege of the Floor.)

Drop-By Voting (*See* Quorum.)

E

Early Organization of the House A 1974 House resolution that subsequently became law permits the Democratic

Caucus and the Republican Conference to meet in December of even-numbered years to take steps that will facilitate the prompt organization of the House in the upcoming Congress. The law also authorizes reimbursement for travel and other expenses connected with these meetings for newly elected as well as reelected members. (*See also* Organization of Congress.)

Earmark To set aside funds for a specific purpose, use, or recipient. Generally speaking, virtually every appropriation is earmarked, and so are certain revenue sources credited to trust funds. In common usage, however, the term is often applied as an epithet for funds set aside for such purposes as research projects, demonstration projects, parks, laboratories, academic grants, and contracts in particular congressional districts or states or for certain specified universities or other organizations. (*See* Appropriation, Trust Funds. *See also* Pork *or* Pork Barrel Legislation.)

Effective Dates Provisions of an act that specify when the entire act or individual provisions in it become effective as law. Most acts become effective on the date of enactment, but it is sometimes necessary or prudent to delay the effective dates of some provisions. The date of enactment may be the date the president signs the act, or the eleventh day after the president has received but neither signed nor returned the act while Congress is in session, or the date on which the president's veto has been overridden. (*See* Act, Override a Veto, Veto. *See* also Pocket Veto.)

Electronic Voting Since 1973 the House has used an electronic voting system to record the yeas and nays and and to conduct recorded votes. Members vote by inserting their voting cards in one of the boxes at several locations in the chamber. They are given at least fifteen minutes to vote.

When several votes occur immediately after each other, the Speaker may reduce the voting time to five minutes on the second and subsequent votes. The Speaker may allow additional time on each vote, but he may also close a vote at any time after the minimum time has expired. Members can change their votes at any time before the Speaker announces the result. The House also uses the electronic system for quorum calls.

While a vote is in progress, a large panel above the Speaker's desk displays how each member has voted. Smaller panels on either side of the chamber display running totals of the votes and the time remaining. The Senate does not have electronic voting. (*See* Cluster Voting, Quorum Call, Recorded Vote, Yeas and Nays.)

Emergency Appropriation Under the Budget Enforcement Act of 1990, a discretionary appropriation designated as an emergency requirement by the president and, in a statute, by Congress. An emergency appropriation results in an adjustment of the cap on its discretionary spending category without causing a sequestration. (*See* Cap, Discretionary Appropriations, Sequestration.)

En Bloc In congressional usage, several amendments offered and considered as a group. Because members normally may offer only one amendment at a time for consideration, they must obtain unanimous consent to offer amendments en bloc. (*See* Amendment, Unanimous Consent.)

En Gros In the House, several amendments reported by the Committee of the Whole and put to a vote as a group instead of individually. The Speaker customarily puts all of them to a vote en gros, but any member may demand a separate vote on one or more of them. (*See* Amendment, Committee of the Whole. *See also* Time Limits for Voting.)

Enacting Clause The opening language of each bill, beginning "Be it enacted by the Senate and House of Representatives of the United States of America in

Congress assembled. . . ." This language gives legal force to measures approved by Congress and signed by the president or enacted over his veto. A successful motion to strike it from a bill kills the entire measure. (*See* Strike Out the Enacting (*or* Resolving) Clause. *See also* Reading for Amendment.)

Enactment Date (*See* Effective Dates.)

Engrossed Bill The official copy of a bill or joint resolution as passed by one chamber, including the text as amended by floor action, and certified by the clerk of the House or the secretary of the Senate (as appropriate). Amendments by one house to a measure or amendments of the other also are engrossed. House engrossed documents are printed on blue paper; the Senate's are printed on white paper. (*See* Amendments Between the Houses. *See also* Blue Slip Resolution, Enrolled Bill.)

Engrossment and Third Reading The question decided by a house, immediately before it votes on passing a bill or joint resolution, ordering the clerk to engross the measure and to read it by title only. It is invariably ordered without objection. (*See* Engrossed Bill, Readings of Bills and Resolutions, Without Objection.)

Enrolled Bill The final official copy of a bill or joint resolution passed in identical form by both houses. An enrolled bill is printed on parchment. After it is certified by the chief officer of the house in which it originated and signed by the House Speaker and the Senate president pro tempore, the measure is sent to the president for his signature. (*See also* Engrossed Bill.)

Entitlement Program A federal program under which individuals, businesses, or units of government that meet the requirements or qualifications established by law are entitled to receive certain payments if they seek such payments. Major examples include Social Security, Medicare, Medicaid, unemployment insurance, and military and federal civilian pensions.

Some entitlements are funded by permanent appropriations, others by annual appropriations. In either case, they are a form of backdoor and mandatory spending. Congress cannot control their expenditures by refusing to appropriate the sums necessary to fund them because the government is legally obligated to pay eligible recipients the amounts to which the law entitles them, and recipients can take legal action if the government fails to do so. Under many entitlement programs, spending automatically increases or decreases over time as the number of recipients eligible for benefits varies. Some entitlement benefits are indexed for inflation; that is, the amount of the benefit is automatically increased by a specified percentage if the national cost-of-living index rises by a specified percentage. The increases are commonly called COLAs, an acronym for cost-of-living allowances. (*See* Appropriated Entitlement, Backdoor Spending Authority, Mandatory Appropriations, One-Year Appropriation, Permanent Appropriation. *See also* Transfer Payment, Trust Funds.)

Equality of the Houses A component of the Constitution's emphasis on checks and balances under which each house is given essentially equal status in the enactment of legislation and in their relations and negotiations. Although the House of Representatives initiates revenue and appropriation measures, the Senate has the right to amend them. Either house may initiate any other legislation and neither can force the other to agree to, or even act on, its measures. Moreover, each house has a potential veto over the other because measures require agreement by both.

Similarly, in a conference to resolve their differences on a measure, each house casts one vote as determined by a majority of its conferees. In most other national bicameral legislatures, the powers of one house are markedly greater than those of the other. (*See* Amendment, Conferees, Conference, General Appropriation Bill, Revenue Legislation.

Equally Divided When debate on a matter is limited to a specific length of time, control of the time is usually divided equally between two individuals or two groups. The individuals may be a proponent and opponent, the majority and minority floor managers, or the majority and minority leaders. The groups may be the two political parties, opponents and proponents, or two committees with an equal interest in the matter.

When more than two committees are involved, the total time may be equally or unequally divided among them, but each committee's time segment will be equally divided between the parties or between proponents and opponents. This practice is usually established in the Senate by unanimous consent and in the House by rule or custom.

A unique situation arises in the House of Representatives when the Committee of the Whole limits debate to a specific period of time or orders the debate to end at a specified time. Immediately after the committee's decision, members who wish to speak during that time rise, their names are noted, and the chairman of the Committee of the Whole customarily divides the time equally among them. If the number of members rising is so large that an equal division would give each of them inadequate time to speak, the chair often divides the total time equally between the majority and minority floor managers and allows them to yield portions of their time to other members. (*See* Committee of the Whole, Floor Manager, Majority Leader, Minority Leader, Rule, Unanimous Consent, Yielding Time.)

Equivalent Question A situation in which the defeat of a question amounts to agreement with its opposite. When a conference report is considered, for example, a motion to agree to it is considered as pending. If that motion is defeated, the effect of the negative vote is equivalent to a positive vote on disagreement. Therefore, a motion to disagree is unnecessary and not permitted. (*See* Conference Report, Motion, Question.)

Ethics Rules Several rules or standing orders in each house that mandate certain standards of conduct for members and congressional employees in finance, employment, franking, and other areas. The Senate Permanent Select Committee on Ethics and the House Committee on Standards of Official Conduct investigate alleged violations of conduct and recommend appropriate actions to their respective houses. (*See also* Code of Official Conduct, Censure, Denounce, Expulsion, Fining a Member, Reprimand, Seniority Loss.)

Ex Officio By virtue of one's office. Under a Senate rule, committee chairmen and ranking minority members may sit ex officio on any of the subcommittees of their committees, but without a vote. Many House committees permit this practice as a matter of custom or committee rule rather than by House rule; some even grant ex officio subcommittee members a vote. (*See* Chairman, Committee, Ranking Minority Member, Subcommittee.)

Exclusion The action of a house in refusing to seat a person nominally elected or appointed to it, on the grounds that the individual does not meet the constitutional qualifications for the office or that the election returns are invalid. Usually a house excludes by agreeing to a privileged resolution of exclusion. It only requires a majority vote, even when the individual has been permitted to take the oath of office pending a decision on their right to the seat. (*See* Oath of Office, Privilege. *See also* Expulsion.)

Exclusive Committee (1) Under the rules of the House Democratic Caucus, a standing committee whose Democratic members usually cannot serve on any other standing committee. As of 1993 the Appropriations, Ways and Means, and Rules committees were designated as exclusive committees.

(2) Under the rules of the two party conferences in the Senate, a standing committee whose members may not simultaneously serve on any other exclusive committee. (*See* Committee Assignments.)

Executive Business The Senate term for nominations and treaties the president has submitted to it for approval, under the Senate's "advice and consent" authority. (*See* Nomination, Treaty. *See also* Advice and Consent, *Executive Calendar*, Executive Session.)

Executive Calendar The Senate's calendar for committee reports on its executive business, namely treaties and nominations. The calendar numbers indicate the order in which items were referred to the calendar but have no bearing on when or if the Senate will consider them. The Senate, by motion or unanimous consent, resolves itself into executive session to consider them. (*See* Executive Session, Motion, Nomination, Treaty, Unanimous Consent. *See also* Advice and Consent.)

Executive Communication A message to Congress from the president or other executive branch official. Among other matters, executive communications communicate vetoes and reports to Congress that are required by law. Each communication is addressed to the Speaker of the House and the president of the Senate. (*See* Veto.)

Executive Document A document, usually a treaty, sent by the president to the Senate for approval. It is referred to a committee in the same manner as other measures. Executive documents are designated as Executive A, 102d Congress, 1st Session; Executive B; and so on. (*See* Bills and Resolutions Referred, Treaty.)

Executive Order A unilateral proclamation by the president that has a policy-making or legislative impact. Members of Congress have challenged some executive orders on the grounds that they usurped the authority of the legislative branch. Although the Supreme Court has ruled that a particular order exceeded the president's authority, it has upheld others as falling within the president's general constitutional powers.

Executive Privilege The assertion that presidents have the right to withhold certain information from Congress. Presidents have based their claim on: (1) the constitutional separation of powers; (2) the need for secrecy in military and diplomatic affairs; (3) the need to protect individuals from unfavorable publicity; (4) the need to safeguard the confidential exchange of ideas in the executive branch; and (5) the need to protect individuals who provide confidential advice to the president. (*See also* Contempt of Congress, Oversight, Subpoena Power.)

Executive Session (1) A Senate meeting devoted to the consideration of treaties and nominations. Normally, the Senate meets in legislative session, but its rules require that it resolve itself into executive session, by motion or by unanimous consent, to deal with those matters. It also keeps a separate *Journal* for executive sessions. They are usually open to the public, but the Senate may choose to close them. (*See Journal*, Legislative Session, Nomination, Treaty, Unanimous Consent. *See also* Secret *or* Closed Session.)

(2) A synonym for a committee meeting that is not open to the public. (*See also* Closed Hearing.)

Expedited Procedures Statutory rules that provide procedures for relatively speedy consideration of certain measures. Usually, these include a deadline for committee consideration, a privileged motion to discharge if the committee fails to meet the deadline, immediate floor consideration under limited debate, and a ban on amendments. Examples include procedures for acting on rescission measures and for joint resolutions repealing legislation passed by the government of the District of Columbia. (*See also* Discharge a Committee, Fast-Track Procedures, Privilege, Rescission, Statutory Rules.)

Expenditures The amount of government spending other than the net amounts disbursed in the form of loans. Appropriations make monies available for spending or obligation; expenditures are the amounts actually spent. These amounts and appropriated amounts are rarely identical in any fiscal year because some expenditures may come from appropriations made available in previous years, and some appropriations for the current year may be obligated but not actually spent in that year. (*See* Appropriation, Direct Loan, Fiscal Year, Obligation. *See also* Balanced Budget, Outlays.)

Expired Account An appropriation or fund account with an unobligated balance that may not be spent or obligated because the time limit for such actions has expired. (*See* Appropriation Account, Obligation, Trust Funds, Unobligated Balance. *See also* Multiyear Appropriation, One-Year Appropriation.)

Explanatory Statement An explanation of a conference report, endorsed by a majority of the conferees of each house, usually prepared by their staffs. The rules of both houses require that such a statement accompany each conference report and that it "shall be sufficiently detailed and explicit to inform the [house] as to the effect which the amendments or propositions contained in such report will have upon the measure to which those amendments or propositions relate." The statement may be organized by section or topic. In either case, it summarizes the House and Senate positions and the conferees' recommendations. It may also include explanations of the intent of recommended language for the guidance of executive agencies and the courts.

The statement is partially couched in jargon intelligible only to the initiated. An explanation may begin as follows: "The Senate amendment to the text of the bill struck out all of the House bill after the enacting clause and inserted a substitute text. The House amendment to the Senate amendment struck out the proposed substitute text and inserted another substitute text. The Senate recedes from its disagreement to the amendment of the House to the amendment of the Senate with an amendment which is a substitute for the House bill, the Senate amendment, and the House amendment to the Senate amendment." The statement then summarizes the differences among all of these versions. (*See* Disagree, Enacting Clause, Recede. *See also* Amendment in the Nature of a Substitute, Amendments Between the Houses, Conference Report.)

Expulsion A member's removal from office by a two-thirds vote of his house; the super majority is required by the Constitution. It is the most severe and most rarely used sanction a house can invoke against a member. Although the Constitution provides no explicit grounds for expulsion, the courts have ruled that it may be applied only for misconduct during a member's term of office, not for conduct before the member's election.

Generally, neither house will consider expulsion of a member convicted of a crime until the judicial processes have been exhausted. At that stage, members sometimes resign rather than face expulsion. In 1977, the House adopted a rule urging members convicted of certain crimes to voluntarily abstain from voting or participating in other legislative business. A rule of the House Democratic Caucus requires a Democratic chairman to step aside in favor of the next ranking member when indicted for a felony that may result in two or more years of imprisonment. (*See* Chairman, Rank, Ranking Member, Super Majority. *See also* Censure, Denounce, Ethics Rules, Exclusion, Fining a Member, Reprimand, Seniority Loss.)

Expunging from the *Record* Deletion from the *Congressional Record* of remarks or other materials that violate the rules of a house, such as derogatory statements about another member, profane remarks, or pornographic material. Expunging requires unanimous consent in the House and unanimous consent or agreement to a motion to do so in the Senate. (*See Congressional Record*, Unanimous Consent. *See also* Decorum, Disorderly Words, Taking Down the Words.)

Extender Congressional jargon for legislation that extends expiring provisions of law, often those involving tax exemptions or levies.

Extensions of Remarks An appendix to the daily *Congressional Record* that contains miscellaneous extraneous material submitted by members. It often includes members' statements not delivered on the floor, newspaper articles and editorials, praise for a member's constituents, and noteworthy letters received by a member, among other material. Representatives supply the bulk of this material, senators submit very little. Extensions of remarks pages are separately numbered, and each number is preceded by the letter *E*.

Materials may be placed in the Extensions of Remarks section only by unanimous consent. Usually, one member of a party makes the request each day on behalf of his party colleagues after the House has completed its legislative business of the day. (*See Congressional Record*, Unanimous Consent. *See also* Debate.)

Extraction Power A term sometimes applied to the authority of the House Rules Committee to report a special rule for the consideration of a measure not yet reported by the committee to which it was referred. In effect, House agreement to such a rule discharges the measure from committee more expeditiously than is possible under the discharge rule. Understandably, the affected committee sometimes condemns the procedure as a usurpation of its rights, but in some circumstances a committee may acquiesce in the action. (*See* Bills and Resolutions Referred, Discharge a Committee, Discharge Rule, Rule.)

Extraordinary Majority (*See* Super Majority. *See also* Constitutional Votes.)

F

Fast-Track Procedures Generally, procedures that circumvent or speed up the usually lengthy legislative process. In the House, these include special procedures in rules reported by the Rules Committee, procedures for dealing with measures on the consent and private calendars, and suspension of the rules. The Senate uses unanimous consent agreements.

Some rulemaking statutes prescribe expeditious procedures for certain measures such as budget resolutions, certain foreign military sales, and trade agreements. (*See* Budget Resolution, Consent Calendar, Private Calendar, Rulemaking Statutes, Suspension of the

Rules (House), Suspension of the Rules (Senate), Unanimous Consent Agreement. *See* also Expedited Procedures.)

Father of the House Unofficial title of the representative with the longest continuous service in the House; also called dean of the House. This member has no official functions but, by custom, administers the oath of office to the Speaker at the beginning of each Congress. No woman has yet reached this rank, so no question has arisen as to what title might be bestowed on such a woman. (*See* Oath of Office.)

Federal Credit Reform Act of 1990 A law that established a system of budgeting for the subsidized cost of federal direct loans and loan guarantees. Under this system, Congress appropriates budget authority or provides indefinite authority equal to the subsidy cost. The budget authority is placed in a program account from which funds are disbursed to a financing account. The Credit Reform Act appears as Title V of the Congressional Budget Act of 1974 where it was inserted by the Budget Enforcement Act of 1990.

The reform act also established new budgetary and accounting rules for federal loans. It put direct and guaranteed loans on an equal footing; provided a means for recognizing a change in the status of loans in the budget and for controlling guaranteed loans at the time the commitments are made; and provided a basis for comparing direct and guaranteed loans with other uses of budgetary resources. (*See* Budget Authority, Budget Enforcement Act of 1990, Budgetary Resources, Congressional Budget Act of 1974, Credit Subsidy Cost, Direct Loan, Financing Account, Loan Guarantee, Program Account. *See also* Credit Authority, Credit Budget.)

Federal Debt The total amount of monies borrowed and not yet repaid by the federal government. Federal debt consists of public debt and agency debt.

Public debt is the portion of the federal debt borrowed by the Treasury or the Federal Financing Bank directly from the public or from another federal fund or account. For example, the Treasury regularly borrows money from the Social Security trust fund. Public debt accounts for about 99 percent of the federal debt.

Agency debt refers to the debt incurred by federal agencies like the Export-Import Bank, but excluding the Treasury and the Federal Financing Bank, which are authorized by law to borrow funds from the public or from another government fund or account. (*See* Borrowing Authority, Debt Limit. *See also* Deficit.)

Federal Regulation of Lobbying Act of 1946 Requires persons attempting to influence the passage or defeat of legislation in Congress to register with the clerk of the House of Representatives or secretary of the Senate and submit quarterly reports on the sources and amounts of money they received and spent for lobbying. The purpose of the law is disclosure, not regulation. The clerk and the secretary compile the information and publish it in the *Congressional Record*.

The Supreme Court has ruled that the law does not apply to (1) persons who spend their own money on lobbying rather than paying someone else to represent them; (2) groups whose principal purpose is something other than lobbying; and (3) persons who do not directly contact members of Congress. Consequently, the law does not effectively provide for disclosure of all lobbying activities. (*See* Lobby.)

Field Hearing A committee or subcommittee hearing held outside of Washington, D.C., often in the district or state of a committee member. The rules of both houses permit committees to "sit and act" anywhere within the United States. (*See* Hearing.)

Fifteen-Minute Rule A House rule that allows members a minimum of fifteen minutes to cast their votes for the yeas and nays and other recorded votes. (*See* Recorded Vote, Yeas and Nays. *See also* Electronic Voting.)

Filed Signifies the official registration of a committee report or conference report at a chamber's rostrum. (*See* Chamber, Committee Report on a Measure, Conference Report.)

Filibuster The use of obstructive and time-consuming parliamentary tactics by one member or a minority of members to delay, modify, or defeat proposed legislation or rules changes. Filibusters are also sometimes used to delay urgently needed measures in order to force the body to accept other legislation. The Senate's rules permitting unlimited debate and the extraordinary majority it requires to impose cloture make filibustering particularly effective in that chamber. Under the stricter rules of the House, filibusters in that body are short-lived and and therefore ineffective and rarely attempted.

Senate filibusters are most likely to succeed when supported by a large minority or when they occur late in a session when time is short and large numbers of must-pass measures are ready for final action. Under those conditions, the threat of a filibuster may force the majority to accept compromises or persuade the leadership to put aside controversial legislation.

Typically, filibusterers give long speeches, offer numerous and lengthy amendments, demand that all amendments be read in full, force time-consuming quorum calls and votes on amendments and procedural motions, object to routine unanimous consent requests, make frequent points of order, and appeal parliamentary rulings. (*See* Cloture, Debate, Must-Pass Bill, Unlimited Debate. *See also* Dilatory Tactics, Postcloture Filibuster, Track System.)

Financing Account An account that receives payments from a credit program account established under the terms of the Federal Credit Reform Act of 1990. The account includes cash flows to and from the government resulting from direct loan obligations or loan guarantee commitments. At least one financing account is established for each credit program account. Financing accounts are excluded from budget totals, however, because they are used to finance only the nonsubsidized portion of federal credit activities. (*See* Budget, Credit Subsidy Cost, Direct Loan, Federal Credit Reform Act of 1990, Loan Guarantee, Program Account.)

Fining a Member In a single instance (1969), the House agreed to a resolution imposing a fine of $25,000 on Rep. Adam Clayton Powell (D-N.Y.) for misbehavior.

Firewall The Budget Enforcement Act of 1990 placed dollar ceilings on three broad categories of federal discretionary spending—defense, international, and domestic—for fiscal years 1991, 1992, and 1993. The act's so-called firewall provisions prevented breaching the spending ceiling of one category by shifting to it funds saved in another category. For example, defense spending could be reduced by a certain amount in order to add that amount to the total available in the domestic category. (*See* Breach. *See also* Discretionary Appropriations.)

First Degree Amendment An amendment offered directly to the text of a measure. (*See also* Amendment in the Nature of a Substitute, Degrees of Amendment, Perfecting Amendment, Strike Out.)

First Reading The required reading to a chamber of a bill or joint resolution by title only after its introduction. The House complies with the first reading by publishing the measure's title in the *Journal* and the *Congressional Record*. (*See Congressional Record, Journal*, Readings of Bills and Resolutions. *See also* Second Reading, Third Reading.)

Fiscal Year The federal government's annual accounting period. It begins October 1 and ends on the following September 30. A fiscal year is designated by the calendar year in which it ends and is often referred to as FY. Thus, fiscal year 1992 began October 1, 1991, ended September 30, 1992, and is called FY92. In theory, Congress is supposed to complete action on all budgetary measures applying to a fiscal year before that year begins. It rarely does so.

From 1884 to 1976, the fiscal year ran from July 1 to June 30 of the following year. The Congressional Budget Act of 1974 changed the dates to accommodate the timetable it established for the new congressional budget process. (*See* Budget Process.)

Five-Minute Rule (1) A House rule that limits debate on an amendment offered in Committee of the Whole to five minutes for its sponsor and five minutes for an opponent. In practice, the committee routinely permits longer debate by two devices: the offering of pro forma amendments, each debatable for five minutes, and unanimous consent for a member to speak longer than five minutes. Consequently, debate on an amendment sometimes continues for hours or, rarely, for more than a day.

At any time after the first ten minutes, however, the committee may shut off debate immediately or by a specified time, either by unanimous consent or by majority vote on a nondebatable motion. The rule, which dates from 1847, is also used in the House as in Committee of the Whole, where debate may be shut off by a motion for the previous question. (*See* Amendment, Committee of the Whole, House as in Committee of the Whole, Nondebatable Motions, Previous Question, Pro Forma Amendment, Unanimous Consent. *See also* Debate-Ending Motion.)

(2) A House rule that limits a committee member to five minutes when questioning a witness at a

hearing until each member has had an opportunity to question that witness. Adopted in 1971, the rule prevents any member from monopolizing so much of the time available for questioning so that others are prevented from asking questions. (*See* Hearing. *See also* Seniority System.)

(3) A House rule limiting debate on a motion to dispense with Calendar Wednesday to five minutes for and five minutes against. (*See* Calendar Wednesday.)

(4) A Senate rule limiting each senator to five minutes of debate on a measure considered during a call of the calendar and five minutes on any amendment to it. (*See* Call of the Calendar.)

Floor (1) The ground level of the House or Senate chamber where members sit and the houses conduct their business. When members are attending a meeting of their house, they are said to be "on the floor."

(2) A member recognized by the presiding officer is said to "have the floor" or "hold the floor." When senators finish what they have to say, they often declare, "Mr. President, I yield the floor." Under certain parliamentary conditions, a member is said to "lose the floor" and may not speak again until recognized. (*See* Recognition. *See also* Decorum, Taking Down the Words.)

(3) "Floor stage" refers to the stage of the legislative process, usually following the committee stage, when a house takes up a measure. (*See* Committee Stage.)

(4) "Floor action" refers to the procedural actions taken during floor consideration, such as deciding on motions, taking up measures, amending them, and voting.

Floor Amendment An amendment offered on the floor by a member. These amendments are distinguished from committee amendments and certain amendments whose consideration is automatically required by a special rule in the House. (*See* Amendment, Committee Amendments, Rule. *See also* Printed Amendment, Reading for Amendment.)

Floor Leader The member elected by each party in each house to be its principal floor spokesman. (*See* Majority Leader, Minority Leader.)

Floor Manager A majority party member responsible for guiding a measure through its floor consideration in a house and for devising the political and procedural strategies that might be required to get it passed. The presiding officer gives the floor manager priority recognition to debate, offer amendments, oppose amendments, and make crucial procedural motions. When debate is under a time limitation, the floor manager controls half of the time in most situations and apportions it among party colleagues, especially to supporters of the measure. In some situations the floor manager controls all of the debate time, but customarily yields half of it to the minority.

In the Senate, the chairman of the reporting committee or of the subcommittee that worked on the measure usually manages it. In the House, a Democratic Caucus rule directs the full committee chairman to permit subcommittee chairmen to handle measures from their panels. In both houses, the ranking minority member of the reporting committee or subcommittee usually acts as the floor manager for his party, and the chair invariably gives him second priority in recognition. (*See* Amendment, Preferential Recognition, Presiding Officer, Ranking Minority Member. *See also* Five-Minute Rule, Hour Rule, Managers, Unanimous Consent Agreement.)

Floor Privileges (*See* Privilege of the Floor.)

Forty-Minute Debate In the House, forty minutes of debate, evenly divided between proponents and opponents, is permitted (1) on a motion to suspend the rules; (2) after the previous question has been ordered on a proposition on which there has been no debate; (3) on a motion to reject a nongermane amendment between the houses; and (4) on a motion to reject a nongermane Senate amendment in a conference report. (*See* Amendments Between the Houses, Conference Report, Germane, Nongermane Senate Amendment, Previous Question, Suspension of the Rules (House).)

Forward Funding A type of multiyear appropriation that is made available in the middle or toward the end of a fiscal year and remains available through the next fiscal year: for example, from July 1 of one year through September 30 of the next. The amount is charged against the budget for the fiscal year in which the appropriation becomes available, not against the budget of the succeeding fiscal year. (*See* Appropriation, Budget, Fiscal Year, Multiyear Appropriation.)

Frank Informally, a member's legal right to send official mail postage free under his or her signature; often called the franking privilege. Technically, it is the autographic or facsimile signature used on envelopes instead of stamps that permits members and certain congressional officers to send their official mail free of charge. The franking privilege has been authorized by law since the first Congress, except for a few months in 1873. Congress reimburses the U.S. Postal Service for the franked mail it handles. In recent years, the House and Senate have set up franking accounts for each of their members and required periodic publication of each member's mail costs.

The frank cannot be used for personal matters or for purposes "unrelated to the official business, activities, and duties" of those who have the privilege. It cannot be used to solicit political support, votes, or financial assistance. Under a House rule adopted in 1993, a representative cannot send any mass mailing outside the congressional district from which he was elected.

A bipartisan Commission on Congressional Mailing Standards advises House members about possible violations of the franking laws and rules and investigates alleged violations. The Senate Select Committee on Ethics performs the same function for senators.

Free Vote In congressional jargon, the vote a member casts for a measure or an amendment, even though he thinks it ill-advised or irresponsible, to enhance his popularity with his constituents, but in the expectation that the other chamber will reject it.

Full Committee An entire committee as distinguished from its subcommittees.

Full Funding (1) An appropriation that finances the full estimated cost of a project or activity that will take several years to complete and that requires periodic or intermittent expenditures over that period of time: for example, a construction project or a procurement program. In contrast, incremental funding refers to instances in which Congress provides funds in each fiscal year for only that year's portion of the estimated total cost of the project or activity. (*See also* Advance Appropriation.)

(2) Sometimes refers to an appropriation that provides the full amount authorized in law for a project or activity for an upcoming fiscal year. (*See* Authorization. *See also* Authorization-Appropriation Process.)

Function or Functional Category A broad category of national need and spending of budgetary significance. A category provides an accounting method for allocating and keeping track of budgetary resources and expenditures for that function because it includes all budget accounts related to the function's subject or purpose. A congressional budget resolution lists all the functional categories and the portion of aggregate budget amounts allocated to each.

As of 1992 there were twenty functional categories, each divided into a number of subfunctions. They included such national-need categories as agriculture, administration of justice, commerce and housing credit, energy, income security, transportation, and national defense. Those not assigned to national needs were net interest and undistributed offsetting receipts. Accounts are placed in the function that best represents their major purpose; consequently, functions do not necessarily correspond with appropriations acts or with the budgets of individual agencies. (*See* Budget Resolution, Budgetary Resources, Expenditures, Offsetting Receipts.)

Funding Gap A term sometimes applied to a period when federal agencies lack authority to obligate or spend funds because their appropriations for that period have not been enacted. Spending gaps occur most frequently at the beginning of a fiscal year, but agencies occasionally run out of money later in the year. During such periods, agencies sometimes furlough many of their employees and shut down many of their operations.

A law permits agencies to classify certain employees as essential for carrying out activities involving the safety of human life and protection of property and to retain them during spending gaps, but it has been alleged that some agencies have applied that classification to employees engaged in routine activities. The Budget Enforcement Act of 1990 amended the law to emphasize that routine activities should not be continued during funding gaps. (*See also* Appropriation, General Appropriation Bill.)

G

Gag Rule A pejorative term for any type of special rule reported by the House Rules Committee that proposes to prohibit amendments to a measure or only permits amendments offered by the reporting committee. Also applied by some members to rules that inhibit the amending process to any marked degree. (*See* Closed Rule, Rule. *See also* Self-Executing Rule.)

Galleries The balconies overlooking each chamber. From different seating areas in the galleries, the public, news media, staff, and others may observe and listen to the floor proceedings.

GAO (*See* General Accounting Office.)

General Accounting Office (GAO) A congressional support agency, often referred to as the investigative arm of Congress. It evaluates and audits federal agencies and programs in the United States and abroad on its own initiative or at the request of congressional committees, their chairmen and ranking minority members, or, occasionally, other members. GAO publishes many of its reports and makes them available to interested members and staff.

The agency's director, the comptroller general of the United States, and GAO's senior staff frequently testify before congressional committees on the results and conclusions of the investigations. Some statutes require GAO to provide legal opinions to Congress, such as on the legality of proposed rescissions and deferrals by the president. The agency also plays a leading role in attempts to improve and standardize federal agency accounting procedures. (*See* Congressional Support Agencies, Comptroller General of the United States, Deferral, Investigative Power, Rescission.)

General Appropriation Bill A term applied to each of the thirteen annual bills that provide funds for most federal agencies and programs and also to the supplemental appropriation bills that contain appropriations for more than one agency or program.

Only general appropriation bills are subject to the rules of the authorization-appropriation process; special appropriation bills are not. Because the House classifies continuing resolutions as special rather than general appropriations, unauthorized appropriations in, or offered as amendments to, such resolutions are not subject to points of order. The Senate, however, classifies continuing resolutions as general bills and permits points of order against such amendments.

The Constitution does not require annual appropriations, but Congress has funded most agencies and programs annually since the first Congress. Because it rarely enacts all the regular annual appropriation bills before the beginning of the fiscal year to which they apply, Congress resorts to one or more stopgap funding measures (that is, continuing resolutions) every year so that all government agencies can continue to function. (*See* Appropriation, Authorization-Appropriation Process, Continuing Resolution, Fiscal Year, Point of Order, Special Appropriation Bill, Supplemental Appropriation Bill, Unauthorized Appropriation. *See also* Budget Process, Three-Day Rule, Two-Day Rule.)

General Debate In the House of Representatives, usually refers to debate at the beginning of proceedings in Committee of the Whole during which amendments may not be offered. Customarily, the time for general debate is controlled by and divided equally between the majority and minority floor managers of a measure. After general debate, amendments are debated under the five-minute rule. The term is applied less often to the hour rule in the House sitting as the House, although debate under that rule may be on a pending measure or on an amendment to it.

Senators seldom use the term and never in the technical sense applied to it in the House. However, the Senate sometimes provides a rough equivalent to general debate under unanimous consent agreements that explicitly set aside time for debate on a bill or on the question of final passage, in addition to time for debate on amendments. As in the House, such time is usually controlled by and divided equally between the floor managers. (*See* Committee of the Whole, Equally Divided, Five-Minute Rule, Floor Manager, Hour Rule, House Sitting as the House, Unanimous Consent Agreement.)

General Leave After the House passes a bill, the floor manager often requests permission or "leave" for all members to insert their statements on it into the *Congressional Record*, usually under a deadline of five legislative days. The manager makes the request as a courtesy to members who were unable to speak during debate or chose not to because all debate in the House is under a time limitation. The same request is often made during periods set aside for eulogizing a recently deceased member or former member, or for praising a member who is leaving the House. General leave requires unanimous consent. (*See* Debate, Floor Manager, Legislative Day, Unanimous Consent. *See also* Leave to Print, Revise and Extend One's Remarks.)

General Legislation The Senate term for legislative provisions as distinguished from appropriation provisions. It is roughly synonymous with the term "changing existing law" in the rules of the House. In both houses, points of order are permitted against such provisions in, or if offered as amendments to, a general appropriation bill. (*See* Authorization-Appropriation Process, Legislation on an Appropriation Bill, Point of Order.)

General Order of Business (*See* Order of Business (House).)

General Orders Calendar (*See* Calendar of General Orders.)

General Pair A voting pair between two absent members that does not indicate their positions on the question.

They may agree or disagree. In the Senate, positions may be inferred when two senators of generally different ideologies announce that they have entered into a general pair. The *Congressional Record* lists House general pairs after the vote: "Mr. Smith with Mr. Jones." (*See* Pairing.)

Gephardt Rule A House rule providing for automatic House passage of a joint resolution increasing the statutory limit on the public debt when the House agrees to a budget resolution that requires such an increase. The amount of the increase in the joint resolution must conform with the level established in the budget resolution. The final House vote on the budget resolution is deemed to be the vote on the joint resolution, thus, a separate direct vote on raising the debt limit is avoided. Rep. Richard A. Gephardt (D-Mo.) was the rule's chief sponsor.

If Congress does not enact legislation to raise the public debt limit when that limit has been reached, the government cannot borrow sufficient monies to pay for all of its commitments and its credit is endangered. Nevertheless, before the first version of this rule was approved in 1979, the House sometimes rejected such legislation because many members feared a direct vote on it would harm them politically or because they opposed it for ideological or political reasons.

In the Senate, which has no such rule, the measure is often the target of numerous riders because it is considered to be virtually veto-proof. (*See* Budget Resolution, Debt Limit, Federal Debt, Joint Resolution, Rider. *See* also Christmas Tree Bill, Must-Pass Bill.)

Germane Basically, on the same subject as the matter under consideration. A House rule requires that all amendments be germane. In the Senate, only amendments proposed to general appropriation bills and budget resolutions or under cloture must be germane.

Germaneness rules can be evaded by suspension of

the rules in both houses, by unanimous consent agreements in the Senate, and by special rules from the Rules Committee in the House. Moreover, presiding officers usually do not enforce germaneness rules on their own initiative; therefore, a nongermane amendment can be adopted if no member raises a point of order against it. Under cloture in the Senate, however, the chair may take the initiative and rule amendments out of order as not being germane, without a point of order being made.

All House debate must be germane except during general debate in the Committee of the Whole, but special rules invariably require that such debate be "confined to the bill." The Senate requires germane debate on a measure only during the first three hours of each daily session.

Under the precedents of both houses, an amendment can be relevant, but not necessarily germane. A crucial factor in determining germaneness in the House is how the subject of a measure or matter is defined. For example, a measure authorizing construction of a naval vessel is defined as the construction of a single vessel, and, therefore, an amendment to authorize an additional vessel is not germane. (*See* Cloture, Committee of the Whole, Debate, General Appropriation Bill, General Debate, Non-Selfenforcing Rules, Pastore Rule, Point of Order, Rider, Rule, Suspension of the Rules (House), Suspension of the Rules (Senate), Unanimous Consent Agreement. *See also* Nongermane Senate Amendment.)

Gerrymandering The manipulation of legislative district boundaries to benefit a particular party, politician, or minority group. The term originated in 1812 when the Massachusetts legislature redrew the lines of state legislative districts to favor the party of Gov. Elbridge Gerry, and some critics said one district looked like a salamander. (*See also* Congressional District, Redistricting.)

Ghost Voting In the House, when someone other than a member casts the member's vote on the floor or records the member as present. In 1980, the House adopted a rule explicitly prohibiting the practice after what the House Manual refers to as "voting anomalies" were discovered in the use of its electronic voting system. (*See* Electronic Voting.)

Government-Sponsored Enterprises (GSEs) Enterprises established by the federal government, but privately owned, that engage in credit activities. Because they are deemed private rather than public entities, they are excluded from the federal budget and their budgets are not reviewed by the president or Congress in the same manner as other programs. However, information about their finances is included in the president's budget.

As of 1992, there were eleven GSEs, among them the Student Loan Marketing Association, the Federal Home Loan Mortgage Corporation, the Farm Credit Banks, and Federal Home Loan Banks. (*See* Budget. *See also* Credit Budget, Federal Credit Reform Act of 1990.)

Gramm-Rudman-Hollings Act of 1985 Common name for the Balanced Budget and Emergency Deficit Control Act of 1985, which established new budget procedures intended to balance the federal budget by fiscal year 1991—a goal subsequently extended to 1993. To achieve that goal, the act set annual maximum deficit targets and mandated automatic across-the-board spending cuts, called sequesters, by the president to enforce the limits. It also extensively amended the Congressional Budget Act of 1974. The act's chief sponsors were senators Phil Gramm (R-Texas), Warren Rudman (R-N.H.), and Ernest Hollings (D-S.C.).

In 1986, the Supreme Court invalidated a provision of the act that authorized the General Accounting Office to determine the sequestrations required of the president. The Court held that the provision violated the Constitution's separation-of-powers doctrine because GAO is a legislative agency. In 1987, Congress assigned the function to the Office of Management and Budget as part of the Balanced Budget and Emergency Deficit Control Reaffirmation Act. (*See* Balanced Budget and Emergency Deficit Control Reaffirmation Act of 1987, Budget Process, Congressional Budget and Impoundment Control Act of 1974, Fiscal Year, General Accounting Office, Maximum Deficit Amounts, Sequestration. *See also* Budget Enforcement Act of 1990.)

Grandfather Clause A provision in a measure, law, or rule that exempts an individual, entity, or a defined category of individuals or entities from complying with a new policy or restriction. For example, a bill that would raise taxes on persons who reach the age of sixty-five after a certain date inherently "grandfathers out" those who are sixty-five before that date. Similarly, a Senate rule limiting senators to two major committee assignments also grandfathers some senators who were sitting on a third major committee prior to a specified date. (*See* Committee Assignments.)

Grants-in-Aid Payments by the federal government to state and local governments to help provide for assistance programs or public services.

H

Hereby Rule In House jargon, another name for a self-executing special rule sometimes used to expedite approval of Senate amendments to House bills. The term is derived from the rule's usual wording that the bill and the amendments are "hereby taken from the Speaker's table . . . and the same are hereby agreed to." (*See* Rule, Self-Executing Rule, Speaker's Table.)

Hearing (1) Committee or subcommittee meetings to receive testimony on proposed legislation during investigations or for oversight purposes. Relatively few bills are important enough to justify formal hearings. Witnesses often include experts, government officials, spokespersons for interested groups, officials of the General Accounting Office, and members of Congress. In hearings on special rules, however, the House Rules Committee takes testimony only from members of Congress. Committees may issue subpoenas to summon reluctant witnesses.

Both houses require that the vast majority of hearings be open to the press and public and, if possible, publicly announced at least a week before they begin. The quorum requirements for hearings are smaller than for business meetings: on Senate committees, not less than one-third of its members must be present; on House committees, not less than two. (*See* Closed Hearing, Investigative Power, Oversight, Quorum. *See also* Business Meeting, Leave to Sit.)

(2) The printed transcripts of hearings. Committees usually try to make these available before the measures they concern come up for floor consideration. A House rule requires that hearings on appropriation bills be available three days before the measure is called up. A Senate rule merely urges its committees "to make every reasonable effort" to make hearings available before floor consideration. (*See* General Appropriation Bill.)

Hearings Announcements The rules of both houses require their committees to announce the date, place, and subject of any hearing at least one week before it begins. The Senate rule exempts its Appropriations and Budget committees; the House exempts its Rules Committee. Senate committees may begin their hearings earlier when they determine "there is good cause." So may House committees, but they must announce the earlier date as soon as possible. They must also promptly publish their announcements in the Daily Digest and enter them in the committee scheduling service of the House Information Systems, a computerized database. (*See* Daily Digest, Hearing.)

Hinds' and Cannon's Precedents of the House of Representatives A monumental, multivolume compilation and detailed explanation of virtually every House precedent from the first Congress (1789-1791) through 1936, arranged by topic. It consists of eleven massive volumes, the last three devoted to the index. The compilers, Asher C. Hinds (R-Maine) and Clarence A. Cannon (D-Mo.), both served the House first as parliamentarians and later as members.

Although some of the precedents cited in the compilation have since been modified or overturned, it is still an invaluable source of information not only about House procedure but also about the chamber's history and development. (*See* Precedent, Procedures. *See also Cannon's Procedure in the House of Representatives, Deschler's Precedents*, House Manual, *Procedure in the U.S. House of Representatives, Riddick's Senate Procedure*.)

Hold A senator's request that his or her party leaders delay floor consideration of certain legislation or presidential nominations. The majority leader usually honors a hold for a reasonable period of time, especially if its purpose is to assure the senator that the matter will not be called up during his or her absence or to give the senator time to gather necessary information. (*See* Majority Leader, Nomination. *See also* Senatorial Courtesy.)

Hold (*or* Have) the Floor A member's right to speak without interruption, unless he violates a rule, after recognition by the presiding officer. At the member's discretion, he or she may yield to another member for a question in the Senate or for a question or statement in the House, but may reclaim the floor at any time. (*See* Floor, Recognition, Yielding. *See also* Lose the Floor, Yield the Floor.)

Hold-Harmless Clause In legislation providing a new formula for allocating federal funds, a clause to ensure that recipients of those funds do not receive less in a future year than they did in the current year if the new formula would result in a reduction for them. Similar to a grandfather clause, it has been used most frequently to soften the impact of sudden reductions in federal grants. (*See* Grandfather Clause.)

Holman Rule A House rule that permits legislation in a general appropriation bill if it is germane to, and clearly retrenches (reduces) amounts in, the bill. Named after its sponsor, Rep. William S. Holman (D-Ind.), it was first adopted in 1876 but has been revised several times since then. The rule has been rarely invoked in recent years. (*See* General Appropriation Bill, Germane, Legislation on an Appropriation Bill, Retrenchment.)

Hopper A box on the clerk's desk in the House chamber into which members deposit bills and resolutions to introduce them. In House jargon, to "drop a bill in the hopper" is to introduce it. (*See* Bills and Resolutions Introduced.)

Hour Rule (1) A House rule that permits members, when recognized, to hold the floor in debate for no more than one hour each. Special rules reported by the Rules Committee are considered under this procedure. The majority party member calling up the rule customarily yields one-half the time to a minority member of the committee.

Although the hour rule applies to general debate in Committee of the Whole as well as in the House, special rules routinely vary the length of time for such debate and its control to fit the circumstances of particular measures. Special order speeches are also subject to the hour rule.

Theoretically, the hour rule could force the House to spend 440 hours on a measure if all members chose to speak, and double that time if even one amendment were offered. But in practice, the first member to speak usually moves the previous question at or near the end of his hour and a majority of the House usually votes for it, thereby shutting off all further debate. (*See* Committee of the Whole, Debate, General Debate, Previous Question, Recognition, Rule, Special Order Speech. *See also* Yielding.)

(2) The hour rule also applies to debate on a conference report, but the hour must be equally divided between the majority and minority parties. If both floor managers support the report, however, an opponent is allotted one-third of the time. (*See* Conference Report, Floor Manager.)

(3) Another House rule permits one hour of debate on a motion to recommit with instructions if the time is demanded by the majority floor manager. The majority floor manager controls half the time; the mover of the motion controls the other half. (*See* Floor Manager, Recommit with Instructions.)

House Always capitalized when referring to the House of Representatives, but usually not when referring to either the House or the Senate, as in "each house" or "the two houses of Congress." (*See* House of Representatives, Senate.)

House as in Committee of the Whole A hybrid combination of procedures from the general rules of the House and from the rules of the Committee of the Whole, sometimes used to expedite consideration of a measure on the floor. Because the House order of business does not provide for a motion to consider measures in this manner, it is normally invoked by unanimous consent or a special rule. However, a House rule requires its use for consideration of private bills.

A bill taken up under these procedures is considered as read, and any part of it is open to amendment. No time is allotted for general debate, but the five-minute rule may be used for that purpose and for debate on amendments, including pro forma amendments. Unlike proceedings in the Committee of the Whole, the Speaker presides; a quorum is 218; and the yeas and nays, the previous question, and a motion to reconsider are permitted. After the amendment process is completed, the Speaker puts the question on the previous question (if it has not already been ordered), then on engrossment and third reading, and finally on passage.

House committees use the basic elements of this procedure when they mark up bills. A Senate rule requiring treaty consideration as in Committee of the Whole was deleted in 1986. (*See* Committee of the Whole, Engrossment and Third Reading, Five-Minute Rule, General Debate, Markup, Motion, Order of Business (House), Passed, Previous Question, Private Bill, Private Calendar, Pro Forma Amendment, Put the Question, Quorum, Reading for Amendment, Readings of Bills and Resolutions, Reconsider a Vote, Rule, Unanimous Consent, Yeas and Nays.)

House Calendar The calendar reserved for all public bills and resolutions that do not raise revenue or directly or indirectly appropriate money or property when they are favorably reported by House committees. (*See* Appropriation, Calendar, Report, Revenue Legislation. *See* also Union Calendar.)

House Manual A commonly used title for the handbook of the rules of the House of Representatives, published in each Congress. Its official title is *Constitution, Jefferson's Manual, and Rules of the House of Representatives.* The text is annotated with pertinent explanations, historical information, and digests of the principal rulings and precedents. Separate sections contain provisions of certain laws applicable to the House and a description of various support services available to members. (*See Jefferson's Manual,* Precedent, Ruling, Standing Rules. *See also* Congressional Support Agencies, Legislative Counsel's Office.)

House of Representatives The house of Congress in which states are represented roughly in proportion to their populations, but every state is guaranteed at least one representative. By law, the number of voting representatives is fixed at 435. Four delegates and one resident commissioner also serve in the House; they may vote in their committees and in Committee of the Whole but not in the House sitting as the House.

Although the House and Senate have equal legislative power, the Constitution gives the House sole authority to originate revenue measures. The House also claims the right to originate appropriation measures, a claim the Senate disputes in theory but concedes in practice. The House has the sole power to impeach, and it elects the president when no candidate has received a majority of the electoral votes. It is sometimes referred to as "the lower body." (*See* Appropriation, Committee of the Whole, Delegate, Floor, House Sitting as the House, Impeachment, Representative, Resident Commissioner from Puerto Rico, Revenue Legislation. *See also* Apportionment, Redistricting.)

House Sitting as the House A phrase that refers to the House of Representatives meeting in its constitutional and legislative role as a house of Congress rather than as a Committee of the Whole. (*See* Committee of the Whole.)

I

Immunity (1) Members' constitutional protection from lawsuits and arrest in connection with their legislative duties. They may not be tried for libel or slander for anything they say on the floor of a house or in committee. Nor may they be arrested while attending sessions of their houses or when traveling to or from sessions of Congress, except when charged with treason, a felony, or a breach of the peace.

(2) In the case of a witness before a committee, a grant of protection from prosecution based on that person's testimony to the committee. It is used to compel witnesses to testify who would otherwise refuse to do so on the constitutional ground of possible self-incrimination. Under such a grant, none of a witness' testimony may be used against him or her in a court proceeding except in a prosecution for perjury or for giving a false statement to Congress. (*See also* Contempt of Congress.)

Impeachment The first step to remove the president, vice president, or other federal civil officers from office and to disqualify them from any future federal office "of honor, Trust or Profit." An impeachment is a formal charge of treason, bribery, or "other high Crimes and Misdemeanors." The House has the sole power of impeachment and the Senate the sole power of trying the charges and convicting. The House impeaches by a simple majority vote; conviction requires a two-thirds vote of all senators present.

The House impeaches by adopting a resolution containing articles of impeachment, usually reported by a committee after an investigation. Although the resolution is privileged for immediate floor consideration, the House usually considers it under a unanimous consent agreement fixing the time for and control of debate. If the resolution is approved, the House appoints managers to present the impeachment articles to the Senate and to act as prosecutors on behalf of the House during the Senate trial.

The Senate tries the impeachment under a separate set of twenty-six rules that appears in its manual. Under the Constitution, the chief justice of the Supreme Court presides over trials of the president. By Senate rule, the chief justice also presides over the trial of a vice president who is temporarily serving as president. The Constitution requires senators to take an oath for the trial. During the trial, senators may not engage in colloquies or participate in arguments. After it concludes, the Senate votes separately on each article of impeachment without debate unless the Senate orders the doors closed. In that case, senators may speak no more than once on a question, not more than ten minutes on an interlocutory question, and not more than fifteen minutes on the final question.

In 1993, no challenge was raised against the seating of then representative-elect Alcee L. Hastings (D-Fla.) who, while serving as a federal judge, had been impeached and convicted in 1989. A federal judge had ruled in 1992 that Mr. Hastings' conviction was not valid because a Senate committee, rather than the full Senate, had held the trial and subsequently reported its recommendations to the Senate for final action, but the judge stayed his order so that the matter could be settled by the Supreme Court. (*See* Privilege, Question, Secret *or* Closed Session, *Senate Manual*, Unanimous Consent.)

Impoundment An executive branch action or inaction that delays or withholds the expenditure or obligation of budget authority provided by law. The Impoundment Control Act of 1974 classifies impoundments as either deferrals or rescissions, requires the president to notify Congress about all such actions, and gives Congress authority to approve or reject them.

The Constitution is unclear on whether a president may refuse to spend appropriated money, but Congress usually expects the president to spend at least enough to achieve the purposes for which the money was provided whether or not he agrees with those purposes. (*See* Budget Authority, Deferral, Expenditures, Rescission.)

Impoundment Control Act of 1974 A title within the Congressional Budget and Impoundment Control Act of 1974 that prescribes procedures for congressional review and control over impoundments proposed by the executive branch. (*See* Impoundment. *See also* Deferral, Rescission.)

Incremental Funding The appropriation by Congress in one fiscal year of only a portion of the estimated total cost of a project or activity that may take several years to complete and require periodic or intermittent expenditures over that period of time. (*See* Appropriation, Fiscal Year. *See also* Full Funding.)

Indefinite Authority (*See* Budget Authority.)

Inflationary Impact Statement A statement of the "inflationary impact on prices and costs in the operation of the national economy" that may result from enactment of a public bill or joint resolution. A House rule requires such statements to appear in its committees' reports on proposed legislation. (*See* Committee Report on a Measure, Public Bill.)

Inquiry (*See* Resolution of Inquiry.)

Insert Add new text to a measure or an amendment by means of an amendment. (*See* Amendment.)

Insertion (*See* Leave to Print, Revise and Extend One's Remarks.)

Insist A motion by a house to reiterate its previous position during the process of amendments between the houses. A house may insist on its amendment after the other house has disagreed to it, or a house may insist on its previous disagreement to an amendment of the other house.

In the sequence of motions permitted during amendments between the houses, insistence precedes adherence. Unlike adherence, it is not an uncompromising position, and it may be accompanied by a request for a conference. (*See* Adhere, Amendments Between the Houses, Concur, Conference, Disagree, Recede. *See* also Stage of Disagreement.)

Inspector General A position created in 1992 to audit the administrative functions of the House of Representatives. Appointed jointly by the Speaker, majority leader, and minority leader, the inspector general reports to them, to the director of non-legislative and financial services, and to the chairman and ranking minority member of the Committee on House Administration. (*See* Director of Non-Legislative and Financial Services.)

Instruct Conferees A formal action by a house urging its conferees to uphold a particular position on a measure in conference. The instruction may be to insist on certain provisions in the measure as passed by that house or to accept a provision in the version passed by the other house. Conferees are not bound by instructions, and a conference report is not subject to a point of order on the ground that instructions were violated. The House has a rule on the subject and occasionally instructs its conferees; the Senate has no such rule and instructs its conferees less often.

Instructions are not binding because the primary responsibility of conferees is to reach agreement on a measure, and they cannot compel the other side to accept particular provisions.

The House permits a motion to instruct after it agrees to a conference but before conferees are appointed. Instructions are also in order if a conference committee has not reported within twenty calendar days or, if appointed during the last six days of a session, if conferees have not reported within thirty-six hours after their appointment. (Under a rule adopted in 1993, a member's motion to instruct conferees who have not reported within twenty calendar days of their appointment must lay over one day before it may be considered.) Minority party members are given priority for offering a motion to instruct. It may be amended and is debated under the hour rule. (*See* Conferees, Conference, Conference Report, Hour Rule, Point of Order.)

Instructions (*See* Instruct Conferees, Recommit with Instructions, Reconciliation.)

International Discretionary Appropriations Appropriations not mandated in law, and therefore made available in appropriation bills in such amounts as Congress chooses, for foreign economic and military aid, the State Department, the U.S. Information Agency, and international financial programs such as the U.S. Export-Import Bank. The Budget Enforcement Act of 1990 established dollar limits on this category of appropriations for fiscal years 1991, 1992, and 1993. If Congress breaches the limits, the excess amounts are subject to presidential sequestration. (*See* Appropriation, Breach, Discretionary Appropriations, Sequestration.)

Intervening Business In the Senate, business that must be transacted after the presence of a quorum has been established before a member may make a point of order that a quorum is no longer present or suggest the absence of a quorum. (*See* Business, Quorum Call.)

Introduction of Bills and Resolutions (*See* Bills and Resolutions Introduced.)

Investigative Power The authority of Congress and its committees to pursue investigations, upheld by the Supreme Court but limited to matters "related to, and in furtherance of, a legitimate task of the Congress." Standing committees in both houses are permanently authorized to investigate matters within their jurisdictions. Major investigations are sometimes conducted by temporary select, special, or joint committees established by resolutions for that purpose.

Some rules of the House provide certain safeguards for witnesses and others during investigative hearings. These permit counsel to accompany witnesses, require that each witness receive a copy of the committee's rules, and order the committee to go into closed session if it believes the testimony to be heard might defame, degrade, or incriminate any person. The committee may subsequently decide to hear such testimony in open session. The Senate has no rules of this kind. (*See* Joint Committee, Select *or* Special Committee. *See also* Contempt of Congress, Hearing, Immunity, Oaths to Witnesses, Oversight, Subpoena Power.)

Investigative Staff Committee staff authorized by annual or biennial resolutions rather than by rule or law; also called temporary staff. They are paid from the contingent fund in their respective houses. The term is somewhat misleading; many staff authorized by resolutions do not perform investigative functions and most continue to serve for indefinite and often extended periods. Since 1981, all Senate committee staff have been authorized by resolutions. (*See* Contingent Fund. *See also* Minority Staff, Permanent Staff, Staff Director.)

Iron Triangle A term sometimes used by scholars and journalists when referring to the alliances often found among a committee, the officials of an agency under its jurisdiction, and lobbyists interested in programs administered by the agency. (*See* Lobby.)

Item Veto A suggested presidential authority to veto a portion of a measure rather than all of it as is now required; sometimes called a line-item veto. Proponents argue that presidents would use the authority to veto pork barrel legislation in appropriations measures or in legislative riders in an appropriations act. Opponents respond that presidents would use such authority for political purposes and that it would seriously erode the congressional power of the purse and the constitutional principle of checks and balances in the legislative process. (*See* Legislation on an Appropriation Bill, Line Item, Pork *or* Pork Barrel Legislation, Power of the Purse, Rider.)

J

Jefferson's Manual Short title of *Jefferson's Manual of Parliamentary Practice*, prepared by Thomas Jefferson for his own guidance when he was president of the Senate from 1797 to 1801. Although it reflects English parliamentary practice in his day, many procedures in both houses of Congress are still rooted in its basic precepts. Under a House rule adopted in 1837, the manual's provisions govern House procedures when applicable and when not inconsistent with its standing rules and orders. The Senate, however, has never officially acknowledged it as a direct authority for its parliamentary procedure. (*See* President of the Senate, Standing Order, Standing Rules.)

Johnson Rule A policy instituted in 1953 under which all Democratic senators are assigned to one major committee before any Democrat is assigned to two. The Johnson Rule is named after its author, Sen. Lyndon B. Johnson (D-Texas), then the Senate's Democratic leader. Senate Republicans adopted a similar policy soon thereafter. (*See* Committee Assignments.)

Joint Committee A committee composed of members selected from each house. The functions of most joint committees involve investigation, research, or oversight of agencies closely related to Congress. Permanent joint committees, created by statute, are sometimes called standing joint committees. Once quite numerous, only four joint committees remained as of 1993: Joint Economic, Joint Taxation, Joint Library, and Joint Printing. None has authority to report legislation. Temporary joint committees are usually established by concurrent resolution. Technically, conference committees are also temporary joint committees, but they are not given that title and are not formed by concurrent resolutions.

The two houses are usually equally represented on joint committees (but not on conference committees). The law establishing a permanent joint committee fixes the number of members from each house and often the number of majority and minority members from each house. Chairmanship of a joint committee usually rotates between the houses from Congress to Congress. (*See* Conference Committee. *See also* Committee Assignments.)

Joint Explanatory Statement (*See* Explanatory Statement.)

Joint Hearings Hearings held jointly by two or more committees (or their subcommittees) of the same house or of both houses. (*See* Hearing.)

Joint Meeting A combined meeting of the House and Senate for some purpose other than that reserved for joint sessions. Usually they are held to welcome or hear an address by a distinguished American or foreign visitor invited by congressional leaders. While joint sessions require adoption of a concurrent resolution, each house merely agrees to recess for a joint meeting. (*See* Joint Session.)

Joint Referral Another term for a multiple referral: the referral of a measure to two or more committees simultaneously. (*See* Multiple and Sequential Referrals.)

Joint Resolution A legislative measure that Congress uses for purposes other than general legislation. Like a bill, it has the force of law when passed by both houses and either approved by the president or passed over the president's veto. Unlike a bill, a joint resolution enacted into law is not called an act; it retains its original title.

Most often, joint resolutions deal with such relatively limited matters as the correction of errors in existing law, continuing appropriations, a single appropriation, or the establishment of permanent joint committees. Unlike bills, however, joint resolutions also are used to propose constitutional amendments; these do not require the president's signature and become effective only when ratified by three-fourths of the states. Furthermore, while preambles are not considered appropriate in a bill, they may be used in a joint resolution to set forth the events or facts that prompted the measure, for example, a declaration of war.

The House designates joint resolutions as H. J. Res., the Senate as S. J. Res. Each house numbers its joint resolutions consecutively in the order of introduction during a two-year Congress. (*See* Bill, Continuing Resolution, Joint Committee, Preamble, Veto.)

Joint Rules Rules governing the procedure of the two houses in matters requiring their concurrent action. Congress adopted a number of joint rules in its early years, but abrogated them in 1876. In the 91st Congress (1969-1971), however, a law specifying that the counting of electoral votes for president and vice president should be conducted in joint session was made a joint rule when it was incorporated in a concurrent resolution by reference (that is, by citation of the law rather than by full text). The House Rules Committee still has explicit jurisdiction over joint rules. (*See* Committee Jurisdiction, Concurrent Resolution, Joint Session, Reference, Rule.)

Joint Session Informally, any combined meeting of the Senate and the House. Technically, a joint session is a combined meeting to count the electoral votes for president and vice president or to hear a presidential address, such as the State of the Union message; any other formal combined gathering of both houses is called a joint meeting.

Joint sessions are authorized by concurrent resolutions and are held in the House chamber because of its larger seating capacity. Although the president of the Senate and the Speaker sit side by side at the Speaker's desk during combined meetings, the former presides over the electoral count and the latter presides on all other occasions and introduces the president or other guest speaker. The president and other guests may address a joint session only by invitation. (*See* Joint Meeting, President of the Senate, Speaker, State of the Union Message.)

Joint Sponsorship Two or more members sponsoring the same measure. (*See* Bills and Resolutions Introduced.)

Journal The official record of House or Senate actions, including every motion offered, every vote cast, amendments agreed to, quorum calls, and so forth.

Unlike the *Congressional Record,* it does not provide reports of speeches, debates, statements, and the like. The Constitution requires each house to maintain a *Journal* and to publish it periodically. The House keeps a single *Journal* but the Senate keeps four: one for its legislative sessions; a second, titled *Executive Proceedings in the Senate,* for its executive business sessions; a third for confidential legislative proceedings; and the fourth for proceedings when it sits as a court of impeachment. (*See* Amendment, *Congressional Record,* Executive Session, Impeachment, *Journal* Approval, Legislative Session, Motion, Quorum Call, Secret *or* Closed Session.)

Journal Approval By rule, each house must approve its *Journal* entry for the previous legislative day at the beginning of its next meeting. Approval is usually routine and expeditious—by unanimous consent in the Senate and automatically by the Speaker's announcement that he has read and approved it in the House.

However, any member may demand a vote on the Speaker's approval, and if the House votes to reject it, any member may offer a nondebatable motion to require a reading of the *Journal.* If that motion carries, the *Journal* is read and open to amendment. The House invariably upholds the Speaker's approval, but members sometimes demand a vote as a substitute for a quorum call to determine which members are present, to interrupt committee meetings, or to vent partisan frustrations.

In the Senate, a rule adopted in 1986 permits a nondebatable motion to waive a reading of the *Journal.* The rule stifles filibuster tactics sometimes used in the past to force a reading. Since the Senate's legislative day often extends over weeks and sometimes months, the reading might take hours. (*See* Filibuster, Legislative Day, Quorum Call, Unanimous Consent.)

Junior Senator The senator who has served for a shorter continuous period in the Senate than the other senator from the same state. (*See also* Senior Senator.)

Junket A member's trip at government expense, especially abroad, ostensibly on official business but, it is often alleged, for pleasure. (*See also* Members' Allowances.)

Jurisdiction (*See* Committee Jurisdiction.)

Justification Materials Documentation in support of an agency's budget request that it submits to the Appropriations committees. Typically the materials attempt to justify differences between the current amounts in an agency's line items and those it is requesting for the next fiscal year. (*See* Agency, Fiscal Year, Line Item.)

K

Killer Amendment An amendment that, if agreed to, might lead to the defeat of the measure it amends, either in the house in which the amendment is offered or at some later stage of the legislative process. Members sometimes deliberately offer or vote for such an amendment in the expectation that it will undermine support for the measure in Congress or increase the likelihood that the president will veto it. (*See also* Free Vote, Rider.)

King of the Mountain (*or* Hill) Rule A special rule from the House Rules Committee that permits votes on a series of amendments, especially complete substitutes for a measure, in a specified order, but directs that the last amendment agreed to shall be the winning one. The usual language states, "If more than one of the amendments . . . has been adopted, only the last such amendment which has been adopted shall be considered as having been finally adopted. . . ."

This kind of rule permits the House to vote directly on a variety of alternatives to a measure, but it also gives the last amendment a potential advantage over the others. In doing so, it sets aside the practice that once an amendment has been adopted no further amendments may be offered to the text it has amended. (*See* Amendment in the Nature of a Substitute, Bigger Bite Amendment.)

L

LA (*See* Legislative Assistant.)

Lame Duck Jargon for a member who has not been re-elected, or did not seek reelection, and is serving the balance of his or her term.

Lame Duck Session A session of a Congress held after the election for the succeeding Congress, so-called after the lame duck members still serving.

Last Train Out Jargon for the last must-pass bill of a session of Congress. (*See* Must-Pass Bill.)

Last Word (*See* Pro Forma Amendment.)

Law An act of Congress that has been signed by the president or passed over the president's veto. (*See* Act, Override a Veto, Veto. *See also* Private Law, Public Law, Slip Law, Statutes at Large, *U.S. Code.*)

Law Revision Counsel A statutory position in the House of Representatives. The counsel's chief function is to develop a codification of U.S. laws. (*See also U.S. Code.*)

Lay on the Table A motion to dispose of a pending proposition immediately, finally, and adversely; that is, to kill it without a direct vote on its substance. Informally referred to as a motion to table, it is not debatable and is adopted by majority vote or without objection. It is a highly privileged motion, taking precedence over all others except the motion to adjourn in the House and all but three additional motions in the Senate. It can kill a bill, resolution, amendment, another motion, a point of order, an appeal, or virtually any other matter.

Tabling an amendment also tables the measure to which it is pending in the House, but not in the Senate. The House does not allow it against the motion to recommit, in Committee of the Whole, and in some other situations. In the Senate, it is the only permissible motion that immediately ends debate on a proposition, but only to kill it. (*See* Adjourn, Amendment, Appeal, Committee of the Whole, Motion, Nondebatable Motions, Point of Order, Precedence of Motions (House), Precedence of Motions (Senate), Privilege, Recommit, Without Objection. *See also* Unlimited Debate.)

Layover Rules Rules that require a specified period of time to elapse before action may be taken on certain measures, motions, or other matters.

Some examples: (1) A House committee report on a bill must be available for at least three days before the House may consider the measure. (2) A Senate committee report on a bill must be available for at least two days before the Senate may consider the measure. (3) In the House, a special rule from the Rules Committee usually must lay over one day before it may be called up for consideration. (4) In the House, a conference report usually may not be considered until the third day after the report and its accompanying statement have been printed in the daily edition of the *Congressional Record*. (5) In the Senate, a cloture motion must lay over one day before it is put to a vote. (6) In the House, a measure on the consent calendar may not be called up unless it has been on that calendar for at least three legislative days. (*See* Cloture, Committee Report on a Measure, Conference Report, *Congressional Record*, Consent Calendar, Explanatory Statement, Legislative Day, Rule. *See* also Discharge Rule, Over Under the Rule.)

Leader (*See* Majority Leader, Minority Leader.)

Leader (*or* Leadership) Time A period of time at the beginning of each daily session of the Senate that (by a Senate standing order) is reserved for statements the majority and minority leaders might wish to make. The order for the 103d Congress authorized each of them up to ten minutes on each calendar day following the prayer and disposition of the *Journal.* (*See Journal,* Majority Leader, Minority Leader, Session.)

(The) Leadership Usually, a reference to the majority and minority leaders of the Senate or to the Speaker and minority leader of the House. The term sometimes includes the majority leader in the House and the majority and minority whips in each house, and, at other times, other party officials as well. (*See* Majority Leader, Minority Leader, Speaker, Whip.)

Leave of Absence A formal grant of permission for a member to be absent during the proceedings of the member's house.

A Senate rule prohibits senators from absenting themselves "from the service of the Senate without leave." In practice, requests for leave are routinely granted. When the party whips announce the names of senators "necessarily absent" before a roll-call vote, they are referring to senators who are temporarily absent, not to those who have been granted leaves of absence.

A House rule requires every member to be "present within the Hall of the House during its sittings, unless excused or necessarily prevented." In practice, two types of absence are permitted: (1) temporary ones granted during the call of the roll; and (2) leaves of absence lasting at least one day, usually granted by unanimous consent at the end of a day's legislative program.

The most frequent reasons given for absences are "official business," personal illness, illness in the member's family, or military service in wartime. In 1973, a member was granted maternity leave. A statute authorizes the sergeant at arms to dock a member's pay for unauthorized absences, but the law has not been enforced since 1914. (*See* Call of the Roll, Unanimous Consent, Yeas and Nays.)

Leave to Print Permission to have remarks not actually delivered on the floor, or other materials, inserted in the *Congressional Record.* It requires unanimous consent. (*See Congressional Record,* Extensions of Remarks, Revise and Extend One's Remarks, Unanimous Consent.)

Leave to Sit Permission for a committee to meet during certain proceedings of its house when most committees are forbidden to meet.

No Senate committee, other than the Appropriations and Budget committees, may meet after the first two hours of the Senate's daily session, or after 2 p.m. while the Senate is in session, unless granted special leave by unanimous consent or by the consent of the majority and minority leaders.

Under a 1993 rule change, all House committees may meet at virtually any time, even when the House or the Committee of the Whole is in session. Before that change, no House committee—except Appropriations, Budget, House Administration, Standards of Official Conduct, and Ways and Means—was permitted to sit without special leave while the House was reading a measure for amendment under the five-minute rule, but a request for leave to sit was granted unless ten or more members objected. However, no House committee may meet during a joint session or joint meeting of Congress. (*See* Five-Minute Rule, Joint

Meeting, Joint Session, Objection, Reading for Amendment.)

Legislation (1) A synonym for legislative measures: bills and joint resolutions.

(2) Provisions in such measures or in substantive amendments offered to them.

(3) In some contexts, provisions that change existing substantive or authorizing law, rather than provisions that make appropriations. (*See* Authorization, Legislation on an Appropriation Bill, Substantive Law. *See also* General Legislation.)

Legislation on an Appropriation Bill A common reference to provisions changing existing law that appear in, or are offered as amendments to, a general appropriation bill. A House rule prohibits the inclusion of such provisions in general appropriation bills unless they retrench expenditures. An analogous Senate rule permits points of order against amendments to a general appropriation bill that propose "general legislation." The intent of both rules is to enforce the separation between substantive legislation and appropriations legislation. (*See* Appropriation, Authorization, Authorization-Appropriation Process, General Appropriation Bill, Retrenchment, Substantive Law.)

Legislative Assistant (LA) A member's staff person responsible for monitoring and preparing legislation on particular subjects and for advising the member on them; commonly referred to as an LA.

Legislative Authority (1) A synonym for an authorization of appropriations. (*See* Authorization.)

(2) A committee's authority to report legislation to its chamber. (*See also* Select *or* Special Committee, Standing Committee.)

Legislative Business A synonym for legislative measures. (*See* Measure. *See also* Business.)

Legislative Calendar Informal title for the Senate's calendar of general orders on which legislative measures are placed.

Legislative Committee (1) A committee authorized to report legislation to its parent body, as distinguished from an investigative, study, or party committee. (*See also* Select *or* Special Committee.)

(2) A term sometimes applied to a committee that reports authorizing legislation rather than appropriation measures. (*See* Appropriation, Authorization, Legislation. *See also* Authorization-Appropriation Process.)

Legislative Counsel's Office In each house, a staff of attorneys who provide nonpartisan, expert assistance in drafting bills, resolutions, and amendments, primarily to committees. The statute authorizing the House Office of the Legislative Counsel defines its function as that of assisting "in the achievement of a clear, faithful, and coherent expression of legislative policies" for both committees and members.

The House Legislative Counsel is appointed by the Speaker, the Senate's by the president pro tempore. In turn, they appoint the other attorneys in their respective offices. The House attorneys often assist their chamber's conferees in preparing conference reports and explanatory statements. (*See* Conference Report, Explanatory Statement.)

Legislative Day The "day" that begins when a house meets after an adjournment and ends when it next adjourns. Because the House of Representatives normally adjourns at the end of a daily session, its legislative and calendar days usually coincide. The Senate, however, frequently recesses at the end of a daily session, and its legislative day may extend over several calendar days, weeks, or months.

Among other uses, this technicality permits the Senate to save time by circumventing its morning hour, a procedure required at the beginning of every legislative day. On occasion, the House or Senate has adjourned in the middle of a calendar day and immediately reconvened in a new legislative "day" to circumvent its one-day layover rules. (*See* Adjourn, Morning Hour, One-Day Rule, Recess.)

Legislative History (1) A chronological list of actions taken on a measure during its progress through the legislative process. (*See* Legislative Process.)

(2) The official documents relating to a measure, the entries in the *Journal*s of the two houses on that measure, and the *Congressional Record* text of its consideration in both houses. The documents include all committee reports and the conference report and joint explanatory statement, if any.

Courts and affected federal agencies study a measure's legislative history for congressional intent about its purpose and interpretation. They pay particular attention to statements in standing and conference committee reports and during floor debates in both houses about the meaning and intended interpretation of individual provisions in the measure and in amendments to it. (*See* Committee Report on a Measure, Conference Report, *Congressional Record*, Explanatory Statement, *Journal*.)

Legislative Measure A bill or joint resolution; a measure that proposes a law. (*See* Measure.)

Legislative Process (1) Narrowly, the stages in the enactment of a law from introduction to final disposition. An introduced measure that becomes law typically travels through reference to committee; committee and subcommittee consideration; report to the chamber; floor consideration; amendment; passage; engrossment; messaging to the other house; similar steps in that house including floor amendment of the measure; return of the measure to the first house; consideration of amendments between the houses or a conference to resolve their differences; approval of the conference report by both houses; enrollment; approval by the president or override of the president's veto; and deposit with the archivist of the United States. (*See* Amendment, Amendments Between the Houses, Bills and Resolutions Introduced, Bills and Resolutions Referred, Committee Report on a Measure, Conference, Conference Report, Engrossed Bill, Enrolled Bill, Hearing, Markup, Message, Override a Veto.)

(2) Broadly, the political, lobbying, and other factors that affect or influence the process of enacting laws. (*See* Lobby.)

Legislative Review (*See* Oversight.)

Legislative Service Organizations (LSOs) The House title for more than 100 unofficial groups of representatives formed to focus attention or advocate action on one or more national policies or on issues important to their constituencies. Smaller, newer groups are formally called congressional member organizations. Both groups are sometimes called informal caucuses.

Most groups consist entirely of House members, a few are for senators only, and a number have bicameral memberships. Many have paid staff, office space, dues-paying members, bylaws, and elected officers. In 1981, the House prohibited the use of space in congressional buildings by informal caucuses that receive funds from outside sources or that charge fees for receipt of their publications. Since then, many groups have created or aligned themselves with private institutes funded by outside sources to provide research and analysis for them. Others have agreed to provide their publications free of charge in return for designation as an LSO.

Some LSOs are partisan and ideological, like the Democratic Study Group and the House Republican Study Committee. Those that focus on the interests of certain population groups or industries are often non-partisan, like the Congressional Rural Caucus, the Congressional Caucus for Women's Issues, the Congressional Textile Caucus, and the Congressional Steel Caucus. Some are racial or ethnic groups, like the Congressional Black Caucus and the Congressional Hispanic Caucus. Geographical groups include the Congressional Sunbelt Caucus and the Northeast-Midwest Congressional Coalition. Their memberships range from under 6 to more than 370.

Legislative Session A Senate meeting to consider legislative business rather than treaties and nominations. The latter are considered in executive session. Under Senate rules, the chamber meets in legislative session unless it agrees by unanimous consent or by motion to go into executive session. It requires the same procedure to return to legislative session. (*See* Executive Session, Legislative Business.)

Legislative Veto A procedure, declared unconstitutional in 1983, that allowed Congress or one of its houses to nullify certain actions of the president, executive branch agencies, or independent agencies. Sometimes called congressional vetoes or congressional disapprovals. Concurrent resolutions were required for vetoes involving both houses, simple resolutions for action by one house. These procedures reversed the usual roles of the two branches, permitting the executive, in effect, to make law subject to a veto by the legislature.

Following the Supreme Court's 1983 decision, Congress amended several legislative veto statutes to require enactment of joint resolutions, which are subject to presidential veto, for nullifying executive branch actions. (*See also* Committee Veto.)

Lie on the Table (*See* Subjects on the Table.)

Lie Over One Day (*See* One-Day Rule, Over Under the Rule.)

Limitation on a General Appropriation Bill Language that prohibits expenditures for part of an authorized purpose from funds provided in a general appropriation bill. Precedents require that the language be phrased in the negative: that none of the funds provided in a paragraph or the act shall be used for a specified activity.

Limitations in general appropriation bills are permitted on the grounds that Congress can refuse to fund authorized programs and, therefore, can refuse to fund any part of them as long as the prohibition does not change existing law. House precedents have established that a limitation does not change existing law if it does not impose additional duties or burdens on executive branch officials, interfere with their discretionary authority, or require them to make judgments or determinations not required by existing law.

The proliferation of limitation amendments in the 1970s and early 1980s prompted the House to adopt a rule in 1983 making it more difficult for members to offer them. The rule bans such amendments during the reading of an appropriation bill for amendments unless they are specifically authorized in existing law. Other limitations may be offered after the reading, but the Committee of the Whole can foreclose them by adopting a motion to rise and report the bill back to the House. The House Appropriations Committee, however, can include limitation provisions in the bills it reports. (*See* Authorization, Committee of the Whole, General Appropriation Bill, Legislation on an Appropriation Bill, Precedent, Reading for Amendment. *See also* Appropriation Limitation, Authorization-Appropriation Process.)

Limitations on Committee Assignments (*See* Committee Assignments.)

Line Item Generally, an amount in an appropriation measure. It can refer to a single appropriation account or to separate amounts within the account. In the congressional budget process, the term usually refers to assumptions about the funding of particular programs or accounts that underlie the broad functional amounts in a budget resolution. These assumptions are discussed in the reports accompanying each resolution and are not binding. (*See* Appropriation Account, Budget Allocation, Budget Process, Function *or* Functional Category.)

Line-Item Veto (*See* Item Veto.)

Liquidating Appropriation An appropriation to pay obligations incurred under contract authority. (*See* Contract Authority, Obligation.)

List of Speakers A list of senators who wish to speak. The list is usually kept at the desk of the presiding officer, who recognizes the senators in the order listed. Although a convenient practice for senators, it has no parliamentary standing, and if no senator has the floor the chair must recognize any senator who rises and demands recognition. (*See* Preferential Recognition, Recognition.)

Live Pair A voluntary and informal agreement between two members on opposite sides of an issue under which the member who is present for a recorded vote withholds or withdraws his or her vote because the other member is absent. Usually, the member in attendance announces that he or she has a live pair, states how each would have voted, and votes "present." (*See* Pairing. *See also* Dead Pair.)

Live Quorum In the Senate, a quorum call to which senators are expected to respond by going to the floor. Usually, senators suggest the absence of a quorum not to force a quorum to appear, but merely to provide a pause in the proceedings during which senators can engage in private discussions or wait for a senator to come to the floor. A senator desiring a live quorum usually announces his or her intention, giving fair warning that there will be an objection to any unanimous consent request that the quorum call be dispensed with. (*See* Objection, Quorum Call, Suggest the Absence of a Quorum, Unanimous Consent.)

Loan Guarantee A statutory commitment by the federal government to pay part or all of a loan's principal and interest to a lender or the holder of a security in case the borrower defaults. The Federal Credit Reform Act of 1990 requires that the cost of guaranteed loans be included in the computation of budget authority and outlays. The congressional budget resolution includes loan guarantee totals. (*See* Budget Authority, Budget Resolution, Credit Budget, Federal Credit Reform Act of 1990, Outlays.)

Lobby To try to persuade members of Congress to propose, pass, modify, or defeat proposed legislation or to change or repeal existing laws. A lobbyist attempts to promote his or her own preferences or those of a group, organization, or industry. Originally the term referred to persons frequenting the lobbies or corridors of legislative chambers in order to speak to lawmakers.

The right to lobby stems from the First Amendment to the Constitution, which bans laws that abridge the right of the people "to petition the government for a redress of grievances." A federal law tries to force disclosure of lobbying activities by requiring persons who receive and spend money for that purpose to register with (and submit quarterly statements to) the clerk of the House or secretary of the Senate.

In a general sense, lobbying includes not only direct contact with members but also indirect attempts to influence them, such as writing to them or persuading others to write or visit them, attempting to mold public opinion toward a desired legislative goal by various means, and contributing or arranging for contributions to members' election campaigns. The Supreme Court has taken a much narrower view of lobbying in its interpretation of federal law.

Some lobbyists focus their efforts on the executive branch and regulatory agencies as well as, or instead of, Congress. (*See* Federal Regulation of Lobbying Act of 1946.)

Locality Rule A custom, rather than a rule, that a member of the House of Representatives should reside in the district he or she represents. (*See* Congressional District.)

Logrolling Jargon for a legislative tactic or bargaining strategy in which members try to build support for their legislation by promising to support legislation desired by other members or by accepting amendments they hope will induce their colleagues to vote for their bill. Occasionally, groups of members deal with other groups this way, for example, when members representing farm areas vote for food stamps in return for farm legislation support by members from urban areas.

Look-Back A procedure that closes sequestration loopholes for pay-as-you-go violations and for breaches of discretionary spending limits.

Under the Budget Enforcement Act of 1990, a deficit increase for a fiscal year caused by direct spending or revenue legislation results in a sequester only once a year—within fifteen days after the end of a session of Congress. When Congress causes such a deficit increase for that fiscal year after the sequester for that year, the look-back procedure requires that the next year's sequestration reduce funding to offset that amount.

Appropriations that breach the discretionary spending limit for the current fiscal year trigger a sequester only if they are enacted before July 1 of that year. When an appropriation enacted after that date causes such a breach, the look-back procedure requires an equivalent reduction in the appropriate spending limits for the next fiscal year. (*See* Breach, Deficit, Direct Spending, Discretionary Appropriations, Fiscal Year, Pay-As-You-Go, Revenue Legislation, Sequestration. *See also* Deficit Neutrality.)

Lose the Floor Members can lose the right to speak on the floor if they violate a rule while speaking. Technically, members also lose the floor when they offer an amendment or other motion. But if the motion is debatable, the member is immediately recognized to speak on it if he or she so chooses. (*See* Floor, Motion, Recognition. *See also* Hold (*or* Have) the Floor, Yield the Floor.)

Lower Body A common reference to the House of Representatives, but one that House members consider pejorative. (*See* Body. *See also* Upper Body.)

LSOs (*See* Legislative Service Organizations.)

M

Mace The symbol of the office of the House sergeant at arms. Under the direction of the Speaker, the sergeant at arms is responsible for preserving order on the House floor by holding up the mace in front of an unruly member, or by carrying the mace up and down the aisles to quell boisterous behavior.

When the House is in session, the mace sits on a pedestal at the Speaker's right; when the House is in Committee of the Whole, it is moved to a lower pedestal.

The mace is 46 inches high and consists of 13 ebony rods bound in silver and topped by a silver globe with a silver eagle, wings outstretched, perched on it. (*See* Sergeant at Arms. *See also* Committee of the Whole.)

Main Question A measure, motion, or proposal under consideration, as distinguished from the amendments to it. In the House, members may speak once on the main question and once on each amendment. (*See also* Put the Question, Question, Questions of Privilege.)

Major Committees The rules of the House Democratic Caucus apply this designation to certain committees and state that no Democratic representative may serve on more than one of them. As of 1993, the major committees were Agriculture; Armed Services; Banking, Finance, and Urban Affairs; Education and Labor; Foreign Affairs; Energy and Commerce; Judiciary; and Public Works and Transportation. (*See* Committee Assignments. *See also* Exclusive Committees, Nonmajor Committees.)

Majority Leader The majority party's chief floor spokesman, elected by that party's caucus—sometimes called floor leader.

In the Senate, the majority leader also develops the party's political and procedural strategy, usually in collaboration with other party officials and committee chairmen. He negotiates the Senate's agenda and committee ratios with the minority leader and usually calls up measures for floor action. The chamber traditionally concedes to the majority leader the right to determine the days on which it will meet and the hours at which it will convene and adjourn.

In the House, the majority leader is the Speaker's deputy and heir apparent. He helps plan the floor agenda and the party's legislative strategy and often speaks for the party leadership in debate. (*See* Committee Ratios, Debate, Minority Leader, Party Caucus.)

Majority Whip (*See* Whip.)

Majority Vote Although not explicitly stated in the rules of either house, both houses decide questions by a majority vote of the members voting except when the Constitution or the rules require otherwise. In all cases, both houses assume that a quorum is present unless the absence of a quorum is determined by the result of a vote or on a point of order. (*See* Absence of a Quorum, Point of Order, Question, Quorum. *See also* Absolute Majority, Cloture, Constitutional Votes.)

Managers (1) The official title of members appointed to a conference committee, commonly called conferees. The ranking majority and minority managers for each house also manage floor consideration of the committee's conference report. (*See* Conferees, Conference Committee, Conference Report, Rank *or* Ranking.)

(2) The members who manage the initial floor consideration of a measure. (*See* Floor Manager.)

(3) The official title of House members appointed to present impeachment articles to the Senate and to act as prosecutors on behalf of the House during the Senate trial of the impeached person. (*See* Impeachment.)

Mandatory Appropriations Amounts that Congress must appropriate annually because it has no discretion over them unless it first amends existing substantive law. Certain entitlement programs, for example, require annual appropriations. (*See* Appropriated Entitlement, Substantive Law. *See also* General Appropriation Bill, Uncontrollable Expenditures.)

Mandatory Spending (*See* Direct Spending.)

Manual Informal title of the official handbooks of the House and Senate containing their rules and other information. (*See* House Manual, *Senate Manual*.)

Markup A meeting or series of meetings by a committee or subcommittee during which members "mark up" a measure by offering, debating, and voting on amendments to it. After a subcommittee marks up a measure and reports it to the full committee, the bill may be put to another markup, normally in full committee. Finally, the committee votes on whether to report the measure to its house recommending approval of any amendments it has adopted.

When a committee has agreed to extensive revisions, it often reports the measure with a single amendment in the nature of a substitute or reports a clean bill. (*See* Amendment, Amendment in the Nature of a Substitute, Clean Bill, Full Committee, Report.)

Maximum Deficit Amounts The maximum amount of the federal budget deficit for each fiscal year specified in the Gramm-Rudman-Hollings Act. Under the Budget Enforcement Act of 1990, the president may make certain adjustments in the maximum deficit level permitted in any year. If the deficit for a particular year is estimated to exceed the adjusted maximum deficit amount by more than a specified margin, a sequester is required to eliminate the excess. (*See* Budget Enforcement Act of 1990, Deficit, Fiscal Year, Gramm-Rudman-Hollings Act of 1985, Sequestration.)

Means-Tested Programs Programs that provide benefits or services to low-income individuals who meet a test of need. Most are entitlement programs, such as Medicaid, food stamps, and Supplementary Security Income. A few—for example, subsidized housing and various social services—are funded through discretionary appropriations. (*See* Discretionary Appropriations, Entitlement Program.)

Measure (1) A bill or joint resolution; a proposed law.

(2) A bill, a joint resolution, a simple resolution, or a concise resolution. Bills and joint resolutions are legislative measures, simple and concurrent resolutions are nonlegislative measures.

Meeting Hour The hour each house establishes for convening its daily meetings. Each does so by agreeing to a standing order: the Senate at the beginning of each Congress and the House at the beginning of each session of Congress.

Although the Senate traditionally fixes noon as its convening hour, the majority leader often alters the time from day to day—by unanimous consent—to cope with the ebb and flow of the chamber's workload.

The House traditionally set noon as its convening hour until 1977 when it formalized the practice of varying the hour to accommodate committee meetings on certain days of the week and to maximize time for floor action on other days. In recent years it has also fixed earlier meeting hours beginning about May 15, the date on which the House may begin to consider annual appropriation bills under the timetable of the budget process. As in the Senate, these times are sometimes altered for particular days by unanimous consent.

In 1993, the House standing order fixed its meeting hour at noon on Mondays and Tuesdays, 2 p.m. on Wednesdays, and 11 a.m. on all other days, until May 15. For the remainder of the session, the daily meeting time was set at noon on Mondays and Tuesdays and 10 a.m. on all other days. (*See* Standing Order. *See also* Continuing Body.)

Member (1) Generic term for one who serves in the House of Representatives or Senate.

(2) One who serves on a committee.

Members' Allowances Official expenses that are paid for or for which members are reimbursed by their houses. Among these are the costs of office space in congressional buildings and in their home states or districts; office equipment and supplies; postage-free mailings (the franking privilege); a set number of trips to and from home states or districts, as well as travel elsewhere on official business; telephone and other telecommunications services; and staff salaries.

All allowances are authorized by law, but each house determines for itself the details and regulations governing many of them. Some allowances are subject to dollar limits, others are not. The two houses sometimes differ on these and other conditions. All allowances are paid from contingent funds. (*See* Appropriation Account, Congressional District, Contingent Fund, Frank.)

Members' Bills Congressional jargon for minor tax bills sponsored by individual members of the House Ways and Means Committee and reported by that committee.

Memorial A communication to Congress, usually from a state legislature, requesting some kind of legislation or expressing the sense of that legislature on some question. (*See also* Petition.)

Message (1) As a noun, an official communication between the houses or from the president to one or both houses. Messages between the houses are used principally to transmit a measure a house has passed or a measure with amendments between the houses. Presidential messages might contain legislative suggestions, a veto, or other information. The Constitution authorizes the president to recommend to Congress "such Measures as he shall judge necessary and expedient." (*See* Amendments Between the Houses, Executive Communication, Veto. *See also* Blue Slip Resolution.)

(2) As a verb, to message is to send such a communication.

Method of Equal Proportions The mathematical formula used since 1950 to determine how the 435 seats in the House of Representatives should be distributed among the 50 states in the apportionment following each decennial census. It minimizes as much as possible the proportional difference between the average district population in any two states.

Because the Constitution guarantees each state at least one representative, fifty seats are automatically apportioned. The formula calculates priority numbers for each state, assigns the first of the 385 remaining seats to the state with the highest priority number, the second to the state with the next highest number, and so on until all seats are distributed. (*See* Apportionment.)

Mid-Session Budget Review A report to Congress that is prepared by the Office of Management and Budget updating the president's budget estimates and economic forecast. The president is required to submit it no later than July 15 each year. (*See* Budget.)

Midterm Election The general election for members of Congress that occurs in November of the second year in a presidential term.

Minority Floor Manager (*See* Floor Manager.)

Minority Leader The minority party's leader and chief floor spokesman, elected by the party caucus; sometimes called minority floor leader. With the assistance of other party officials and the ranking minority members of committees, the minority leader devises the party's political and procedural strategy.

Because the Senate's rules allow the minority to obstruct the chamber's proceedings in numerous ways, the majority leader usually negotiates with the minority leader on decisions about the legislative schedule and other institutional matters.

In the House, whose rules severely limit dilatory tactics, the minority leader's influence on the chamber's agenda usually depends on his or her personal relationship with the Speaker, the number of minority party members, and the coalitions built with like-minded majority party factions. Customarily, the Speaker consults the minority leader on legislative matters more as a matter of courtesy than of necessity, except when nonpartisan institutional matters arise. (*See* Dilatory Tactics, Party Caucus, Ranking Minority Member, Speaker. *See also* Majority Leader.)

Minority Staff The staff who assist the minority party members of a committee. The Senate's rules on minority staff are more generous than those of the House. Its regulation declares that a committee's staff should reflect the relative number of the committee's majority and minority members and guarantees the minority at least one-third of the funds available for staff.

In the House, a majority of a standing committee's minority members are authorized to select six of its eighteen professional staff and four of its twelve clerical permanent staff, but these selections are subject to approval by the full committee in each individual case. The rule also permits the ranking minority member of a standing subcommittee to appoint one staff member to serve at his or her pleasure. However, House rules do not guarantee minority members control over the hiring of any investigative staff. (*See* Investigative Staff. *See also* Permanent Staff, Staff Director.)

Minority Views (*See* Supplemental, Minority, and Additional Views.)

Minority Whip (*See* Whip.)

Modified Rule A special rule from the House Rules Committee that permits only certain amendments to be offered to a measure during its floor consideration or that bans certain specified amendments or amendments on certain subjects.

A House Democratic Caucus rule directs that no committee chairman shall seek and no Democratic members of the Rules Committee shall support any special rule prohibiting any germane amendment to any bill reported from the committee until four legislative days after the chairman gives notice in the *Congressional Record* of an intention to do so. If within those four days fifty or more Democrats give that chairman and the chairman of the Rules Committee notice that they wish to offer a particular germane amendment, the chairman may not seek and the Democratic members of the Rules Committee may not support the proposed rule until the caucus decides whether such a rule should be allowed. (*See* Party Caucus, Rule.)

Modifying an Amendment A member's action in altering his or her pending amendment. In the House, members may not modify their amendments except by unanimous consent, nor offer amendments to their own amendments. Senators may modify their amendments unless the Senate has taken some action on them, for example, by amending them or ordering the yeas and nays on them. (*See* Amendment, Yeas and Nays. *See also* Withdrawal of Motions.)

Morning Business In the Senate, routine business transacted at the beginning of the morning hour at the demand of any senator. The business consists, first, of laying before the Senate, and referring to committees, messages from the president and the House, federal agency reports, and unreferred petitions, memorials, bills, and joint resolutions. Next, senators may present additional petitions and memorials, then committees may present their reports, and then senators may introduce bills and resolutions. Finally, resolutions coming over from a previous day are taken up for consideration.

In practice, the Senate adopts standing orders that permit senators to introduce measures and file reports at any time, but only if there has been a morning business period on that day. Because the Senate often remains in the same legislative day for several days, weeks, or months at a time, it orders a morning business period almost every calendar day for the convenience of senators who wish to introduce measures or make reports. (*See* Bills and Resolutions Introduced, Executive Communication, Legislative Day, Memorial, Morning Hour, Over Under the Rule, Petition. *See also* Leader (*or* Leadership) Time, Special Order Speech.)

Morning Hour A two-hour period at the beginning of a new legislative day during which the Senate is supposed to conduct routine business, call the calendar on Mondays, and deal with other matters described in a Senate rule. In practice, it often does not occur because the Senate frequently recesses, rather than adjourns, at the end of a daily session and therefore the rule does not apply when it next meets.

The rule reserves the first hour for morning business, but a Senate order permits senators to deliver so-called morning hour speeches on any subject for up to five minutes (or longer by unanimous consent) during this period. The rule then requires a call of the calendar until the end of the two-hour period. In contemporary practice, the calendar is usually called at a more convenient time during the day's proceedings and under a unanimous consent order. Senate committees are allowed to meet during the morning hour without special leave but not during the rest of a Senate session unless the two floor leaders jointly grant permission.

After the completion of morning business, or at the end of the first hour, the rules permit a motion to proceed to the consideration of a measure on the calendar out of its regular order (except on Mondays). Because that normally debatable motion is not debatable if offered during the morning hour, the majority leader sometimes uses this procedure when he anticipates a filibuster on the motion to consider. If the Senate agrees to the motion, it can consider the measure until the end of the morning hour, and if there is no unfinished business from the previous day it can continue considering it after the morning hour. But if there is unfinished business, a motion to continue consideration is necessary, and that motion is debatable. (*See* Call of the Calendar, Consider, Debate, Filibuster, Legislative Day, Morning Business, Order of Business (Senate), Recess, Unfinished Business.)

Motion A formal proposal for a procedural action, such as to consider, to amend, to lay on the table, to reconsider, to recess, or to adjourn. It has been estimated that at least eighty-five motions are possible under various circumstances in the House of Representatives, somewhat fewer in the Senate.

Usually, a motion is offered or moved by a member when he or she is recognized, but in some parliamentary situations certain motions are considered as pending. By rule or custom, the chair recognizes particular individuals, such as floor managers, the majority leader, or a minority member, to offer some types of motions.

Most motions may be offered under some circumstances but not others. For instance, in the House, a motion to lay on the table or to adjourn is not permitted in Committee of the Whole. Furthermore, an amendable proposition must be pending before a member may offer an amendment to it. House rules permit the Speaker to deny recognition for dilatory motions; Senate rules forbid dilatory motions under cloture.

Generally, a motion takes effect only after the body agrees to it by a vote or by unanimous consent. However, by unanimous consent in either house or by a special rule in the House, a chamber may agree in advance that a particular motion will automatically go into effect at a certain stage of the proceedings. Many special rules, for example, require automatic imposition of the previous question when the House acts on a measure reported from the Committee of the Whole.

Not all motions are created equal; some are privileged or preferential and enjoy a priority over others. And some motions are debatable, amendable, or divisible, while others are not. (*See* Adjourn, Amendment, Committee of the Whole, Consider, Dilatory Tactics, Division of a Question for Voting, Floor Manager, Lay on the Table, Majority Leader, Nondebatable Motions, Preferential Motion, Preferential Recognition, Previous Question, Privilege, Recess, Recognition, Reconsider a Vote, Rule, Unanimous Consent. *See also* Debate-Ending Motion.)

Move The act of offering a motion, as in "Mr. Speaker, I move that the House do now adjourn," or "Mr. President, I move that the Senate proceed to the consideration of S. 135."

Multiple and Sequential Referrals The practice of referring a measure simultaneously to two or more committees for concurrent consideration (multiple or joint referral), or successively to several committees in sequence (sequential referral). A measure may also be divided into several parts, each referred to a different committee or to several committees sequentially (split referral). In theory, this gives all committees that have jurisdiction over parts of a measure the opportunity to consider and report on them.

Prior to 1975, House precedents banned such referrals. A 1975 rule requires the Speaker to make concurrent and sequential referrals "to the maximum extent feasible." On sequential referrals, the Speaker may set deadlines for reporting the measure. The Speaker has ruled that this provision authorizes him to discharge a committee from further consideration of a measure and place it on the appropriate calendar of the House if the committee fails to meet his deadline. The Speaker may also use a combination of concurrent and sequential referrals on a measure.

In the Senate, before 1977, concurrent and sequential referrals were only permitted by unanimous consent. In that year, a rule authorized a privileged motion for such referrals if offered jointly by the majority and minority leaders. Debate on the motion and all amendments to it is limited to two hours. The motion may set deadlines for reporting and provide for discharging the committees involved if they fail to meet the deadlines. To date, this procedure has never been invoked; multiple referrals in the Senate continue to be made by unanimous consent. (*See* Bills and Resolutions Referred, Calendar, Discharge a Committee. *See also* Committee Jurisdiction, Division of Bills for Referral.)

Multiyear Appropriation An appropriation that remains available for spending or obligation for more than one fiscal year; the exact period of time is specified in the act making the appropriation. Some multiyear appropriations are made available for periods that do not coincide with the beginning or end of a fiscal year. (*See* Appropriation, Fiscal Year, Forward Funding, Obligation.)

Multiyear Authorization (1) Legislation that authorizes the existence or continuation of an agency, program, or activity for more than one fiscal year.

(2) Legislation that authorizes appropriations for

an agency, program, or activity for more than one fiscal year. (*See* Appropriation, Fiscal Year.)

Must-Pass Bill Congressional jargon for a bill whose passage is critically important, often because it is needed to continue the operations of the federal government, to pay for its obligations, or to protect its credit. Chief among must-pass bills are the regular annual appropriation bills, continuing resolutions, and bills to raise the federal debt ceiling.

Because the president is usually reluctant to veto such measures, members often try to attach riders to them that the president might reject if sent to him as separate measures. And because a must-pass bill is so urgently needed, a senator's threat to filibuster it often persuades the Senate to accept the rider or take some other action that is demanded. The last major must-pass bill of a session, sometimes called "the last train out of the station," invariably attracts many riders. Hence, such bills are sometimes called "Christmas tree bills," with the riders as ornaments. (*See* Debt Limit, Filibuster, General Appropriation Bill, Rider, Veto. *See also* Christmas Tree Bill, Omnibus Bill.)

N

Negative Outlay (*See* Offsetting Receipts.)

Nomination A proposed presidential appointment to a federal office submitted to the Senate for confirmation. Approval is by majority vote.

The Constitution explicitly requires confirmation for ambassadors, consuls, "public Ministers" (department heads), and Supreme Court justices. By law, other federal judges, all military promotions of officers, and many high-level civilian officials must be confirmed. Nominations lapse if the Senate does not approve them before sine die adjournment or before it adjourns or recesses for more than thirty days. If the president wants a decision on these nominations, they must be resubmitted during the next session.

In any year, the Senate processes almost 40,000 nominations, most of them for military positions and the vast bulk with little debate or objection. Usually, but not always, the Senate gives the president the benefit of the doubt on cabinet and Supreme Court nominations. The Senate often rejects nominations to federal positions in states when the nominations are opposed by senators of the president's party from those states. Presidents often withdraw nominations that the Senate refuses to act on or that arouse considerable controversy. (*See also* Advice and Consent, Courtesy Calls, *Executive Calendar*, Recess Appointment, Senatorial Courtesy.)

Nondebatable Motions Motions that must be put to an immediate vote without discussion. Both houses prohibit debate on the motions to adjourn, recess, and lay on the table. Other major nondebatable motions in the Senate include those to consider conference reports, to consider measures during the morning hour, and to close the doors. Other nondebatable House motions include a call of the House, to order the previous question, to resolve into the Committee of the Whole, that the Committee of the Whole rise and report, to close general debate, and to close debate on amendments in Committee of the Whole. (*See* Adjourn, Amendment, Committee of the Whole, Conference' Report, Lay on the Table, Morning Hour, Previous Question, Recess, Secret *or* Closed Session. *See also* Debate-Ending Motion.)

Nongermane Senate Amendment A Senate amendment to a House bill that would be held nongermane if offered in the House. A 1970 House rule, which was subsequently revised and expanded, permits a point of order against such an amendment if it is included in a conference report or reported in disagreement by a conference committee. If the point is upheld, any member may offer a motion to reject it. If the House agrees to reject one or more nongermane provision in a conference report, the entire report is automatically rejected, and the House may then send to the Senate whatever remains of the conference report in the form of an amendment between the houses.

If the House rejects a nongermane Senate amendment *not* contained in a conference report, it may take further steps permitted under the procedure of amendments between the houses.

In either situation, debate on motions to reject is limited to forty minutes divided equally between proponents and opponents.

Before 1970, the House was not allowed to amend or reject a part of a conference report; it could only accept or reject the whole report. The 1970 rule gives the House a procedure for circumventing the all-or-nothing approach and gives its conferees leverage in refusing to agree to Senate riders.

Generally, a sustained point of order immediately prevents the violation of a rule; under the 1970 rule, a sustained point of order permits the House to decide whether it wants to prevent or permit a violation. (*See* Amendments Between the Houses, Amendments in Disagreement, Concur, Conferees, Conference Committee, Conference Report, Germane, Point of Order, Rider, Sustained.)

Nonlegislative Period The Senate term for a scheduled congressional recess during which senators can visit their states and meet with constituents. (*See* Recess. *See* also District Work Period.)

Nonmajor Committees The rules of the House Democratic Caucus apply this designation to ten committees and state that no Democratic representative can serve on more than two of them. A member who serves on a major committee is limited to one nonmajor committee assignment. As of 1993, the following committees were considered nonmajor: Budget; District of Columbia; Government Operations; House Administration; Merchant Marine and Fisheries; Natural Resources; Post Office and Civil Service; Science, Space, and Technology; Small Business; and Veterans' Affairs. (*See* Committee Assignments, Major Committees.)

Non-Selfenforcing Rules A term sometimes applied to rules that the chair usually does not enforce on his own initiative. He is required to enforce rules only when a member makes a timely and valid point of order or demands the regular order.

For example, most of the rules concerning the authorization-appropriation process, budget process, required contents of committee reports on measures, and prohibitions relating to conference reports are non-selfenforcing. The fact that a house has taken an action that violates one of these rules does not invalidate that action. If members want such rules enforced, they must demand enforcement. (*See* Authorization-Appropriation Process, Budget Process, Committee Report on a Measure, Conference Report, Point of Order, Regular Order, Rule.)

Not in Order (*See* Out of Order.)

Notice Quorum (*See* Short Quorum.)

No-Year Appropriation An appropriation that is obligated for an indefinite period. The unobligated balances of one-year and multiyear appropriations revert to the Treasury at the end of the period for which they are provided. (*See* Appropriation, Obligation, Unobligated Balance.)

Numbered Amendments In the Senate, amendments submitted for printing are numbered sequentially through a Congress. Unprinted amendments are similarly numbered. (*See* Printed Amendment, Unprinted Amendment.)

O

Oath of Office Upon taking office, members of Congress must swear or affirm that they will "support and defend the Constitution ... against all enemies, foreign and domestic," that they will "bear true faith and allegiance" to the Constitution, that they take the obligation "freely, without any mental reservation or purpose of evasion," and that they will "well and faithfully discharge the duties" of their office. The oath is required by the Constitution; the wording is prescribed by a statute.

All House members must take the oath at the beginning of each new Congress. Usually, the member with the longest continuous service in the House swears in the Speaker, who then swears in the other members. The president of the Senate or a surrogate administers the oath to newly elected senators. (*See also* Father of the House.)

Oaths to Witnesses A statute empowers House and Senate chairmen and members of select or standing committees to administer oaths to witnesses. It also gives the same power to the Speaker and to chairmen of the Committee of the Whole in the House, an authority not exercised in recent times. Violation of such an oath is subject to prosecution and criminal penalty. (*See also* Hearing, Investigative Power.)

Objection (1) In parliamentary usage, a formal objection forestalls an action that violates or circumvents a rule or practice. By definition, a single objection prevents acceptance of a unanimous consent request. In the

House, objections by three or more members prevent consideration of a measure on the consent calendar under certain circumstances. (*See* Consent Calendar, Unanimous Consent Request. *See also* Leave to Sit, Reserving the Right to Object.)

(2) In the plural, the constitutional term for the reasons offered by the president in a veto message. (*See* Veto.)

Objectors (*See* Official Objectors.)

Obligated Balance The amount of an appropriation that has been obligated but not spent. Usually this balance is carried forward to succeeding fiscal years until the obligations are paid. (*See* Obligation. *See also* Unobligated Balance.)

Obligation A binding agreement by a government agency to pay for goods, products, services, studies, and the like, either immediately or in the future. When an agency enters into such an agreement, it incurs an obligation. As the agency makes the required payments, it liquidates the obligation.

Appropriation laws usually make funds available for obligation for one or more fiscal years but do not require agencies to spend their funds during those specific years. The actual outlays can occur years after the appropriation is obligated; for example, a contract for payment for a submarine when it is delivered in the future. Such obligated funds are often said to be "in the pipeline." Under these circumstances, an agency's outlays in a particular year can come from appropriations obligated in previous years as well as from its current-year appropriation. Consequently, the money Congress appropriates for a fiscal year rarely coincides with the total amount of appropriated money the government will actually spend in that year. (*See* Appropriation, Fiscal Year, Outlays. *See also* Backdoor Spending Authority, Balanced Budget.)

Off-Budget Entities Specific federal entities whose budget authority, outlays, and receipts are excluded by law from the calculation of budget totals, although they are part of government spending and income. As of early 1993, these included the Social Security trust funds (Federal Old-Age and Survivors Insurance Fund and the Federal Disability Insurance Trust Fund) and the Postal Service. Government-sponsored enterprises are also excluded from the budget because they are considered private rather than public organizations. (*See* Budget, Budget Authority, Government-Sponsored Enterprises, Outlays.)

Offer To propose. In congressional parlance, members offer amendments and either offer, make, or move a motion. (*See* Amendment, Motion.)

Office of Technology Assessment (OTA) A support agency that assists Congress by producing or contracting for expert studies on the beneficial and adverse affects of the application of current and prospective technologies. It was established by the Technology Assessment Act of 1971. (*See* Congressional Support Agencies.)

Officers of Congress The Constitution refers to the Speaker of the House and the president of the Senate as officers and declares that each house "shall chuse" its "other Officers," but does not name them or indicate how they should be selected. A House rule refers to its clerk, sergeant at arms, doorkeeper, and chaplain as officers.

Officers are not named in the Senate's rules, but *Riddick's Senate Procedure* lists the president pro tempore, secretary of the Senate, sergeant at arms, chaplain, and the secretaries for the majority and minority parties as officers. A few appointed officials are sometimes referred to as officers, including the parliamentarians and the legislative counsels.

The House elects its officers by resolution at the beginning of each Congress. The Senate also elects its officers, but once elected they serve from Congress to Congress until their successors are chosen. (*See* Clerk of the House, Doorkeeper of the House, Legislative Counsel's Office, Parliamentarian, President of the Senate, President Pro Tempore, *Riddick's Senate Procedure*, Secretary of the Senate, Sergeant at Arms.)

Official Conduct (*See* Code of Official Conduct.)

Official Objectors House members who screen measures on the consent calendar or private calendar. They object to those measures that violate certain generally accepted criteria and also to other measures at the request of a party colleague. The leader of each party appoints three objectors for each of the two calendars at the beginning of every Congress. Shortly thereafter, the six objectors for the calendars announce or publish in the *Congressional Record* the criteria they will enforce.

The consent calendar objectors usually oppose measures that (1) involve more than $1 million, (2) change national or international policy, or (3) the membership is not fully informed about. The private calendar objectors do not permit consideration of a private measure until it has been on the calendar at least seven days. They also eliminate measures that provide unfair relief, set undue precedents, or contain controversial provisions. (*See Congressional Record*, Consent Calendar, Majority Leader, Minority Leader, Objection, Private Calendar.)

Official Title A concise statement of a measure's subject and purposes, which appears above the enacting clause. (*See* Enacting Clause, Title.)

Offsetting Receipts Funds collected by the federal government that are not counted as revenue. Instead, they are deducted from outlays and are called negative outlays.

Some receipts are proprietary ones from the public such as flat premiums for supplementary medical insurance, monies from timber and oil leases, and proceeds from the sale of electric power. Others are intragovernmental transactions such as payments by federal agencies to retirement and other funds.

Some offsetting receipts are deducted from specific budget accounts; others, called undistributed offsetting receipts, are deducted from total outlays. (*See also* Budget Receipts, Function *or* Functional Category.)

Omnibus Bill A measure that combines the provisions of several disparate subjects into a single and often lengthy bill. Examples include reconciliation bills, continuing resolutions that contain all or most of the thirteen general appropriation bills, and omnibus claims bills that combine several private bills into a single measure. (*See* Continuing Resolution, General Appropriation Bill, Private Bill, Reconciliation. *See also* Christmas Tree Bill, Conferees, Must-Pass Bill.)

One-Day Rule (1) A Senate rule that requires measures to lie over on the calendar for at least one legislative day before the Senate may consider them. The rule is often waived by unanimous consent. (*See* Calendar, Legislative Day, Unanimous Consent.)

(2) A House rule prohibits consideration of a special rule reported by the Rules Committee until it lies over for at least one legislative day, but the House, by a two-thirds vote, can permit consideration of the rule on the day it is reported. However, a special rule waiving the three-day rule on committee reports and hearings may be considered immediately. (*See* Committee Report on a Measure, Hearing, Legislative Day, Rule, Three-Day Rule.)

(3) Another House rule requires that the printed report on a resolution to fund committee expenses, reported by the House Administration Committee, must be available for at least one calendar day before

the resolution may be considered. (*See also* Contingent Fund.)

One-Hour Rule (*See* Hour Rule.)

One-Minute Speeches Addresses by House members on any subject but limited to one minute each, usually permitted at the beginning of a daily session after the chaplain's prayer and approval of the *Journal*. They are a customary practice, not a right granted by rule. Consequently, recognition for one-minute speeches requires unanimous consent and is entirely within the Speaker's discretion. The Speaker sometimes refuses to permit them when the House has a heavy legislative schedule, or limits or postpones them until a later time of the day.

Since 1984, the Speaker has alternated recognition between majority and minority members. Since 1990, the Speaker has recognized members suggested by their party's leadership before others. Traditionally, the Speaker limits a member to one one-minute speech before the House takes up legislative business each day. (*See Journal* Approval, Recognition, Unanimous Consent.)

One-Speech Rule (1) A House rule limits members to one speech on any question unless the House permits otherwise. A member may speak once on a measure, once on each amendment to it, and once on any debatable motion because the limitation applies to each question. However, the member who has moved or proposed the pending matter and has spoken once on it may speak again after all other members have had an opportunity to speak once. In Committee of the Whole, members circumvent the limitation by offering pro forma amendments. (*See* Amendment, Committee of the Whole, Measure, Motion, Pro Forma Amendment, Question.)

(2) A Senate rule limits senators to one speech of no more than five minutes on a measure and five minutes on each amendment to it during a call of the calendar. (*See* Call of the Calendar. *See also* Two-Speech Rule.)

One-Year Appropriation An appropriation made available for spending or obligation during a single year, usually the fiscal year specified in the enacting clause of the appropriation act. General appropriation acts usually provide one-year appropriations. Any portion of an agency's one-year appropriation that it does not spend or obligate during that fiscal year is said to lapse, and the agency loses it. (*See* Appropriation, Enacting Clause, Fiscal Year, General Appropriation Bill, Obligation.)

Open Hearing A committee hearing that the press and public can attend. (*See* Closed Hearing, Hearing. *See also* Sunshine Rules.)

Open Rule A special rule from the House Rules Committee that permits members to offer as many floor amendments as they wish as long as the amendments are germane and do not violate other House rules. (*See* Amendment, Floor, Germane, Rule.)

Open to Amendment at Any Point A procedural situation in which members may offer amendments to any part of a pending measure in no particular order. This contrasts with situations in which a measure is considered for amendment section by section, or title by title, and only amendments to the pending section or title are permitted. In the Senate, all measures are open to amendment at any point. The same is true in the House sitting as the House, but not when the House is in Committee of the Whole. (*See* Committee of the Whole, House Sitting as the House, Reading for Amendment, Section, Title.)

Order (1) As a noun, a continuing or temporary regulation or directive not incorporated into a chamber's standing rules. Continuing orders are called standing orders. Temporary ones are sometimes called special orders. Both types are created either by unanimous consent or by adopting a resolution.

The most notable types of temporary orders are unanimous consent agreements for the consideration of measures in the Senate and special rules for the same purpose reported by the House Rules Committee. Examples of other temporary orders include those that direct the chamber to adjourn at the conclusion of certain business, or recess for a certain period of time during the day, or reconvene at a specified hour the next day.

The House uses few standing orders, and those it adopts expire at the end of a Congress because the House is not a continuing body. Senate standing orders continue from one Congress to the next, like its standing rules, unless changed or the order states otherwise. Some Senate orders establish permanent entities such as the Select Ethics Committee, the Select Intelligence Committee, the U.S. Senate Commission on Art, and the Office of Deputy President Pro Tempore. These and others appear in the *Senate Manual* under the title "Nonstatutory Standing Orders Not Embraced in the Rules. . . ." (*See* Adjourn, Continuing Body, Recess, Rule, *Senate Manual,* Standing Rules, Unanimous Consent Agreement. *See also* Special Order, Special Order Speech.)

(2) Compliance with the rules and practices of appropriate parliamentary behavior during meetings' of a house or a committee. (*See also* Call to Order, Decorum, Out of Order, Regular Order, Speak Out of Order.)

(3) Precedence of certain actions, such as the order of business or the voting order on amendments. (*See* Order of Business (House), Order of Business (Senate),

Voting Order on Amendments. *See also* Special Order of Business.)

(4) As a verb, the term used for approval of certain actions, such as to order the yeas and nays, the previous question, or engrossment and third reading of a measure. (*See* Engrossment and Third Reading, Previous Question, Yeas and Nays. *See also* Approval Terminology, Ordered Reported.)

Order of Business (House) The sequence of events during the meeting of the House on a new legislative day prescribed by a House rule; also called the general order of business. The sequence consists of (1) the chaplain's prayer; (2) approval of the *Journal*; (3) correction of the reference of public bills; (4) disposal of business on the Speaker's table; (5) unfinished business; (6) the morning hour call of committees and consideration of their bills (largely obsolete); (7) motions to go into Committee of the Whole; and (8) orders of the day (also obsolete).

In practice, on days specified in the rules, the items of business that follow approval of the *Journal* are supplanted in part by the special order of business (for example, the consent, discharge, or private calendars) and on any day by other privileged business (for example, general appropriation bills and special rules) or measures made in order by special rules.

By this combination of an order of business with privileged interruptions, the House gives precedence to certain categories of important legislation, brings to the floor other major legislation from its calendars in any order it chooses, and provides expeditious processing for minor and noncontroversial measures. (*See* Bills and Resolutions Referred, Committee of the Whole, Consent Calendar, Discharge Calendar, General Appropriation Bill, *Journal* Approval, Private Calendar, Privileged Interruptions, Rule, Speaker's Table, Special Order of Business, Unfinished Business.)

Order of Business (Senate) The sequence of events at the beginning of a new legislative day prescribed by Senate rules. The sequence consists of (1) the chaplain's prayer; (2) *Journal* reading and correction; (3) morning business in the morning hour; (4) call of the calendar during the morning hour; and (5) unfinished business. (*See* Call of the Calendar, *Journal* Approval, Morning Business, Morning Hour, Unfinished Business. *See* also Over Under the Rule.)

Ordered Reported A committee's formal action of agreeing to report a measure to its house for floor consideration. (*See* Floor, Report.)

Organization of Congress The actions the two houses take at the beginning of a Congress that are necessary to their operations. These include swearing in newly elected members, notifying the president that a quorum of each house is present, making committee assignments, and fixing the hour for daily meetings. Because the House of Representatives is not a continuing body, it must also elect its Speaker and other officers and adopt its rules. (*See* Committee Assignments, Congress, Meeting Hour, Officers of Congress, Rule. *See also* Early Organization of the House.)

Original Bill (1) A bill drafted by a committee and introduced by its chairman, or by a subcommittee chairman, when the committee reports the measure to its house. Unlike a clean bill, it is not referred back to the committee after introduction. The Senate permits all its standing committees to report original bills. In the House, only the Appropriations Committee has that authority, and it is strictly confined to general appropriation bills and continuing resolutions. (*See* Clean Bill, Continuing Resolution, General Appropriation Bill, Report, Standing Committee. *See also* Bills and Resolutions Introduced, Bills and Resolutions Referred, Original Jurisdiction, Report at Any Time.)

(2) In the House, special rules reported by the Rules Committee often require that an amendment in the nature of a substitute be considered as an original bill for purposes of amendment, meaning that the substitute, like a bill, may be amended in two degrees. Without that requirement, the substitute may only be amended to one degree. The Senate's synonymous term is "original text." Under the Senate's precedents, a committee amendment in the nature of a substitute is always considered as original text for purposes of amendment. (*See* Amendment in the Nature of a Substitute, Degrees of Amendment, Rule.)

Original Jurisdiction The authority of certain committees to originate a measure and report it to the chamber. For example, general appropriation bills reported by the House Appropriations Committee are original bills, and special rules reported by the House Rules Committee are original resolutions. (*See* General Appropriation Bill, Original Bill, Rule. *See also* Report at Any Time.)

Origination Clause Clause 1 of Article I, Section 7 of the Constitution, which grants the House the sole prerogative to originate revenue legislation. (*See* Revenue Legislation.)

OTA (*See* Office of Technology Assessment.)

Other Body A commonly used reference to a house by a member of the other house. Congressional comity discourages members from directly naming the other house during debate. (*See* Comity. *See also* Body, Decorum, Lower Body, Upper Body.)

Out of Order (1) Improper behavior by a member during a meeting: for example, such as addressing remarks directly to another member instead of to the chair. (*See also* Call to Order, Decorum, Regular Order, Speak Out of Order.)

(2) An action or proposal, such as a motion, that is not permitted at a particular time. For example, in the Committee of the Whole it is not in order to demand the yeas and nays or to move the previous question. (*See* Committee of the Whole, Previous Question, Yeas and Nays.)

Outlays Amounts of government spending. They consist of payments, usually by check or in cash, to liquidate obligations incurred in prior fiscal years as well as in the current year, including the net lending of funds under budget authority. In federal budget accounting, net outlays are calculated by subtracting the amounts of refunds and various kinds of reimbursements to the government from actual spending. (*See* Budget Authority, Direct Loan, Fiscal Year, Obligation. *See also* Offsetting Receipts, Unexpended Balances.)

Outyears Years that follow an upcoming fiscal year. The Congressional Budget Act of 1974 requires both the president and Congress to make projections of economic conditions and budget estimates for several outyears. In addition, committee reports on measures are required to contain cost estimates of that measure for the upcoming fiscal year and the following five fiscal years. (*See* Congressional Budget and Impoundment Control Act of 1974, Cost Estimates, Fiscal Year.)

Over Under the Rule A Senate procedure for considering simple and concurrent resolutions without first referring them to committees; seldom used in recent years. Except by unanimous consent, such resolutions may not be considered on the day they are submitted and must "lie over" for at least one day. If unanimous consent is refused, the resolution goes on the calendar in a section titled "Resolutions and Motions Over, Under the Rule." On the next legislative day, the chair lays resolutions over under the rule before the Senate at the end of morning business in the order that they appear on the calendar, and the chamber considers them.

If the Senate does not complete action on a pending resolution by the end of the morning hour, it goes on the calendar of general orders where it is subject to the normal rules for bringing measures to the floor. Resolutions not called up during the morning hour maintain their status as over under the rule and are called up during the next morning hour. (*See* Calendar of General Orders, Legislative Day, Morning Business, Morning Hour, Unanimous Consent.)

Overlapping Jurisdiction (*See* Committee Jurisdiction.)

Override a Veto Congressional enactment of a measure over the president's veto. A veto override requires a recorded two-thirds vote of those voting in each house, a quorum being present. Because the president must return the vetoed measure to its house of origin, that house votes first, but neither house is required to attempt an override, whether immediately or at all. If an override attempt fails in the house of origin, the veto stands and the measure dies.

The question put to each house is: "Shall the bill [or joint resolution] pass, the objections of the president to the contrary notwithstanding?" The question is highly privileged in both houses. In the House, it is considered under the hour rule. In the Senate, the motion to consider and the question itself are debatable. (*See* Consider, Hour Rule, Privilege, Question, Quorum, Recorded Vote, Veto. *See also* Unlimited Debate.)

Overrule To decide against a point of order; an adverse ruling. A chair is said to sustain a point of order when he or she upholds one. (*See* Chair, Point of Order. *See also* Ruling.)

Oversight Congressional review of the way in which federal agencies implement laws to ensure that they are carrying out the intent of Congress and to inquire into the efficiency of the implementation and the effectiveness of the law. The Legislative Reorganization Act of 1946 defined oversight as the function of exercising continuous watchfulness over the execution of the laws by the executive branch.

The rules of both houses assign this responsibility to their standing committees and direct them to determine, on the basis of their reviews, whether laws within their respective jurisdictions should be changed or if additional laws are necessary. The function is also sometimes called legislative review.

The House requires each of its committees with twenty or more members to establish an oversight subcommittee or direct all its subcommittees to conduct oversight on subjects within their jurisdictions. Furthermore, a House committee report on a measure must include its relevant oversight findings. Senate committees must submit a report on their oversight activities by March 31 of each odd-numbered year. (*See* Committee Report on a Measure. *See also* General Accounting Office, Investigative Power.)

P

Page and Line Identification The system used to identify the location of text in bills and resolutions. The lines on each page of a measure, as well as the pages, are sequentially numbered. This permits precise identification of the text for the purpose of amendment. Typical amendments may read: "On page 53, strike out lines 5 through 14." "On page 12, strike out the sentence beginning on line 10, and insert in lieu thereof. . . ." "On page 104, line 7, after the first comma, insert. . . ." (*See* Amendment.)

Pairing A procedure that permits two or three members to enter into voluntary arrangements that offset their votes so that one or more of the members can be absent without changing the result. The names of paired members and their positions on the vote (except on general pairs) appear in the *Congressional Record*. Members can be paired on one vote or on a series of votes.

Pairs take three forms: (1) In a live pair, a member on one side who is present withholds his vote when his pair partner on the other side is absent. On a two-thirds vote, two members in favor withhold their votes to offset the absence of one opponent, or one opponent withholds his vote when two favoring the question are absent.

(2) In a specific pair, sometimes called a special or dead pair, both members (or all three) are absent, and the *Record* identifies how they would have voted.

(3) In a general pair, absent members are listed as paired with no indication how either might have voted. Therefore it no longer has any practical purpose.

In the House, party pair clerks help arrange these informal agreements. Leadership staff handle them in the Senate. Pairs are not enforceable because they are informal arrangements.

Pairs are not counted in tabulating the final results of recorded votes so the outcomes are not affected by specific and general pairs; if the members had been present, their votes would have added equally to both sides. But a live pair subtracts a vote that might otherwise have been counted, and several of them, or even one, may affect the outcome of a close vote.

Pairing is one of the many practices Congress copied from the British House of Commons, where it had been used at least as early as 1743. When a pair resulted in the defeat of a resolution in the House in 1840, John Quincy Adams denounced it as a violation of the Constitution and unsuccessfully tried to outlaw the practice. The House did not permit pairing in Committee of the Whole until 1975. (*See* Committee of the Whole, *Congressional Record*, General Pair, Leadership, Live Pair, Specific Pair.)

(The) Papers Certain documents that are passed back and forth between the houses as they attempt to resolve their differences on a measure. These include the original engrossed copy of the measure, the engrossed amendments of one house to the other's measure or amendments, any special acts concurring with amendments, the messages transmitting them, and, later, the conference report signed by the managers. (*See* Amendments Between the Houses, Conference Report, Custody of the Papers, Engrossed Bill, Message.)

Paragraph by Paragraph In the House, the method by which appropriation bills are read for amendment in Committee of the Whole. (*See* Reading for Amendment. *See also* Open to Amendment at Any Point, Section by Section.)

Parallel Jurisdiction (*See* Committee Jurisdiction.)

Parliamentarian The official advisor to the presiding officer in each house on questions of procedure. The parliamentarian and his assistants also answer procedural questions from members and congressional staff, refer measures to committees on behalf of the presiding officer, and maintain compilations of the precedents. The House parliamentarian revises the House Manual at the beginning of every Congress and usually reviews special rules before the Rules Committee reports them to the House.

Either a parliamentarian or an assistant is always present and near the podium during sessions of each house. To help them anticipate points of order, parliamentary inquiries, and other procedural questions, the parliamentarians review most measures before they come to the floor. The Senate parliamentarian is also the Senate's official timekeeper when debate is under time limitations.

The Speaker appoints the House parliamentarian. Nominally, the secretary of the Senate appoints its parliamentarian, but always with the approval of the majority leader.

Unofficial parliamentarians advised the presiding officers during most of the nineteenth and early twentieth centuries. The House formally recognized the position in 1927, the Senate not until 1937. In 1977, the House established an office of the parliamentarian and directed that it be managed, supervised, and administered by a nonpartisan parliamentarian appointed by the Speaker. (*See* Bills and Resolutions Referred, Majority Leader, Parliamentary Inquiry, Point of Order, Precedent, Procedures, Rule, Secretary of the Senate. *See also Deschler's Precedents,* Officers of Congress, *Riddick's Senate Procedure.*)

Parliamentary Inquiry A member's question, posed to the presiding officer, about a pending procedural situation. Although not required to answer such questions, the chair usually does if they are proper inquiries and properly made. A proper inquiry deals only with questions of procedure on a pending matter, not on the interpretation or consistency of amendments or on hypothetical situations. To make a parliamentary inquiry, a member must have the floor or the member having the floor must yield it for that purpose. (*See* Floor, Hold (*or* Have) the Floor, Yielding.)

Parliamentary Law The formal rules governing the methods of procedure, discussion, and debate in deliberative bodies and organized assemblies. The House of Representatives follows general parliamentary law at the beginning of a new Congress before it adopts its own rules. As understood in the House, this law is founded in *Jefferson's Manual* as modified by the practice of U.S.

legislative assemblies, especially the House itself. (*See Jefferson's Manual.*)

Party Caucus Generic term for each party's official organization in each house. Only House Democrats officially call their organization a caucus. House and Senate Republicans and Senate Democrats call their organizations conferences.

The party caucuses elect their leaders, approve committee assignments and chairmanships (or ranking minority members, if the party is in the minority), establish party committees and study groups, and discuss party and legislative policies. On rare occasions, they have stripped members of committee seniority or expelled them from the caucus for party disloyalty. In the past, the House and Senate Democratic caucuses had so-called binding rules that required their members to support a party position adopted by a super majority of the caucus on threat of expulsion.

Caucus rules of both parties in both houses place certain limitations on the number of chairmanships or ranking minority positions a member may hold and on members' assignments to certain types of committees. House Democratic Caucus rules require certain procedures for the election of subcommittee chairmen and members and limit the number of such chairmanships any member can hold.

Some House Democratic Caucus rules have a direct impact on House floor and committee procedures. Under one rule, if at least fifty Democrats oppose a special rule that prohibits a germane amendment, Democratic members of the Rules Committee may not support that rule unless the caucus decides otherwise. Another rule limits the kinds of measures the Speaker may schedule for suspension of the rules. Still another rule directs committee chairmen to permit subcommittee chairmen to handle floor consideration of legislation from their respective subcommittees.

Democratic Caucus rules also require a minimum of three Democrats for each two Republican members on standing committees, limit the number of subcommittees on those committees, and prescribe the maximum sizes for subcommittees. Finally, a caucus rule directs that the ratio of Democratic to Republican conference managers be at least as favorable as their ratio on the committee from which they are selected. (*See* Closed Rule, Committee Assignments, Committee Ratios, Conferees, Floor Manager, Managers, Rule, Subcommittee, Super Majority, Suspension of the Rules (House). *See also* Caucus.)

Party Leader (*See* Majority Leader, Minority Leader.)

Party Ratios (*See* Committee Ratios, Conferees.)

Party Tables Tables in the House chamber on the Democratic and Republican sides of the aisle that are reserved for the use of their respective party members. Those who do not wish to speak from the well of the House use the microphones attached to their party tables. Party tables are also called committee tables because the committee floor managers of a measure sit at them during House consideration of the measure. (*See* Aisle, Floor Manager, Well.)

Pass Over Without Prejudice In the House, a request to defer action on a measure called up from the consent or private calendar without affecting the measure's position on its calendar. It requires unanimous consent. The request usually implies that members need time to deal with some problem connected with the measure. (*See* Consent Calendar, Private Calendar, Unanimous Consent.)

Passed The term applied to bills and joint resolutions that have been approved by a house. (*See also* Approval Terminology.)

Pastore Rule Familiar title of a Senate rule requiring that "all debate shall be germane and confined to the specific question then pending" during the first three hours of a day. The three hours begin after the morning hour on a new legislative day or after the Senate takes up business on any calendar day. Germane debate in the Senate is not required under any other circumstances. The rule's author was Sen. John O. Pastore (D-R.I.). (*See* Business, Germane, Legislative Day, Morning Hour.)

Pay-As-You-Go (PAYGO) A requirement of the Budget Enforcement Act of 1990, effective for fiscal years 1991-1995, that congressional action on revenue legislation and legislation on entitlement or other mandatory programs should not add to the budget deficit. Increased spending for such programs resulting from new legislation and revenue losses from legislation reducing taxes or fees are supposed to be offset by legislated spending reductions in other programs subject to PAYGO or by legislated increases in other taxes.

If Congress fails to enact the appropriate offsets, the act requires presidential sequestration of sufficient offsetting amounts in specific direct spending accounts. Congress and the president can circumvent the requirement if both agree that an emergency makes a particular action necessary or if a law is enacted declaring that deteriorated economic circumstances make it necessary to suspend the requirement. (*See* Direct Spending, Entitlement Program, Fiscal Year, Revenue Legislation, Sequestration.)

Pending Amendment(s) In the singular, the amendment on which the next vote will occur. In the plural, all amendments that have been offered but not yet voted on, withdrawn, or temporarily laid aside. The number of pending amendments to a measure usually does not exceed four or five, but Senate practices permit as many as seven, and nine are possible in the House.

The Senate's possible seven pending amendments are: (1) an amendment in the nature of a substitute (ANS); (2) a first degree substitute for it; (3) a second degree amendment to the first degree substitute; (4) a perfecting amendment to the ANS; (5) a second degree amendment to that perfecting amendment; (6) a perfecting amendment to the text of the measure; and (7) a second degree amendment to the perfecting amendment. While one or more of these is pending, a senator also may offer a motion to recommit with instructions; the instructions are subject to a first and second degree amendment.

Although the situation rarely occurs, the nine simultaneously pending amendments permitted in the House are: (1) an amendment in the nature of a substitute; (2) a first degree amendment to it; (3) a second degree amendment to the first degree amendment; (4) a substitute for the first degree amendment; (5) a perfecting amendment to the substitute; (6) a first degree amendment to the text of the measure; (7) a second degree amendment to the first degree amendment; (8) a substitute for the first degree amendment; and (9) an amendment to that substitute. (*See* Amendment, Amendment in the Nature of a Substitute, Degrees of Amendment, Perfecting Amendment, Recommit with Instructions, Substitute. *See also* Original Bill, Voting Order on Amendments.)

Pending Business A measure or matter that a house is considering. In both houses, certain rules apply only to pending business. For example, a cloture motion in the Senate applies only to pending business. (*See* Business, Cloture, Measure. *See also* Unfinished Business.)

Perfect a Measure or Amendment Procedural terminology for the process of amending a measure or amendment. *Jefferson's Manual* declares that "the friends of [a text] are first to make it as perfect as they can by amendments. . . ."

The implication that those offering amendments are friendly to the text is not necessarily true. On the contrary, opponents of the text can try to perfect it with amendments that eviscerate its intent or make it so grotesque as to be unacceptable to its friends. (*See* Amendment, *Jefferson's Manual. See also* Perfecting Amendment, Substitute.)

Perfecting Amendment An amendment other than a substitute. It alters language in a bill or another amendment but does not replace the entire text of either one. (*See* Amendment, Substitute. *See also* Voting Order on Amendments.)

Permanent Appropriation An appropriation that remains continuously available, without current action or renewal by Congress, under the terms of a previously enacted authorization or appropriation law. One such appropriation provides for payment of interest on the public debt and another the salaries of members of Congress. (*See* Appropriation, Authorization, Public Debt.)

Permanent Authorization An authorization without a time limit. It usually does not specify any limit on the funds that may be appropriated for the agency, program, or activity that it authorizes, leaving such amounts to the discretion of the appropriations committees and the two houses. A permanent authorization continues in effect unless, or until, Congress changes or terminates it. (*See* Appropriation, Authorization. *See also* Annual Authorization, Multiyear Authorization.)

Permanent *Record* The permanent, hardbound editions of the *Congressional Record* published some time after the conclusion of a session of a Congress. Members sometimes ask that errors in the daily *Record* be corrected in the permanent edition. (*See Congressional Record.*)

Permanent Select *or* Special Committee (*See* Select *or* Special Committee.)

Permanent Staff Committee staff authorized by rule or law, as distinguished from temporary or investigative staff authorized by annual or biennial resolutions. All but two House standing committees may appoint a maximum of thirty permanent staff (eighteen professional and twelve clerical staff). The House Appropriations and Budget committees may appoint any number of staff, subject to the amount of funds appropriated for them in the annual legislative branch appropriations act. The Senate eliminated the distinction between permanent and investigative staff in 1981. (*See* Investigative Staff. *See also* Minority Staff, Staff Director.)

Personal Privilege A question of privilege relating to members individually. (*See* Questions of Privilege.)

Personally Obnoxious (*or* Objectionable) A characterization a senator sometimes applies to a president's nominee for a federal office in that senator's state to justify his or her opposition to the nomination. (*See* Nomination, Senatorial Courtesy.)

Petition A formal plea from a citizen, group, or organization that asks Congress to take some legislative action or oppose an action. (*See also* Memorial, Private Bill.)

Pigeonhole In a committee, to put a measure aside indefinitely with the intention of ignoring it. Thousands of bills are pigeonholed in every Congress for a variety of reasons. (*See* Committee, Measure.)

Pipeline Appropriations obligated in one fiscal year that will not be spent until some year in the future are often said to be in the pipeline. (*See* Obligation, Unexpended Balance.)

Pocket Veto The indirect veto of a bill as a result of the president withholding approval of it until after Congress has adjourned sine die. A bill the president does not sign, but does not formally veto while Congress is in session, automatically becomes a law ten days (excluding Sundays) after it is received. But if Congress adjourns its annual session during that ten-day period, the measure dies even if the president does not formally veto it. (*See* Adjournment Sine Die, Veto.)

Point of No Quorum A point of order that a quorum is not present. It is used in the House but rarely in the Senate where the practice is to suggest the absence of a quorum. (*See* Point of Order, Quorum Call, Suggest the Absence of a Quorum.)

Point of Order A parliamentary term used in committee and on the floor to object to an alleged violation of a rule and to demand that the chair enforce the rule. The objecting member must explain the nature of the violation. A point of order immediately halts the proceedings until the chair decides whether the contention is valid. If the chair sustains a point of order against a measure or an amendment, it may not be considered; against a provision in a measure, it is immediately deleted; against a conference report, it is automatically rejected; and if against unparliamentary remarks by another member, that member must sit down or proceed in order.

If the floor manager of a bill concedes a point of order, the chair immediately sustains it. Otherwise, the chair usually permits members to present arguments for and against it before announcing a ruling, but is not required to do so and can cut off discussion whenever he or she chooses.

With some exceptions in the House, a member may appeal the chair's ruling. Appeals are rarely demanded in the House and even more rarely upheld. They are demanded more often in the Senate and are occasionally successful. The Senate's presiding officer has the option of submitting the point to the decision of the Senate, but must do so when the objection involves a constitutional question or certain Senate rules. (*See* Amendment, Appeal, Call to Order, Conference Report, Constitutionality, Ruling, Sustained, Unparliamentary. *See also* Nongermane Senate Amendment, Non-Selfenforcing Rules, Objection, Point of No Quorum, Quorum, Regular Order, Timeliness.)

Point of Personal Privilege (*See* Questions of Privilege.)

Policy Committees The political party committees in each house that review legislative proposals and provide recommendations or advice on party action and policy. Majority party policy committees advise their leaders on the scheduling of measures for floor action. In the House, these functions are performed for the Democratic Party by its Steering and Policy Committee. (*See* Steering and Policy Committee.)

Popular Titles The informal, unofficial names by which bills and laws are better known. For example, the Balanced Budget and Emergency Deficit Control Act of 1985 is usually referred to as the Gramm-Rudman-Hollings Act or merely as Gramm-Rudman. (*See* Title.)

Pork *or* Pork Barrel Legislation Pejorative terms for federal appropriations, bills, or policies that provide funds to benefit a legislator's district or state, with the implication that the legislator presses for enactment of such benefits to ingratiate himself or herself with constituents rather than on the basis of an impartial, objective assessment of need or merit.

    The terms are often applied to such benefits as new parks, post offices, dams, canals, bridges, roads, water projects, sewage treatment plants, and public works of any kind, as well as demonstration projects, research grants, and relocation of government facilities. Funds released by the president for various kinds of benefits or government contracts approved by him allegedly for political purposes are also sometimes referred to as pork. (*See also* Earmark.)

Postcloture Filibuster A filibuster conducted after the Senate invokes cloture. It employs an array of procedural tactics rather than lengthy speeches to delay final action.

The Senate curtailed the postcloture filibuster's effectiveness by closing a variety of loopholes in the cloture rule in 1979 and 1986, principally by fixing a time limitation on all proceedings following a Senate vote to invoke cloture. Moreover, under the Senate's precedents, the chair may rule dilatory and nongermane amendments out of order on his own initiative once cloture is invoked. (*See* Cloture, Dilatory Tactics, Filibuster, Germane, Precedent.)

Postpone A motion to postpone a proposal indefinitely kills it. Postponing to a day certain brings the proposal back for consideration on the specified day. Both motions are debatable. The House does not allow either motion in Committee of the Whole. Motions to postpone are rarely made in either house. (*See also* Precedence of Motions (House), Precedence of Motions (Senate).)

Power of the Purse A reference to the constitutional power Congress has over legislation to raise revenue and appropriate monies from the Treasury. Article I, Section 8, states that Congress "shall have Power To lay and collect Taxes, Duties, Imposts and Excises, [and] to pay the Debts. . . ." Section 9 declares: "No Money shall be drawn from the Treasury, but in Consequence of Appropriations made by Law. . . ." (*See* Appropriation, Revenue Legislation. *See also* Authorization-Appropriation Process.)

PPA (*See* Program, Project, or Activity.)

Preamble Introductory language describing the reasons for and intent of a measure, sometimes called a whereas clause. It occasionally appears in joint, concurrent, and simple resolutions but rarely in bills. In a bill it is placed before the enacting clause, in a joint resolution before the resolving clause, and in other resolutions above the text.

Like other parts of a measure, preambles may be amended. The Senate permits amendments to a preamble only after the bill or resolution has been passed; the House follows that practice only on simple and concurrent resolutions. When the House is considering a bill or joint resolution in Committee of the Whole, it permits amendments to a preamble after finishing with all amendments to the text of the measure. After the Committee of the Whole reports the measure to the House, the Speaker puts the question on any amendments to the preamble after the vote on engrossment but before the vote on the third reading. (*See* Committee of the Whole, Concurrent Resolution, Enacting Clause, Engrossed Bill, Engrossment and Third Reading, Joint Resolution, Put the Question, Resolution, Resolving Clause, Third Reading.)

Precedence The order in which amendments and other motions may be offered and acted on. The priorities in the two houses differ somewhat. When a motion is pending, a motion of higher precedence may be offered and must be disposed of first. For example, a second degree amendment has precedence over a first degree amendment, but a motion to lay on the table takes precedence over both of them. (*See* Amendment, Degrees of Amendment, Lay on the Table, Motion, Precedence of Motions (House), Precedence of Motions (Senate).)

Precedence of Motions (House) The order in which motions are given priority in the House of Representatives. When a question is under debate in the House, the motions usually having the highest precedence (in order of priority) are those to adjourn, to lay on the table, for the previous question, to postpone to a day certain, to refer, to amend, and to postpone indefinitely. The first three are not debatable.

One exception to this order gives a motion to recommit precedence over all other motions after the previous question has been ordered on the passage of a bill or joint resolution. Another exception gives two nondebatable motions equal priority with the motion to adjourn, but only if the Speaker, at his discretion, entertains them: (1) a motion that the Speaker be authorized to declare a recess; and (2) a motion that, when the House adjourns, it stand adjourned to a day and time certain. These priorities do not apply in Committee of the Whole where none of these motions, except the one to amend, is permitted. (*See* Adjourn, Adjournment to a Day Certain, Amendment, Commit, Committee of the Whole, Lay on the Table, Motion, Nondebatable Motions, Postpone, Previous Question, Recess, Recommit.)

Precedence of Motions (Senate) The order in which motions are given priority in the Senate. When a question is pending in that chamber, the motions having the highest precedence (in order of priority) are those to adjourn, to adjourn to a day certain, to recess, to proceed to consider executive business, to lay on the table, to postpone indefinitely, to commit, and to amend. The first five motions are not debatable. A cloture motion also has a very high precedence in the Senate. (*See* Adjourn, Adjournment to a Day Certain, Amendment, Cloture, Commit, Executive Business, Lay on the Table, Motion, Nondebatable Motions, Postpone, Recess.)

Precedent A previous ruling on a parliamentary matter or a long-standing practice or custom of a house. Before a presiding officer makes a ruling, he or she is expected to consider prior rulings on the same, similar, or analogous questions. Precedents serve to control arbitrary rulings and serve as the common law of a house. Each house compiles and publishes its precedents from time to time. (*See* Presiding Officer, Ruling. *See also Deschler's Precedents, Hinds' and Cannon's Precedents of the House of Representatives*, House Manual, *Procedure in the U.S. House of Representatives, Riddick's Senate Procedure*, Stare Decisis.)

Preferential Motion A motion whose precedence requires that it be dealt with before another. (*See also* Precedence of Motions (House), Precedence of Motions (Senate), Strike Out the Enacting (*or* Resolving) Clause.)

Preferential Recognition The practice of granting priority of recognition to certain members. In the Senate, the chair gives preferential recognition to the majority leader, the minority leader, the floor manager of a pending measure, and the minority floor manager, in that order.

In the House, a measure's floor manager is entitled to prior recognition for motions that expedite the measure's consideration at all stages of the legislative process. If the House or the Committee of the Whole rejects one of the floor manager's essential motions, the chair recognizes the member leading the opposition. The Speaker also gives preferential recognition to the leading minority party opponent of a measure for a motion to recommit. By long-standing custom, during the amendment process in Committee of the Whole, the chairman gives priority of recognition to the floor manager, then to the minority floor manager, and finally to other members of the committee that reported the bill, in the order of their seniority on that committee, alternating between the majority and the minority. (*See* Committee of the Whole, Floor Manager, Recognition, Recommit, Seniority.)

Present (1) A member's response to a quorum call, vocally in the Senate, vocally or through the electronic voting system in the House. (*See* Electronic Voting, Quorum Call.)

(2) A member's response during a vote when (a) he has a live pair with an absent colleague; (b) his vote would involve a conflict of interest; or (c) he does not wish to vote. (*See* Live Pair. *See also* Recorded Vote, Voting.)

President of the Senate The vice president of the United States in his constitutional role as presiding officer of the Senate. Senators address him and his surrogates as "Mr. President." The Constitution permits the vice president to cast a vote in the Senate only to break a tie, but he is not required to do so. This vote is sometimes called a casting vote. The Senate usually authorizes the vice president, by unanimous consent, to appoint senators to conference committees and to some commissions and boards, but he normally appoints those recommended by the Senate's party leaders or by the chairman and ranking minority member of the committee with jurisdiction over the measure.

Modern vice presidents usually preside only when their vote may be needed, on ceremonial occasions, or to rule on some crucial procedural questions. The president pro tempore or a senator designated by him presides over the Senate during the vice president's frequent absences. (*See* Casting Vote, Chairman, Conferees, Conference Committee, President Pro Tempore, Ranking Minority Member, Unanimous Consent.)

President Pro Tempore Under the Constitution, an officer elected by the Senate to preside over it during the absence of the vice president of the United States. Often referred to as "the pro tem," he is usually the majority party senator with the longest continuous service in the chamber and also, by virtue of his seniority, a committee chairman. When attending to committee and other duties, the president pro tempore appoints other senators to preside. Whoever presides is formally addressed as Mr. or Madam President. In 1890, the Senate decided that a president pro tempore should continue in that office until it determines otherwise. (*See also* Seniority System.)

President's Budget (*See* Budget.)

Presiding Officer In a formal meeting, the individual authorized to maintain order and decorum, recognize members to speak or offer motions, and apply and interpret the chamber's rules, precedents, and practices. The Speaker of the House and the president of the Senate are the chief presiding officers in their respective houses. Other presiding officers include the chairmen of committees (including Committee of the Whole), subcommittees, task forces, boards, commissions, and their surrogates. A presiding officer is often referred to as "the chair." (*See* Chairman, Committee of the Whole, Decorum, Order, Precedent, Recognition.)

Previous Question A nondebatable motion which, when agreed to by majority vote, usually cuts off further debate, prevents the offering of additional amendments, and brings the pending matter to an immediate vote. It is a major debate-limiting device in the House; it is not permitted in Committee of the Whole or in the Senate. If the previous question is ordered on a debatable proposal before any debate has occurred on it, the proposal may be debated for forty minutes.

When the House considers a special rule from the Rules Committee, the measure's floor manager usually moves the previous question toward the end of the first hour of debate. The motion rarely fails, but when it does the Speaker recognizes a member who opposed it to offer and debate an amendment. That member then moves the previous question on the resolution and the amendment to it. Special rules invariably provide automatic imposition of the previous question during House consideration of a measure reported from Committee of the Whole. (*See* Amendment, Committee of the Whole, Forty-Minute Debate, Hour Rule, Motion, Nondebatable Motions, Pending Business, Rule. *See also* Debate-Ending Motion, Precedence of Motions (House).)

Previously Noticed Amendment In the House, an amendment printed in the *Congressional Record* at least one day before it is offered in Committee of the Whole. (*See* Printed Amendment.)

Printed Amendment (1) In the House, an amendment printed in the Congressional Record at least one day before it is offered in Committee of the Whole; sometimes called a previously noticed amendment. Unlike other amendments, a printed amendment offered to a part of a bill on which the committee has closed debate may nevertheless be debated by its sponsor for five minutes, and another member may speak five minutes in opposition. No further debate is permitted. (*See* Amendment, Committee of the Whole, *Congressional Record*, Five-Minute Rule. *See also* Debate-Ending Motion.)

(2) In the Senate, an amendment submitted for printing in the Congressional Record under the heading Amendments Submitted. The printing gives other senators an opportunity to examine the amendment but gives it no special parliamentary standing or status. Once printed, any senator, not only the senator who submitted the amendment, may call it up for consideration. Senate printed amendments are numbered sequentially in the order of their submission through an entire Congress. (*See* Amendment, *Congressional Record*. *See also* Cloture.)

Private Bill A bill that applies to one or more specified persons, corporations, institutions, or other entities, usually to grant relief when no other legal remedy is available to them. Many private bills deal with claims against the federal government, immigration and naturalization cases, and land titles. The title of a private bill usually begins, "For the relief of. . . ."

Congress has considerably reduced its private claims workload since the mid-nineteenth century by authorizing executive branch agencies to settle them. Occasionally, Congress refers private claims to the U.S. Court of Claims for advisory findings. (*See also* Public Bill.)

Private Calendar Commonly used title for a calendar in the House reserved for private bills and resolutions favorably reported by committees. The private calendar is officially called the Calendar of the Committee of the Whole House. The calendar must be called on the first Tuesday of the month unless dispensed with by a two-thirds vote; it may also be called on the third Tuesday of the month at the Speaker's discretion.

Members appointed by each party, called official objectors, monitor the calendar to determine whether any measures on it raise problems. If two or more members object to the consideration of a private measure after the clerk reads its title, the measure is stricken from the calendar and recommitted to committee. Often, a member obtains unanimous consent to pass over the measure "without prejudice," permitting it to remain on the calendar while members try to clear up whatever problem it presents. If there are no problems, the measure is considered in the House as in Committee of the Whole and usually passed with little or no debate.

When the calendar is called on the third Tuesday of the month, preference is given to omnibus bills containing some of the measures previously stricken from the calendar, but such bills have rarely been used in recent decades. Members may not object to the consideration of these bills, but amendments may be offered to strike out any provision, reduce amounts, or impose limitations. No amendment adding another claim is permitted. After the House passes the bill, its components are divided into separate bills and resolutions and processed as if separately passed. (*See* Calendar, Call Up, House as in Committee of the Whole, Official Objectors, Omnibus Bill, Private Bill, Recommit. *See also* Special Order of Business.)

Private Law A private bill enacted into law. Private laws are numbered in the same fashion as public laws. (*See* Public Law.)

Privilege An attribute of a motion, measure, report, question, or proposition that gives it priority status for consideration. That status may come from provisions of the Constitution, standing rules, precedents, or statutory rules. Privileged questions are those given priority in the order of business; questions of privilege concern the rights and safety of a house and of its individual members.

Privileged motions and motions to bring up privileged questions are not debatable. Some motions are privileged in both houses, others are privileged in only one house. House rules refer to some motions as highly privileged or of the highest privilege; Senate rules do not, but its precedents cite some matters as highly privileged.

The houses differ radically in the way they bring up privileged questions for consideration and in the extent to which they grant privileged status to measures and other matters. Except on certain constitutional matters such as veto messages, the Senate requires agreement to a nondebatable motion to consider privileged matters. In the House, privileged measures, reports, questions, and propositions are called up without a motion; the Speaker must recognize an authorized or qualified member who seeks to call one up, subject to one-day or three-day layover rules.

Except by unanimous consent, the House rarely considers a matter unless it is a privileged one or granted privilege by a special rule, a procedural system it calls privileged interruptions of the order of business. The Senate has no procedure for granting privileged status to nonprivileged matters; it typically brings them up by debatable motion or by unanimous consent. (*See* One-Day Rule, Precedence of Motions (House), Precedence of Motions (Senate), Precedent, Privileged Business, Privileged Report, Question, Questions of Privilege, Rule, Standing Rules, Statutory Rules, Three-Day Rule, Unanimous Consent. *See also* Order of Business (House).)

Privilege of the Floor In addition to the members of a house, certain individuals are admitted to its floor while it is in session. The rules of the two houses differ somewhat, but both extend the privilege to the president and vice president, Supreme Court justices, cabinet members, state governors, former members of that house, members of the other house, certain officers and officials of Congress, certain staff of that house in the discharge of official duties, and the chambers' former parliamentarians. They also allow access to a limited number of committee and members' staff when their presence is necessary. House customs and practices permit selected individuals who do not have floor privileges to go to the floor during joint meetings of Congress. (*See* Floor, Joint Meeting.)

Privilege of the House A question of privilege affecting a house collectively. (*See* Questions of Privilege.)

Privileged Business Business that has priority over the daily order of business; also called privileged interruptions in the House. Some items of business are privileged in both houses, but the House confers that status on more items than does the Senate.

Both houses grant privilege to conference reports; vetoed bills; concurrent resolutions for adjournment and for certain joint sessions; budget resolutions; administering the oath of office to members-elect; resolutions electing members to committees; and questions of privilege (for example, contempt citation resolutions).

In the House, the consent, discharge, and private calendars, District Day, Calendar Wednesday, and suspension of the rules are privileged on certain days. Business privileged on any day includes general appropriation bills; privileged reports from committees that have the right to report at any time, including special rules from the Rules Committee; and reported resolutions of inquiry. Any other matter may be given privileged status by unanimous consent or by a special rule.

Amendments between the houses are always privileged in the Senate. The House gives privilege only to amendments in disagreement and Senate amendments that do not require consideration in Committee of the Whole. (*See* Adjourn, Amendments Between the Houses, Amendments in Disagreement, Budget Resolution, Business, Calendar Wednesday, Committee of the Whole, Concurrent Resolution, Consent Calendar, District Day, General Appropriation Bill, Joint Session, Oath of Office, Order of Business (House), Order of Business (Senate), Private Calendar, Privileged Report, Questions of Privilege, Resolution of Inquiry, Rule, Stage of Disagreement, Suspension of the Rules (House), Unanimous Consent. *See also* Special Order of Business.)

Privileged Interruptions In the House, business that may interrupt or has priority over the daily order of business. (*See* Business, Order of Business (House), Privilege, Privileged Business.)

Privileged Motion (*See* Precedence of Motions (House), Precedence of Motions (Senate), Privilege.)

Privileged Question (*See* Privilege, Privileged Business, Questions of Privilege.)

Privileged Report In the House, a committee report that may be filed from the floor at any time because it deals with a privileged measure or matter. A report's privilege may stem from a constitutional provision, as in the case of vetoed measures and impeachment proceedings, or it may be provided in the standing rules.

One such rule grants specified committees the right to report certain privileged measures at any time: the Appropriations Committee on general appropriation bills and certain continuing resolutions; the Budget Committee on budget resolutions and certain other budget-related matters; the House Administration Committee on enrolled bills, contested elections, printing measures, contingent fund expenditures, and House records; the Rules Committee on rules and the order of business; and the Standards of Official Conduct Committee on its recommendations concerning the official conduct of House members and employees. Under the rule on questions of privilege, committee reports recommending contempt citations are privileged. (*See* Budget Resolution, Constitutional Rules, Contempt of Congress, Contingent Fund, Continuing Resolution, Enrolled Bill, Filed, Floor, General Appropriation Bill, Impeachment, Order of Business (House), Overriding a Veto, Privilege, Privileged Business, Questions of Privilege, Report at Any Time, Rule, Standing Rules. *See also* Code of Official Conduct.)

Pro Forma Amendment In the House, an amendment that ostensibly proposes to change a measure or another amendment by moving "to strike the last word" or "to strike the requisite number of words." A member offers it not to make any actual change in the measure or amendment but only to obtain time for debate.

Pro forma amendments are permitted in the House of Representatives under the five-minute rule, either in Committee of the Whole or in the House as in Committee of the Whole, but not in the Senate. In modern practice, pro forma amendments are not put to a vote and are considered as withdrawn when the time has expired of the member who has offered one. A member who has proposed a substantive amendment and has debated it for five minutes cannot extend his or her time by offering a pro forma amendment because this would violate the rule that a member may not amend his own amendment except by unanimous consent. (*See* Amendment, Committee of the Whole, Five-Minute Rule, House as in Committee of the Whole, Unanimous Consent.)

Pro Forma Session A brief meeting of a house held to satisfy the constitutional requirement that it must obtain the consent of the other house if it adjourns for more than three days. It is understood that little or no business will be conducted during such meetings because most members are absent. The unofficial record for the shortest session of a house is two seconds, set by the Senate in 1963.

Pro Tem A common reference to the president pro tempore of the Senate or, occasionally, to a Speaker pro tempore. (*See* President Pro Tempore, Speaker Pro Tempore.)

Procedure in the U.S. House of Representatives A single-volume summary of the modern precedents and practices of the House. The most recent edition, published in 1987, was prepared under the direction of Wm. Holmes Brown, parliamentarian of the House. (*See* Precedent. *See also Deschler's Precedents.*)

Procedures The methods of conducting business in a deliberative body. The procedures of each house are governed first by applicable provisions of the Constitution, then by its standing rules and orders, precedents, traditional practices, and any statutory rules that apply to it. The authority of the houses to adopt rules in addition to those specified in the Constitution is derived from Article I, Section 5, Clause 2 of the Constitution, which states: "Each House may determine the Rules of its Proceedings. . . ."

By rule, the House of Representatives also follows the procedures in *Jefferson's Manual* that are not inconsistent with its standing rules and orders. Many Senate procedures also conform with Jefferson's provisions, but by practice rather than by rule. At the beginning of each Congress, the House uses procedures in general parliamentary law until it adopts its standing rules. (*See* Constitutional Rules, *Jefferson's Manual*, Parliamentary Law, Rulemaking Statutes, Standing Order, Standing Rules, Statutory Rules.)

Proceed to Consider The most common Senate motion for bringing up a matter for consideration; it is rarely used in the House. (*See* Call Up, Consider.)

Program Account An account to which an appropriation is made for the subsidy cost of a direct loan or loan guarantee program under the terms of the Federal Credit Reform Act of 1990. (*See* Direct Loan, Federal Credit Reform Act of 1990, Loan Guarantee. *See also* Credit Authority, Credit Subsidy Cost.)

Program, Project, or Activity (PPA) An element within a federal budget account. In annually appropriated accounts, PPAs are defined by the appropriations acts and their accompanying reports and documentation. For accounts not funded by annual appropriations, PPAs are defined by the program listings in the program and financing schedule in the president's budget.

The sequestration process established by the Gramm-Rudman-Hollings Act requires that equal percentages be taken from each PPA that is not exempted from the process. (*See* Appropriation, Budget, General Appropriation Bill, Report, Sequestration.)

Proxy Voting The practice of permitting a member to cast the vote of an absent colleague in addition to his own vote. Proxy voting is prohibited on the floors of the House and Senate, but both houses permit their committees to authorize proxy voting, and most do.

When authorized by a House committee, members must submit signed proxy authorizations limited to a specific measure, amendments to it, and motions relating to it. General proxies on procedural motions are also permitted.

The Senate rule declares that "proxies may not be voted when the absent member has not been informed of the matter on which he is being recorded and has not affirmatively requested that he be so recorded." (*See also* Ghost Voting.)

Public Bill A bill dealing with general legislative matters having national applicability or applying to the federal government or to a class of persons, groups, or organizations. (*See also* Bills and Resolutions Introduced, Private Bill.)

Public Debt Federal government debt incurred by the Treasury or the Federal Financing Bank by the sale of securities to the public or borrowings from a federal fund or account. (*See also* Agency Debt, Debt Limit, Federal Debt.)

Public Law A public bill or joint resolution enacted into law. It is cited by the letters P.L. followed by a hyphenated number. The digits before the hyphen indicate the number of the Congress in which it was enacted; the digits after the hyphen indicate its position in the numerical sequence of public measures that became law during that Congress. For example, the Budget Enforcement Act of 1990 became P.L. 101-508 because it was the 508th measure in that sequence for the 101st Congress. (*See also* Private Law.)

Put the Question The procedure for initiating a vote on a proposal. The chair puts the question to a vote when all the time for debate on the question has expired, when no member seeks recognition to debate it further, or when no debate is permitted. When that appropriate time arrives, the chair states, "The question is on the [motion, amendment, resolution, passage of the bill, or some other matter]. As many as are in favor will say 'aye'." And then, "As many as are opposed, will say 'no'." A House rule requires the Speaker to rise when he puts the question, "but may state it sitting." (*See* Debate, Question, Recognition, Time Limits on Debate. *See also* Cloture, Division Vote, Nondebatable Motions, Rule, Voice Vote, Yeas and Nays.)

Q

Question A parliamentary term for a pending proposition, such as a measure, motion, or amendment when the chair puts it to a vote by stating, "The question is on the [type of proposition]." (*See also* Main Question, Put the Question.)

Question of Privilege Two classes of privileged questions, one relating to a house collectively, the other to members individually. A House rule defines the first, called privilege of the House, as questions affecting the rights of the House and the safety, dignity, and integrity of its proceedings. The second, called personal privilege, refers to questions affecting the rights, reputation, and conduct of individual members in their representative capacity only. Generally, both types of questions have precedence over all others in the House except motions to adjourn.

A privilege of the House question must be considered as a simple resolution. A question of personal privilege may be put in a resolution, a question, or a point of personal privilege, but the member must explain the grounds on which it is based.

Under a House rule adopted in 1993, the Speaker may postpone consideration of certain questions of privilege of the House for up to two days. Exempted from the two-day delay are questions raised in resolutions offered by the majority or minority leader or reported by committees, and resolutions relating to the right of the House to originate revenue bills. Exempted questions and questions of personal privilege may be raised at almost any time except in Committee of the Whole. When a member raises a question of privilege, the Speaker determines whether it is admissible under the rule and the precedents before recognizing the member to debate it.

If the Speaker accepts the question, the member is recognized under the hour rule and the matter is considered under the normal rules of the House. If a resolution is involved, it is subject to the usual motions—the previous question may be moved and the resolution may be tabled or referred.

Although the Senate has no rule on either of the two classes of questions, its precedents indicate that personal privilege questions may be raised almost any time a senator is recognized and that the senator must confine his or her remarks to that question.

The Senate's precedents provide no clues about the proper basis for raising a personal privilege question. House precedents cite numerous examples, including a member impugning the motives or veracity of another in statements to the press and newspaper charges of vote-selling or illegal acts. One case involved a majority leader's statement to the press that "there is nothing to stop a man from making a damn fool of himself if he wants to," a remark one member took personally.

Privilege of the House questions have included such subjects as invasions of House jurisdiction or prerogatives by the Senate or the courts, the proper attire of members, certain derogatory material in the *Congressional Record*, and the possible threat to members' safety in the Capitol. (*See* Committee of the Whole, Hour Rule, Lay on the Table, Majority Leader, Minority Leader, Precedent, Previous Question, Privilege, Question, Recognition, Resolution, Revenue Legislation. *See also* Privileged Business.)

Quorum The minimum number of members required to be present for the transaction of business. Under the Constitution, a quorum in each house is a majority of its members: 218 in the House and 51 in the Senate when there are no vacancies. By House rule, a quorum in Committee of the Whole is 100. In practice, both houses usually assume a quorum is present even if it is not, unless a member makes a point of no quorum in the House or suggests the absence of a quorum in the Senate. Consequently, each house transacts much of its business, and even passes bills, when only a few members are present.

A majority quorum must actually be present in a Senate committee when it reports a measure or recommendation. The same rule applied to House committees until 1993 when it was changed in two respects. First, a majority quorum need not actually be present during a roll-call vote to report; the only requirement is that a majority of the committee's members must respond to the vote. Thus, members who have voted need not remain to establish the physical presence of a majority quorum during the vote; it is sufficient that the records of the committee establish that a majority of its members responded. This is sometimes referred to as a "rolling quorum" or "drop-by voting."

Second, on measures reported by unanimous consent or voice votes, no point of order against the measure on the ground that a majority quorum was not present during such actions is permitted on the House floor unless such a point of order was made in the committee at the time of such action.

As few as one-third of a committee's members may transact other business. Senate committees may fix a number less than one-third for taking sworn testimony; House committees may take testimony with a quorum of two.

When the House chooses a president, the Constitution requires a quorum of at least one member each from two-thirds of the states. The Constitution also mandates a quorum of two-thirds of the Senate when that body elects a vice president. (*See* Absence of a Quorum, Business Meeting, Committee of the Whole, Point of No Quorum, Report, Roll Call, Rolling Quorum, Suggest the Absence of a Quorum. *See also* Automatic Roll Call, Counting a Quorum, Hearing, Live Quorum, Quorum Call, Short Quorum, Timeliness.)

Quorum Call A procedure for determining whether a quorum is present in a chamber. In the Senate, a clerk calls the roll (roster) of senators. The House usually employs its electronic voting system.

A senator can force a quorum call any time he or she has the floor by suggesting the absence of a quorum, except under certain cloture situations and provided that business has intervened since a quorum was last established.

The more restrictive House rules limit points of no quorum essentially to situations in which the chair has put a pending question to a vote. However, the Speaker may recognize any member to move a call of the House at any time. When the House is in Committee of the Whole, one quorum call is permitted when no vote is pending but only if a quorum has not previously been established that day; moreover, the chairman may refuse to entertain such a call during general debate. (*See* Absence of a Quorum, Business, Call of the House, Call of the Roll, Committee of the Whole, Electronic Voting, Floor, Point of No Quorum, Put the Question, Quorum, Suggest the Absence of a Quorum. See also Automatic Roll Call, Counting a Quorum, Live Quorum, Short Quorum.)

R

Ramseyer Rule A House rule that requires a committee's report on a bill or joint resolution to show the changes the measure, and any committee amendments to it, would make in existing law. That part of the report is often called "the Ramseyer."

The rule requires the report to present the text of any statutory provision that would be repealed and a comparative print showing, through typographical devices such as stricken-through type or italics, other changes in existing law. On the floor, a valid point of order that the report fails to comply with the rule automatically recommits the measure, and it may not be considered until the committee submits a proper report or if the House agrees to a special rule waiving the requirement.

The rule, adopted in 1929, is named after its sponsor, Rep. Christian W. Ramseyer (R-Iowa). The Senate's analogous rule is called the Cordon Rule. (*See* Committee Report on a Measure, Cordon Rule, Point of Order, Recommit, Rule.)

Randolph Rule A reference to a Senate resolution adopted in 1984 that requires senators to vote from their seats. Sen. Jennings Randolph (D-W.Va.) sponsored the resolution. (*See* Voting.)

Rank *or* Ranking A member's position on the list of his party's members on a committee or subcommittee.

When first assigned to a committee, a member is placed at the bottom of the list, then moves up as those above leave the committee. On subcommittees, however, a member's rank may not have anything to do with the length of his service on it. At committee and subcommittee meetings, a member's rank determines where he sits, and the chairman usually recognizes members in the order of their ranking, alternating between the parties to question witnesses, make motions, and for other purposes.

By House rule, the majority member next in rank to the chairman of a standing committee or subcommittee is given the title of vice chairman. In the absence of the chairman and vice chairman, the highest ranking majority member presides over meetings. The higher a member's committee ranking, the greater the likelihood that he is the chairman or ranking minority member of a subcommittee. (*See* Ranking Minority Member, Vice Chairman. *See also* Seniority, Seniority System.)

Ranking Member (1) Most often a reference to the minority member with the highest ranking on a committee or subcommittee.

(2) A reference to the majority member next in rank to the chairman or to the highest ranking majority member present at a committee or subcommittee meeting. (*See* Rank *or* Ranking, Ranking Minority Member.)

Ranking Minority Member The member whose name appears at the head of the list of minority members on a committee or subcommittee. The ranking minority member usually appoints the minority staff, acts as minority floor manager on committee measures, and recommends minority members for appointment as conferees on such measures.

In the House, the rules of the Republican Conference prohibit its members from serving as ranking minority member on more than one committee or, except with conference approval, on more than one subcommittee. Senate Republicans may hold that position on one standing and one joint committee.

On December 8, 1992, the House Republican Conference adopted a rule that prohibits any of its members from holding any full committee's ranking position for more than six consecutive years; subcommittee positions are not affected. The rule went into effect in 1993 and is not retroactive.

The ranking minority member on Senate committees is always the minority senator with the longest continuous service on that panel unless he or she holds that position on another committee. When there is a dispute about which Republican should hold the position, the Republican members of a committee nominate their candidate, subject to a vote by the full party conference.

House Republican ranking committee members are elected by the Republican Conference on nominations submitted by its Committee on Committees. The rules of the Conference require those members to floor manage a bill in accordance with any position the Conference might have taken on it. (*See* Committee on Committees, Conferees, Conference, Floor Manager, Full Committee, Minority Staff. *See also* Rank *or* Ranking, Seniority, Seniority System.)

Ratification (1) The president's formal act of promulgating a treaty after the Senate has approved it. The resolution of ratification agreed to by the Senate is the procedural vehicle by which the Senate gives its consent to ratification. (*See* Resolution of Ratification, Treaty.)

(2) A state legislature's act in approving a proposed constitutional amendment. Such an amendment becomes effective when ratified by three-fourths of the states.

Reading for Amendment In Committee of the Whole, the House practice of completing action on all amendments to a section or paragraph of a measure, after a clerk has read or designated it, before permitting amendments to the next section or paragraph. A full reading of a section's text is often waived by unanimous consent or by a special rule from the Rules Committee, in which case the clerk reads only the the section's number or designates the paragraph. Sometimes, by unanimous consent or special rule, a measure is read or designated by title rather than by section or paragraph.

Generally, an amendment may not be offered to a part of a measure until the clerk has read that part or after the clerk has read the next part, but a member may offer an amendment in the nature of a substitute to the whole measure after the first or last section has been read. A motion to strike out the enacting clause may be offered at almost any time.

The Senate's rules do not require that a measure be read for amendment; therefore, senators may offer amendments to any part of a measure and in any order. The same is true in the House when it takes up a measure in the House as in Committee of the Whole. (*See* Amendment in the Nature of a Substitute, Committee of the Whole, Enacting Clause, House as in Committee of the Whole, Rule, Strike Out the Enacting (*or* Resolving) Clause, Unanimous Consent.)

Reading of Amendments Both houses require that a clerk read each amendment in full to the chamber before the amendment is debated, amended, or brought to a vote. The reading is often waived by unanimous consent or by a special rule from the Rules Committee in the House.

In addition, the House permits a nondebatable motion to dispense with the reading of certain amendments in Committee of the Whole. The motion may apply to committee amendments printed in the bill as reported and to any member's amendment printed in the *Congressional Record* and submitted to the reporting committee (or committees) at least one day before floor consideration. Also, a Senate rule waives the reading, after cloture is invoked, of amendments that have been printed and available at senators' desks for at least twenty-four hours. (*See* Cloture, Committee Amendment, Committee of the Whole, Desk, Nondebatable Motions, Rule, Unanimous Consent, Unanimous Consent Agreement.)

Readings of Bills and Resolutions Both houses require three so-called readings of bills and joint resolutions before passage, but in the House the first and third readings are by the title of the measure only and in the Senate all three are by title only. The House requires a complete second reading but usually dispenses with it by unanimous consent for a measure considered only in the House or by special rule for measures considered in Committee of the Whole.

In the Senate, each reading must be on a different legislative day, except by unanimous consent. The first two readings occur before the measure is referred to committee, and the third comes before action on final passage. Under House practices, the first reading comes after introduction of the measure and before referral to committee, and it is satisfied by publishing the title in the *Journal* and *Congressional Record.* The third reading occurs immediately before the vote on final passage.

By custom, the House requires one reading of simple and concurrent resolutions before they are considered. In the Senate, they are read only on demand.

These readings stem from British parliamentary practice, probably begun in the fifteenth century for the benefit of the many legislators who could not read.

(*See* Committee of the Whole, Concurrent Resolution, *Congressional Record, Journal,* Legislative Day, Resolution, Rule, Title, Unanimous Consent)

Reapportionment (*See* Apportionment.)

Reappropriation Congressional action that permits all or part of the unobligated portion of an appropriation that has expired, or would otherwise expire, to remain available for obligation for the same or different purposes.

Except for public works in progress, the rules of both houses prohibit reappropriation of unexpended balances of appropriations, but only when they appear in, or are offered as amendments to, general appropriation bills. The prohibition does not apply to special appropriation bills, and it may also be circumvented by other means. Furthermore, the Gramm-Rudman-Hollings Act permits the House Appropriations Committee to transfer unexpended balances within the department or agency for which they were originally appropriated. (*See* Appropriation, Expired Account, General Appropriation Bill, Gramm-Rudman-Hollings Act of 1985, Obligation, Special Appropriation Bill, Unexpended Balance, Unobligated Balance.)

Recapitulation of a Vote A repetition of a vote to verify its result. The chair may order it when he or she is in doubt of the result. On a recapitulation after the vote has been announced, members may not change their previous vote nor may they vote if they did not do so on the original vote.

In the House, members have no right to a recapitulation; the Speaker has complete discretion on whether or not to order it. The Speaker declines to do so unless the vote is very close, usually by a margin of fewer than four votes. The Speaker refuses recapitulation requests on division votes, votes by tellers, and electronic votes. In the Senate, the chair has some discretion in granting recapitulation requests. (*See* Division Vote, Electronic Voting, Objection, Teller Vote.)

Recede A motion by a house to withdraw from its previous position during the process of amendments between the houses. It may recede from its amendment or from its disagreement to an amendment of the other house. In the latter case, it can simply concur in the amendment or concur with a further amendment to it. (*See* Adhere, Amendments Between the Houses, Concur, Disagree, Insist.)

Recess (1) A temporary interruption or suspension of a meeting of a chamber or committee. Unlike an adjournment, a recess does not end a legislative day. Because the Senate often recesses from one calendar day to another, its legislative day may extend over several calendar days, weeks, or even months. A motion to recess in the Senate takes precedence over most other motions and is not debatable.

In the House, an ordinary motion to recess has no special privilege; under a rule adopted in 1991, however, the Speaker may entertain a nondebatable motion authorizing him to declare a recess, and that motion has equal privilege with a motion to adjourn. In addition, under a rule adopted in 1993, the Speaker is authorized to declare a recess "for a short time" when no question is pending before the House. (*See* Adjourn, Chamber, Legislative Day, Nondebatable Motions, Precedence of Motions (House), Precedence of Motions (Senate), Privilege, Question.)

(2) A period of adjournment for more than three days to a day certain, especially over a holiday or in August during odd-numbered years. (*See* Adjournment for More Than Three Days, Adjournment to a Day (and Time) Certain, August Adjournment. *See also* District Work Period, Nonlegislative Period.)

Recess Appointment A presidential appointment to a vacant federal position made after the Senate has adjourned sine die or has adjourned or recessed for more than thirty days. If the president submits the recess appointee's nomination during the next session of the Senate, that individual can continue to serve until the end of the session even though the Senate might have rejected the nomination. When appointed to a vacancy that existed thirty days before the end of the last Senate session, a recess appointee is not paid until confirmed. (*See* Adjournment Sine Die, Nomination, Recess.)

Recognition Permission by the presiding officer to a member to speak or propose a procedural action. A member seeking recognition must rise and address the chair, but may not do so while another member holds the floor unless that member has violated a rule.

In the Senate, the chair must recognize for purposes of debate the first senator who addresses him or her unless a unanimous consent agreement requires otherwise. When several senators simultaneously seek recognition, the chair may choose among them, subject, however, to the preferential recognition practices of the Senate or, again, to the terms of a unanimous consent agreement.

Generally, recognition in the House is within the chair's discretion. Under some circumstances, the chair's discretion is absolute; under others, the chair may be required to recognize a member eventually but not necessarily the first time the member seeks recognition. Under still other circumstances, the chair is required to recognize certain members for specific purposes. Frequently the chair refuses to recognize a member, or first asks, "For what purpose does the gentleman [gentlewoman] rise?" and then decides whether to recognize.

However, the Speaker must recognize members for privileged business and motions, but when several members seek recognition on business of equal privilege the Speaker has discretion in deciding whom to recognize first. Furthermore, by tradition and practice, both the Speaker and the chairman of the Committee of the Whole follow certain priorities of recognition during debate.

In both houses, the chair's recognition authority is not subject to appeal. A Speaker remarked in 1881 that the power of recognition "is just as absolute in the Chair as the judgment of the Supreme Court . . . is absolute as to the interpretation of the law." (*See* Floor, Preferential Recognition, Presiding Officer, Privileged Business. *See also* List of Speakers.)

Recommit To send a measure back to the committee that reported it; sometimes called a straight motion to recommit to distinguish it from a motion to recommit with instructions. A successful motion to recommit kills the measure unless it is accompanied by instructions. The motion is allowed in the Senate and the House but not in Committee of the Whole. In the Senate, a motion to recommit a measure may be offered any time before the measure's passage or adoption. In the House, the motion may be offered just before the vote on final passage or adoption.

The House permits only one motion to recommit a measure; the Senate's rules impose no limit on the number. In the House, the Speaker gives priority of recognition for offering the motion, in order, to minority members of the reporting committee, to any other minority party member, to majority members of the committee, and finally to any other majority party member, but only to those who declare that they oppose the measure. A House rule precludes the Rules Committee from reporting a special rule that prevents the motion. (*See also* Commit, Precedence of Motions (House), Precedence of Motions (Senate), Recommit with Instructions.)

Recommit a Conference Report To return a conference report to the conference committee for renegotiation of some or all of its agreements. A motion to recommit may be offered with or without instructions. It is in order only if the other house has not yet agreed to the report because agreement by one chamber automatically discharges its conferees and dissolves the conference committee. (*See* Conferees, Conference Committee, Conference Report. *See also* Discharge of Conferees, Instruct Conferees.)

Recommit with Instructions To send a measure back to a committee with instructions to take some action on it. Invariably in the House and often in the Senate, when the motion recommits to a standing committee, the instructions require the committee to report the measure "forthwith" with specified amendments. In that case, the majority floor manager immediately reports it back to the chamber with the required amendments; the committee does not physically receive the measure or convene to act on it. Once reported, the amendments must still be voted on by the chamber. The motion is not allowed in Committee of the Whole.

The House permits only one such motion during action on a measure; the Senate's rules impose no such limit. In the House, the Speaker follows the same priorities of recognition as on a straight motion to recommit (that is, without instructions), but only recognizes members who declare their opposition to the measure in its entirety or "in its present form." Moreover, the instructions may not propose nongermane amendments or any that violate other House rules or precedents. Although the Rules Committee may not report a special rule that prevents a motion to recommit, the rule may forbid certain instructions or any instructions. However, the rule may permit instructions that violate House rules, usually doing so by permitting a recommital motion "with or without instructions."

In the Senate, the motion to recommit with instructions and to report forthwith without any amendments has the effect of stripping the measure of all floor amendments previously agreed to. Accordingly, unanimous consent agreements often restrict its use and it is rarely offered. (*See* Committee of the Whole, Floor Amendment, Floor Manager, Germane, Precedent, Recommit, Rule, Standing Committee, Unanimous Consent Agreement.)

Reconciliation A procedure for changing existing revenue and spending laws to bring total federal revenues and spending within the limits established in a budget resolution.

Reconciliation begins with directives in the budget resolution instructing specific committees to report legislation adjusting revenues or spending within their respective jurisdictions by specified amounts, usually by a specified deadline. Although the total amount for each committee is based on program assumptions usually printed in the House and Senate Budget committees' reports on the budget resolution, an instructed committee is not bound by them and can decide for itself how the total should be allocated.

When several committees are instructed, the Budget Committee in each house consolidates their proposals in an omnibus reconciliation bill that the Budget Committee brings to the floor without changes but to which it may offer amendments. Amendments to the bill must be germane and deficit neutral. Debate on reconciliation bills is limited in both houses.

Congress has applied reconciliation chiefly to revenues and mandatory spending programs, especially entitlements. Discretionary spending is controlled through annual appropriation bills. (*See* Budget Allocation, Budget Resolution, Debate, Deficit Neutrality, Discretionary Appropriations, Entitlement Program, General Appropriation Bill, Germane, Omnibus Bill,

Report, Revenue Legislation. *See* also Byrd Rule, Direct Spending.)

Reconciliation Resolution A concurrent resolution directing the clerk of the House or the secretary of the Senate, as appropriate, to make specified changes in bills and resolutions that have been passed but have not yet been enrolled to make them conform with the terms of the budget resolution. Under the Congressional Budget Act, a budget resolution can contain a provision delaying the enrollment of certain measures should such changes be necessary. As of 1992, no budget resolution has contained such a provision. (*See* Budget Resolution, Concurrent Resolution, Enrolled Bill.)

Reconsider a Vote A parliamentary practice that gives a house one opportunity to review its action on a motion, amendment, measure, or any other proposition. Killing a motion to reconsider an action by laying the motion on the table makes that action final and blocks any future attempt to reverse it.

In the House, immediately after the result of a vote has been announced, the Speaker usually declares, "Without objection, a motion to reconsider is laid on the table." Alternatively in the House, and invariably in the Senate, a member who voted on the winning side offers the motion to reconsider, another moves to lay it on the table, and the chair states that the motion to table is agreed to without objection.

Any member can object to this headlong approach and thereby force a vote on the tabling motion. This is usually done when the original vote on the proposition is so close that enough members might be persuaded to change their minds or absent members might appear, vote against tabling, vote for reconsideration, and finally reverse the original vote.

In the House, only a member who voted on the prevailing side can offer a motion to reconsider. It must be moved on the same day as the original vote or on the next legislative day.

In the Senate, either a member who voted on the prevailing side or one who did not vote at all can offer the motion. It must be moved on the same day or the next two days of actual session.

The House does not allow a motion to reconsider in Committee of the Whole. The motion is debatable in both houses only when offered to a proposal that was debatable. (*See* Committee of the Whole, Debate, Lay on the Table, Legislative Day, Nondebatable Motions, Without Objection.)

Record Familiar title for the *Congressional Record.*

Recorded Teller Vote *(See Recorded Vote by Clerks.)*

Recorded Vote (1) Generally, any vote in which members are recorded by name for or against a measure; also called a record vote or roll-call vote. The only recorded vote in the Senate is a vote by the yeas and nays and is commonly called a roll-call vote. (*See* Roll Call, Yeas and Nays.)

(2) Technically, a recorded vote is one demanded in the House of Representatives and supported by at least one-fifth of a quorum (forty-four members) in the House sitting as the House or at least twenty-five members in Committee of the Whole. Only one demand for a recorded vote on a pending question is permitted, but a member can make the demand before or immediately after a voice or division vote. (*See* Committee of the Whole, Division Vote, House Sitting as the House, Question, Quorum, Voice Vote. *See also* Cluster Voting, Electronic Voting, Teller Vote, Yeas and Nays.)

Recorded Vote by Clerks A voting procedure in the House where members pass through the appropriate "aye" or "no" aisle in the chamber and cast their votes by depositing a signed green (yea) or red (no) card in a ballot box. These votes are tabulated by clerks and reported to the chair.

A demand for a recorded vote, whether by clerks or by the electronic voting system, requires the support of one-fifth of a quorum (forty-four members) in the House or twenty-five members in Committee of the Whole. The electronic voting system is much more convenient and has largely supplanted this procedure. (*See* Committee of the Whole, Recorded Vote, Teller Vote.)

Redistricting The redrawing of congressional district boundaries within a state after a decennial census. Redistricting may be required to re-equalize district populations or to accommodate an increase or decrease in the number of a state's House seats that might have resulted from the decennial apportionment.

The state governments determine the district lines, but they are subject both to Supreme Court decisions that district populations should be as nearly equal as practicable and to federal laws that prohibit districting intended to dilute the voting power of minorities or that produce discriminatory results. (*See* Apportionment, Congressional District. *See also* At-Large, Gerrymandering.)

Reestimates Changes made in executive branch or congressional budget estimates to reflect changes in economic conditions, spendout rates, workload, and other factors, but not the effects of changes in policy. From time to time, the reestimates are entered into budget baseline projections and scorekeeping reports. (*See* Baseline, Scorekeeping. *See also* Mid-Session Budget Review.)

Reference (1) A synonym for referral. (*See* Referral. *See also* Bills and Resolutions Referred.)

(2) "By reference" refers to a method by which a statute converts a simple or concurrent resolution into

law merely by citing its designation number rather than reproducing its full text. In the same manner, some resolutions convert statutory provisions into rules by citing the section or title of the law. (*See* Concurrent Resolution, Resolution. *See also* Joint Rules.)

Referral The assignment of a measure to one or more committees for consideration. Under a House rule, the Speaker can refuse to refer a measure he believes is "of an obscene or insulting character." (*See* Bills and Resolutions Referred, Multiple and Sequential Referrals.)

Regional Whip (*See* Whip, Zone Whip.)

Regular Meeting Day The day or days during a month that a committee designates for regular meetings to transact its business. Both houses require their standing committees to fix at least one day a month for that purpose. The establishment of regular committee meeting days is intended to circumvent chairmen who refuse to call meetings in order to prevent the committee from considering legislation they oppose. The Senate, however, exempts its Appropriations Committee from that requirement. (*See also* Special Committee Meeting, Business Meeting.)

Regular Order (1) The proper sequence of daily business under the rules and practices of each house, including unanimous consent agreements and special rules. That sequence may not be violated if any member demands the regular order. (*See* Order of Business (House), Order of Business (Senate), Rule, Unanimous Consent Agreement.)

(2) The proper execution of certain rules or procedures. For example, upon a demand for the regular order, a member may not reserve either a point of order or the right to object to a unanimous consent request; the member must either make the point of order or objection or remain silent. Senators sometimes

demand the regular order when they believe the presiding officer is improperly delaying announcement of the result of a roll-call vote. (*See* Objection, Order of Business (House), Order of Business (Senate), Point of Order, Reserving a Point of Order, Reserving the Right to Object, Roll Call.)

Regulatory Impact Statement An evaluation of the regulatory impact of a proposed bill or joint resolution. It is required to appear in Senate committee reports.

A regulatory impact statement must include: (1) an estimate of the number and types of individuals and businesses that would be regulated by the measure; (2) the economic impact of the measure on individuals, consumers, and businesses; (3) the measure's impact on personal privacy; and (4) how much additional paperwork the measure would require and the paperwork costs in time and money. The statement may be omitted if the report explains why the evaluations are impracticable. (*See also* Committee Report on a Measure, Inflationary Impact Statement.)

Relevancy in Debate (*See* Debate, Germane, Pastore Rule.)

Report (1) As a verb, a committee is said to report when it submits a measure or other document to its parent chamber. Both houses require a committee's chairman to report an approved measure promptly and to take whatever steps are necessary to bring it to a vote. If a chairman fails to report a measure promptly, a majority of the committee can force its filing. (*See* Chairman. *See also* Report at Any Time.)

(2) A clerk is said to report when he or she reads a measure's title, text, or the text of an amendment to the body at the direction of the chair. (*See* Reading for Amendment, Reading of Amendments, Readings of Bills and Resolutions.)

(3) As a noun, a committee document that accompanies a reported measure. It describes the measure, the committee's views on it, its costs, and the changes it proposes to make in existing law; it also includes certain impact statements. These reports are required in the House; although they are optional in the Senate, its committees usually provide them. (*See* Committee Report on a Measure. *See also* Adverse Report, Conference Report, Cordon Rule, Cost Estimates, Inflationary Impact Statement, Privileged Report, Ramseyer Rule, Regulatory Impact Statement.)

(4) A committee document submitted to its parent chamber that describes the results of an investigation or other study or provides information it is required to provide by rule or law. (*See* Investigative Power. *See also* Oversight.)

Report at Any Time In the House, the right of certain committees to file a report from the floor on certain privileged matters. These reports may be called up for consideration at any time, subject to the three-day or one-day rules on availability of reports. (*See* Filed, One-Day Rule, Privileged Report, Three-Day Rule.)

Representative An elected and duly sworn member of the House of Representatives who is entitled to vote in the chamber. The Constitution requires that a representative be at least twenty-five years old, a citizen of the United States for at least seven years, and an inhabitant of the state from which he or she is elected. Customarily, the member resides in the district he or she represents. Representatives are elected in even-numbered years to two-year terms that begin the following January. (*See* House of Representatives, Locality Rule.)

Reprimand A formal condemnation of a member for misbehavior, considered a milder reproof than censure. The House of Representatives first used it in 1976 when it approved a resolution accepting a reprimand recommendation reported by its Standards of Official Conduct Committee. Adoption of the report usually constitutes the reprimand, but the Speaker can administer it verbally. The Senate has not used the term. (*See also* Censure, Code of Official Conduct, Denounce, Ethics Rules, Expulsion, Fining a Member, Seniority Loss.)

Reprogramming An executive agency's shift of funds from one purpose to another within the same appropriation account. Reprogramming does not require specific statutory authority, but agencies usually consult with the appropriate congressional committees before taking such an action. Agencies often are required to give those committees formal notification and, in some instances, are expected to obtain their approval. (*See* Appropriation Account.)

Request a Conference A formal action by one house requesting the other house to agree to a meeting between their representatives in order to resolve their differences on a measure.

A house can request a conference only when it has custody of the papers and only after it has disagreed with the most recent action of the other body on that measure or insisted on its own most recent position. One house cannot force the other to agree to a conference, but requests are rarely rejected.

A House rule permits a privileged motion to send a measure to conference if authorized by the appropriate committee and if the Speaker recognizes for the purpose of offering that motion. (*See* Conference, Custody of the Papers, Disagree, Insist, (The) Papers, Privilege, Recognition. *See also* Amendments Between the Houses, Stage of Disagreement.)

Requisite Number of Words (*See* Pro Forma Amendment.)

Re-referral The transfer of an erroneously referred measure from one committee to another. Measures are re-referred by unanimous consent or by motion. (*See* Bills and Resolutions Referred, Motion, Referral, Unanimous Consent.)

Rescind A seldom used motion to annul or invalidate a previously taken action. On rare occasions, the House has nullified proceedings by rescinding the records of them in the *Journal* and both houses have rescinded or expunged entries in the *Journal*s of preceeding Congresses. (*See also* Congress, Expunging from the *Record, Journal*, Rescission, Vacate Proceedings.)

Rescission A provision of law that repeals previously enacted budget authority in whole or in part. Under the Impoundment Control Act of 1974, the president can impound such funds by sending a message to Congress requesting one or more rescissions and the reasons for doing so. If Congress does not pass a rescission bill for the programs requested by the president within forty-five days of continuous session after receiving the message, the president must make the funds available for obligation and expenditure. If the president does not, the comptroller general of the United States is authorized to bring suit to compel the release of those funds. A rescission bill may rescind all, part, or none of an amount proposed by the president, and may rescind funds the president has not impounded.

The term "continuous session" means days on which either house is in actual session. The houses rarely meet seven days a week; therefore, the forty-five-day deadline usually takes a longer period of calendar days to expire. Rescission bills are privileged in both houses and time for debate on them is limited. (*See* Budget Authority, Comptroller General of the United States, Debate, Impoundment, Obligation, Privilege, Time Limits on Debate.)

Reservation A statement added to a Senate resolution of ratification of a treaty. It usually limits the obligations of the United States under the treaty. (*See* Treaty.)

Reserve the Balance of One's Time A member's conservation of whatever remaining time for debate he or she controls.

When debate time on a pending matter is limited and divided between proponents and opponents (or between the parties), the member controlling the time for the proponents (or for the majority party) speaks first, then usually reserves the balance of his time, if any, to permit his opposite member to make a statement. The latter speaks, then reserves his remaining time to permit the other side to use additional portions of its time. Debate continues in this fashion until all time has expired or until the controlling members yield back the time remaining to them.

Usually the member who speaks first reserves some time to make the last statement in the debate. Members are not permitted to reserve the balance of their time when debate is under the five-minute rule in Committee of the Whole. (*See* Committee of the Whole, Debate, Five-Minute Rule. *See also* Equally Divided, Yield Back the Balance of One's Time.)

Reserving a Point of Order In the House, a member's declaration that he may make a point of order against a pending matter at some indefinite future time. By reserving a point of order, a member attempts to circumvent the requirement that points of order must be made against a matter before debate on that matter begins.

A member reserves a point of order either (1) to get an explanation of a pending motion or amendment before deciding whether to press for a point of order or withdraw his or her reservation; (2) to gain time to study a provision or amendment to determine whether a point of order will lie; or (3) as a courtesy to a colleague who has offered a proposition and wishes to explain it before the point of order is made. Points of order against provisions in a general appropriation bill are usually reserved when the measure is reported to the House.

Recognition to reserve a point of order in the House is within the discretion of the chair and does not require unanimous consent. Nevertheless, reserving a point of order violates the regular order, and any member can prevent it, or prevent its continuation, by demanding the regular order. If that happens, the reserver still has the right to make a point of order.

The practice of reserving a point of order is not followed in the Senate because a senator is allowed to make a point of order against a matter at any time it is under consideration. However, when debate on a proposition is under a time limit, a point of order may be made only when debate on it has ended. (*See* Amendment, Committee of the Whole, Conference Report, Debate, Explanatory Statement, General Appropriation Bill, Point of Order, Recognition, Regular Order, Time Limits on Debate. *See also* Authorization-Appropriation Process, Non-Selfenforcing Rules, Reserving the Right to Object.)

Reserving the Right to Object A member's declaration that at some indefinite future time he or she may object to a unanimous consent request. It is an attempt to circumvent the requirement that a member may prevent such an action only by objecting immediately after it is proposed.

In the House, recognition for a reservation is within the discretion of the chair. However, the chair invariably recognizes for that purpose unless he or she believes the reservation is dilatory. Even if the chair permits it, however, a reservation violates the regular order, and any member can prevent it or prevent its continuation by demanding the regular order. If that happens, the reserver still has the right to object. (*See* Dilatory Tactics, Objection, Recognition, Regular Order, Unanimous Consent Request. *See also* Non-Selfenforcing Rules, Reserving a Point of Order.)

Resident Commissioner from Puerto Rico A nonvoting member of the House of Representatives, elected to a four-year term. The resident commissioner has the same status and privileges as delegates. Like the delegates, the resident commissioner may not vote in the House, but a rule adopted in 1993 allows him to vote in Committee of the Whole. (*See* Committee of the Whole, Delegate.)

Resolution (1) A simple resolution; that is, a nonlegislative measure effective only in the house in which it is proposed and not requiring concurrence by the other chamber or approval by the president. Simple resolutions are designated H. Res. in the House and S. Res. in the Senate and are consecutively numbered in the order of their introduction during a two-year Congress.

Simple resolutions express nonbinding opinions on policies or issues or deal with the internal affairs or prerogatives of a house. For example, they are used to establish select and special committees, appoint the members of standing committees, and amend the standing rules. In the House, the Rules Committee reports its special rules in the form of simple resolutions. (*See* Bills and Resolutions Introduced, Committee Assignments, Congress, Measure, Rule, Select *or* Special Committee, Standing Rules. *See also* Resolution of Inquiry, Resolution of Ratification.)

(2) Any type of resolution: simple, concurrent, or joint. (*See* Concurrent Resolution, Joint Resolution.)

Resolution of Inquiry A resolution—usually simple rather than concurrent—calling on the president or the head of an executive agency to provide specific information or papers to one or both houses. It is a privileged measure in the House, but not in the Senate. Resolutions of inquiry have sometimes caused conflicts between the branches of government, especially when they call for papers relating to foreign affairs. (*See* Concurrent Resolution, Privileged Business, Resolution. *See also* Executive Privilege.)

Resolution of Ratification The Senate vehicle for agreeing to a treaty. The constitutionally mandated vote of two-thirds of the senators present and voting applies to the adoption of this resolution. However, it may also contain amendments, reservations, declarations, or understandings that the Senate had previously added to it by majority vote. (*See* Advice and Consent, Treaty.)

Resolutions and Motions Over, Under the Rule A section in the Senate's *Calendar of Business* that lists simple and concurrent resolutions denied immediate consideration by an objection. (*See Calendar of Business*, Objection, Over Under the Rule.)

Resolving Clause The first section of a joint resolution that begins "Resolved by the Senate and House of Representatives of the United States of America in Congress assembled.... " This language gives legal force to the measure when approved by Congress and signed by the president or when a veto is overridden by Congress. A successful motion to strike the resolving clause kills the entire measure. (*See* Override a Veto, Strike Out the Enacting (*or* Resolving) Clause.)

Retrenchment A reduction in an amount of money contained in a general appropriation bill. Under the Holman Rule in the House of Representatives, a germane provision in, or amendment to, such a bill is permitted if it changes existing law by reducing the amount of money covered by the bill.

During consideration of a general appropriation bill in Committee of the Whole, retrenchment amendments may be offered only after the reading for amendments has been completed, and then only if the committee does not prevent their offering by adopting a motion to rise and report the bill back to the House. Members have seldom used the Holman Rule in recent decades, relying instead on limitation amendments. (*See* Changing Existing Law, Committee of the Whole, General Appropriation Bill, Germane, Holman Rule, Legislation on an Appropriation Bill, Limitation on a General Appropriation Bill, Reading for Amendment. *See also* Authorization-Appropriation Process.)

Revenue Legislation Measures that levy new taxes or tariffs or change existing ones. Under Article I, Section 7, Clause 1 of the Constitution, the House of Representatives originates federal revenue measures, but the Senate can propose amendments to them. The House Ways and Means Committee and the Senate Finance Committee have jurisdiction over such measures, with a few minor exceptions.

A House rule adopted in 1983 prohibits the reporting of a tax or tariff measure by a committee not having that jurisdiction; if the chair sustains a point of order on that basis, the offending provision is automatically stricken from the bill. The rule also prohibits a tax or tariff proposal offered as an amendment to a bill reported by a committee not having jurisdiction over such measures.

On various occasions, the House has refused to consider Senate bills that, in its view, violated House prerogatives on revenue measures. Any House member may rise to a question of privilege on such a measure and introduce a resolution (often called a blue slip resolution) to return it. The House has also returned a nonrevenue House bill to which the Senate added a revenue amendment—the 1983 House rule prohibits consideration of such a Senate amendment to a House measure reported by a committee not having revenue jurisdiction. (*See* Amendments Between the Houses, Blue Slip Resolution, Committee Jurisdiction, Point of Order, Questions of Privilege.)

Revise and Extend One's Remarks A unanimous consent request to publish in the *Congressional Record* a statement a member did not deliver on the floor, a longer statement than the one made on the floor, or miscellaneous extraneous material. Members frequently make such requests, and these are rarely objected to, because debate time is limited in the House. (*See Congressional Record*, Debate, Floor, Objection, Unanimous Consent Request. *See also* Extensions of Remarks.)

Revolving Fund A trust fund or account whose income remains available to finance its continuing operations without any fiscal year limitation. (*See* Fiscal Year, Trust Funds.)

Riddick's Senate Procedure A single-volume digest of Senate precedents, procedures, and practices originally compiled by Floyd M. Riddick, a parliamentarian emeritus. The fourth edition, revised and edited by Alan S. Frumin, parliamentarian of the Senate, was published as a Senate document in 1992. It is arranged alphabetically by subject, each introduced by a short explanation and the text of the relevant rules as of that date. An appendix presents Senate terminology in various procedural situations. (*See* Precedent. *See also Senate Manual.*)

Rider Congressional slang for an amendment unrelated or extraneous to the subject matter of the measure to which it is attached. Riders often contain proposals that are less likely to become law on their own merits as separate bills, either because of opposition in the committee of jurisdiction, resistance in the other house, or the probability of a presidential veto.

Riders are more common in the Senate, where the rules permit unrelated amendments on most legislation, than in the House, where a rule requires amendments to be germane. Nevertheless, House bills often carry riders because no point of order is made against them or because points of order are waived by a special rule.

Riders sometimes take the guise of limitation provisions in general appropriation bills. Must-pass measures usually attract large numbers of riders. (*See* Amendment, Committee Jurisdiction, Germane, Limitation on a General Appropriation Bill, Must-Pass Bill, Rule, Veto. *See also* Christmas Tree Bill, Omnibus Bill.)

Rifleshot Congressional slang for a tax provision that provides a special tax benefit for an individual, corporation, industry, or limited group. (*See also* Pork *or* Pork Barrel Legislation, Revenue Legislation.)

Rise In congressional jargon, a committee is said to rise when it ends a meeting. When a Committee of the Whole completes its work on a measure, it rises and its chairman immediately reports its recommendations to the full House. (*See* Committee of the Whole.)

Roll The official roster of members in each house. (*See also* Call of the Roll, Roll Call.)

Roll Call A call of the roll to determine whether a quorum is present, to establish a quorum, or to vote on a question.

Usually, the House uses its electronic voting system for a roll call, but when the system is malfunctioning the Speaker directs the clerk to read the names. The Senate does not have an electronic voting system; its roll is always called by a clerk. After the entire roll has been called, the clerk calls the names of those who did not respond and the names of members who indicate they now wish to respond.

Before the chair has announced the result of a roll-call vote in the Senate, senators are permitted to ask how they are recorded on the vote and to change the way they are recorded, if they so desire. Sometimes, a number of senators rise in turn to ask how they are recorded in order to delay the announcement of the vote's result until one or more absent senators can come to the floor and cast their votes. Representatives can change their votes by presenting themselves in the well of the House and seeking recognition for that purpose before the chair has announced the result of the vote. (*See* Electronic Voting, Quorum, Recognition, Roll, Well, Yeas and Nays. *See also* Automatic Roll Call, Regular Order, Voting.)

Rolling Quorum The method by which each house complies with the requirements for establishing the "presence" of a quorum during a quorum call or recorded vote without requiring the actual presence of a majority of its members in the chamber at the same time. Under this practice, it is sufficient that the required number of members arrive in the chamber and record their presence at some time during the call or vote, after which they may leave.

In 1993, the House adopted a rule that, in effect, applied the same practice to the requirement that a majority quorum be present when a committee orders a measure to be reported to its house. (*See* Quorum.)

Rule (1) A permanent regulation that a house adopts to govern its conduct of business, its procedures, its internal organization, behavior of its members, regulation of its facilities, duties of an officer, or some other subject it chooses to govern in that form. In addition to its standing rules, a house is subject to precedents, constitutional rules, statutory rules, standing orders, and, in the House of Representatives, certain rules in *Jefferson's Manual*.

Under the Constitution, each house determines the rules of its proceedings, an authority called the rulemaking power. Generally, when two or more rules are in conflict, the most recently adopted rule is followed. The same practice applies to a conflict between a standing rule and a statutory rule. Under its rulemaking power, either house can, at any time, unilaterally supersede a statutory rule as it applies to that house. (*See* Constitutional Rules, Constitutional Votes, Precedent, Standing Order, Standing Rules, Statutory Rules. *See also* Party Caucus, Rule Citations.)

(2) In the House, a privileged simple resolution reported by the Rules Committee that provides methods and conditions for floor consideration of a measure or, rarely, several measures. The resolution is also called a special rule, special order, or special order of business resolution. With few exceptions, major nonprivileged bills are taken up under the terms of such resolutions. Explicitly or implicitly, a rule can temporarily waive any rule of the House or any statutory rule during consideration of a measure, but it may not set aside Calendar Wednesday, a motion to recommit, or a constitutional requirement.

The common terms for different types of rules usually reflect their treatment of amendments. An open rule puts no limit on the number of amendments that may be offered, providing the amendments do not violate a rule or practice of the House. A closed rule, sometimes called a gag rule, permits no amendments or only those offered by the reporting committee. A modified rule permits some amendments but not others. According to *Deschler's Precedents,* a modified open rule permits any germane amendment except certain designated ones, while a modified closed rule prohibits the offering of amendments except those it designates. Some rules ban amendments to certain parts of a measure but not to other parts.

A waiver rule may refer to one consisting only of a ban on points of order against a privileged measure, usually a general appropriation bill, or to a rule on a nonprivileged measure that, among other conditions, waives points of order against the bill or against certain amendments that may be offered to it. Sometimes the waiver only exempts a measure or amendment from points of order that are permitted under certain specified House rules; in other cases, the rule provides a blanket waiver against all points of order.

A typical rule implicitly waives the regular order of business by permitting the House to consider a nonprivileged measure, usually in Committee of the Whole. It limits general debate in the committee, customarily to one or more hours equally divided and controlled by the chairman and ranking minority member of the reporting committee, and then requires consideration of the measure for amendment under the five-minute rule. When that process is completed, the rule orders the committee to rise and report the measure to the House with the amendments it has adopted. It then imposes the previous question on House consideration of the bill and on the committee's amendments until final passage, banning all other motions except one motion to recommit. (*See* Amendment, Calendar Wednesday, Committee of the Whole, Constitutional Rules, Five-Minute Rule, General Appropriation Bill, General Debate, Germane, Order of Business (House), Point of Order, Previous Question, Privilege, Ranking Minority Member, Recommit, Recommit with Instructions, Resolution, Rise, Statutory Rules. *See also* Amendment in the Nature of a Substitute, Discharge a Committee, King of the Mountain (*or* Hill) Rule, Party Caucus, Self-Executing Rule.)

Rule Citations The two houses differ somewhat in their terminology for citing subdivisions of their standing rules. The progression in a House rule is: Rule I, clause 1, paragraph (a), subparagraph (a). The Senate prefers: Rule I, paragraph 1, subparagraph (a). (*See* Standing Rules.)

Rule Twenty-Two A common reference to the Senate's cloture rule. (*See* Cloture.)

Rulemaking Power The constitutional authority of each house to determine the rules of its proceedings. In accordance with this authority, a house may change its rules at any time, may change any statutory rule as it applies to that house, or may adopt a rule that supercedes a statutory rule. Moreover, a house may waive or suspend any of its rules by unanimous consent or by a two-thirds vote, except those rules explicitly exempted. (*See* Rule, Standing Rules, Statutory Rules, Unanimous Consent.)

Rulemaking Statutes Laws that apply rules of procedure to one or both houses. (*See* Statutory Rules. *See also* Rule, Rulemaking Power.)

Ruling The decision of the presiding officer on a parliamentary matter. (*See also* Appeal, Precedent.)

S

Scope of Differences The limits within which a conference committee is permitted to resolve the disagreements between the two houses on a measure. For example, if the disagreement is between an authorization of one million dollars for a particular program proposed by house A and two million dollars for that program proposed by house B, the conference may agree to one million, two million, or any amount between. If the conference committee's report proposes an amount larger than two million or smaller than one million, that proposal goes beyond the scope of the differences between the houses, and the report can be killed in either house by a point of order.

In matters involving differences over complex legislative language, it is often more difficult to define precisely the scope within which those differences can be legitimately resolved. Conferees sometimes consult the parliamentarians of their respective houses in such cases. (*See* Authorization, Conferees, Conference Committee, Conference Report, Parliamentarian, Point of Order. *See also* Amendment in the Nature of a Substitute.)

Scorekeeping The process of calculating the budgetary effects of pending and enacted legislation and assessing their impact on the targets or limits in the budget resolution, as required by the Congressional Budget Act of 1974. The Congressional Budget Office (CBO) produces detailed scorekeeping reports, and the Budget committees issue summarized versions at least once a month and often more frequently. By using these reports and CBO's cost estimates on proposed legislation, members can determine whether approval of a particular amendment or bill would breach the spending ceilings, revenue floor, or deficit limit established by the budget resolution or the allocations of budget resolution amounts made to committees.

Scorekeeping reports tabulate congressional actions affecting budget authority, receipts, outlays, the surplus or deficit, and the public debt limit. CBO derives its scorekeeping estimates from analyses of the president's budget, baseline budget projections, and bill cost estimates. (*See* Baseline, Breach, Budget Allocation, Budget Authority, Budget Receipts, Budget Resolution, Congressional Budget Office, Cost Estimates, Debt Limit, Deficit, Outlays, Surplus.)

Seat A position on a committee or subcommittee.

Second A member who indicates formal support of a motion or other parliamentary action so that it can be discussed, put to a vote, or implemented. The term also refers to the number of members required to indicate formal support in certain situations. To "second a motion" is to indicate such formal support.

Long ago, both houses of Congress discarded the requirement of a second for ordinary motions, and in

1991 the House eliminated the requirement for a seconding vote by a majority (determined by tellers) for certain motions to suspend the rules. Currently, the only second mentioned in the rules of the House refers to one by a majority of members present for a motion to adjourn after an automatic roll call, and the only second required by the Senate's rules applies to a motion to close its doors.

Nevertheless, other support requirements in the rules and in the Constitution, although not explicitly called seconds, amount to the same thing: the support of one-fifth of the members for the yeas and nays, of one-fifth of a quorum for a recorded vote in the House, of twenty-five members for a recorded vote in Committee of the Whole, by the signatures of a majority of House members on a discharge petition, and by the signatures of sixteen senators on a cloture motion. (*See* Adjourn, Automatic Roll Call, Cloture, Committee of the Whole, Discharge Rule, Motion, Quorum, Recorded Vote, Secret *or* Closed Session, Suspension of the Rules (House), Teller, Yeas and Nays.)

Second Degree Amendment An amendment to an amendment in the first degree. It is usually a perfecting amendment. (*See* Degrees of Amendment, Perfecting Amendment. *See* also Pending Amendment, Substitute, Voting Order on Amendments.)

Second Reading A required reading of a bill or joint resolution to a chamber: in the Senate, by title only before referral to a committee; in the House, in full before floor consideration in the House or in Committee of the Whole. The House usually dispenses with the full reading before consideration in the House by unanimous consent and in Committee of the Whole by a special rule. (*See* Committee of the Whole, Readings of Bills and Resolutions, Rule, Title, Unanimous Consent.)

Secret *or* Closed Session A session of either house that is
held behind closed doors to discuss business deemed to
require secrecy. Only members and necessary staff may
attend.

  The Senate immediately closes its doors upon a
motion by any senator that is seconded by another, and
it then determines whether the matter to be discussed
warrants keeping them closed. Any senator who dis-
closes the confidential business discussed is subject to
expulsion from the Senate, and any staff person who
does so can be dismissed and punished for contempt.

  In the House, a motion to resolve into secret
session is not debatable, but the chamber must first
agree to it before the doors can be closed. (*See* Expulsion, Motion, Second. *See also* Business Meeting, Closed
Hearing, Executive Session.)

Secretary of the Senate The chief administrative and budgetary officer of the Senate. The secretary manages a
wide range of functions that support the operation of
the Senate as an organization as well as those functions
necessary to its legislative process, including
recordkeeping, document management, certifications,
housekeeping services, administration of oaths, and
lobbyist registrations. In the absence of the vice president and pending the election of a president pro
tempore, the secretary presides over the Senate.
Elected by resolution or order of the Senate, the
secretary is invariably the candidate of the majority
party and usually of the majority leader. (*See* Lobby,
Majority Leader, President of the Senate, President Pro
Tempore. *See also* Clerk of the House, Director of Non-
Legislative and Financial Services, Sergeant at Arms.)

Section A subdivision of a bill or statute. By law, a section
must be numbered and, as nearly as possible, contain
"a single proposition of enactment."

  When a measure is not divided into titles, its
sections are numbered 1, 2, 3, and so on. Within a title,

the first one or two digits of each section's number corresponds with its title's roman number: Title I begins with section 101, title II with section 201, and so forth. (*See* Title.)

Section by Section In the House, the sequence in which a bill is read for amendment in Committee of the Whole. (*See* Committee of the Whole, Reading for Amendment, Section.)

Select *or* Special Committee A committee established by a resolution in either house for a special purpose and, usually, for a limited time. Most select and special committees are assigned specific investigations or studies, but are not authorized to report measures to their chambers. During the past several decades, however, both houses created several permanent select and special committees and gave legislative reporting authority to a few of them: the Ethics and the Indian Affairs committees in the Senate and the Intelligence committees in both houses.

There is no substantive difference between a select and a special committee; it merely depends on whether the resolution creating the committee calls it one or the other. Usually, the Speaker appoints the members of temporary select and special committees in the House, and a rule adopted in 1993 authorizes the Speaker, at any time, to remove members from them or appoint additional members. The president of the Senate or the president pro tempore is authorized to appoint select and special committee members in that chamber. (*See* Resolution. *See also* Ad Hoc Select Committee, Standing Committee.)

Self-Executing Rule A special rule from the House Rules Committee stipulating that upon the adoption of the rule, the House is deemed to have passed a measure, adopted an amendment, or taken some other action. The rule precludes a separate vote on the measure, amendment, or action. It has the same effect as a closed rule or gag rule because it also precludes the offering of floor amendments to the proposition at issue.

Once used to expedite consideration of Senate amendments to House-passed bills or to make technical, minor, or noncontroversial amendments to a bill, self-executing rules have been applied more recently to measures and provisions that are more substantive and controversial. (*See* Amendments Between the Houses, Closed Rule, Floor Amendment, Rule, Speaker's Table.)

Semi-Closed *or* Semi-Open Rule (*See* Modified Rule.)

Senate The house of Congress in which each state is represented by two senators; each senator has one vote. Article V of the Constitution declares that "No State, without its Consent, shall be deprived of its equal Suffrage in the Senate." The Constitution also gives the Senate equal legislative power with the House of Representatives. Although the Senate is prohibited from originating revenue measures, and as a matter of practice it does not originate appropriation measures, it can amend both.

Only the Senate can give or withhold consent to treaties and nominations from the president. It also acts as a court to try impeachments by the House and elects the vice president when no candidate receives a majority of the electoral votes. It is often referred to as "the upper body," but not by members of the House. (*See* Amendment, Appropriation, Impeachment, Nomination, Revenue Legislation, Treaty.)

Senate Calendar Commonly used title for the Senate's *Calendar of Business.*

Senate Manual The handbook of the Senate's standing rules and orders and the laws and other regulations that apply to the Senate, usually published once each Congress. It also contains several historical documents, including the Constitution, and lists of all senators and

other Senate officials from the First Congress to date.
(*See* Congress, Standing Order, Standing Rules. *See also*
House Manual, Senate Procedure.)

Senate Procedure Commonly used title of *Riddick's Senate
Procedure,* a single-volume digest of Senate procedure
and precedents. (*See Riddick's Senate Procedure. See also*
Precedent, *Senate Manual.*)

Senator A duly sworn elected or appointed member of the
Senate. The Constitution requires that a senator be at
least thirty years old, a citizen of the United States for
at least nine years, and an inhabitant of the state from
which he or she is elected. Senators are usually elected
in even-numbered years to six-year terms that begin
the following January.

When a vacancy occurs before the end of a term,
the state governor can appoint a replacement to fill the
position until a successor is chosen at the state's next
general election or, if specified under state law, the
next feasible date for such an election, to serve the
remainder of the term. Until the Seventeenth Amendment was ratified in 1913, senators were chosen by
their state legislatures. (*See* Senate. *See also* Classes of
Senators, Junior Senator, Senior Senator.)

Senatorial Courtesy The Senate's practice of declining to
confirm a presidential nominee for an office in the
state of a senator of the president's party unless that
senator approves. Sometimes called "the courtesy of
the Senate," the practice is a customary one and not
always adhered to. A senator sometimes invokes the
custom by declaring that the nominee is personally
obnoxious or personally objectionable to him.

The Senate usually confirms the nomination of a
sitting or former senator at once, without referring it to
a committee. And it also usually complies with a
senator's request for a temporary delay in considering

a nomination, a request referred to as a hold. (*See* Hold, Nomination.)

Senior Senator Of the two senators from a state, the one with the longer continuous service in the Senate. (*See also* Junior Senator.)

Seniority The priority, precedence, or status accorded members according to the length of their continuous service in a house or on a committee. (*See also* Seniority System.)

Seniority Loss A type of punishment that reduces a member's seniority on his or her committees, including the loss of chairmanships. Party caucuses in both houses have occasionally imposed such punishment on their members, for example, for publicly supporting candidates of the other party.

A 1980 rule of the House Democratic Caucus requires automatic loss of committee and subcommittee chairmanships for a censured member or one indicted or convicted of a felony carrying a sentence of at least two years. (*See also* Caucus, Censure, Denounce, Ethics Rules, Expulsion, Fining a Member, Reprimand.)

Seniority Rule The customary practice, rather than a rule, of assigning the chairmanship of a committee to the majority party member who has served on the committee for the longest continuous period of time. (*See also* Seniority System.)

Seniority System A collection of long-standing customary practices under which members with longer continuous service than their colleagues in their house or on their committees receive various kinds of preferential treatment. Although some of the practices are no longer as rigidly observed as in the past, they still pervade the organization and procedures of Congress.

Usually, the majority party member with the greatest seniority on a committee serves as its chairman, although in recent decades the House Democratic Caucus has occasionally chosen members with less seniority to replace a chairman or to fill a vacant chairmanship. Committee members are ranked among their party colleagues according to their committee seniority, and chairmen usually recognize them to question witnesses and to offer motions and amendments in the order of their ranking. The parties also take seniority in their houses into account when filling vacancies on committee rosters. Committee seniority is also a factor in the selection of subcommittee chairmen and of conferees.

The parties also follow the custom that members may not be removed from their committees, or have their rankings on them reduced, without their consent, except under extraordinary circumstances, such as publicly supporting a presidential candidate of the other party or if a change in party ratios on a committee or a reduction in the committee's size requires it.

Larger and more conveniently located offices are assigned according to members' seniority in their houses. The Senate invariably chooses the most senior majority party senator as its president pro tempore, and the most senior member of the House normally swears in the Speaker at the beginning of each Congress. (*See* Amendment, Chairman, Committee, Committee Assignments, Committee Ratios, Motion, Party Caucus, Preferential Recognition, President Pro Tempore, Rank *or* Ranking, Subcommittee, Subcommittee Assignments. *See also* Committee on Committees, Father of the House.)

Sense of Congress Resolution (*See* Concurrent Resolution.)

Sequential Referrals (*See* Multiple and Sequential Referrals.)

Sequestration A procedure for canceling budgetary resources—that is, money available for obligation or spending—to enforce budget limitations established in law. Sequestered funds are no longer available for obligation or expenditure.

Automatic sequestration occurs by presidential order following a report from the Office of Management and Budget (OMB) declaring that a specified budget limit has been breached. The procedure was first established in the Gramm-Rudman-Hollings Act and subsequently modified by the Balanced Budget and Emergency Deficit Control Reaffirmation Act of 1987 and the Budget Enforcement Act of 1990.

If OMB determines that a discretionary category's spending cap has been breached, a presidential sequestration cancels enough budgetary resources in that category in order to bring the total within the cap. If legislation that reduces revenues or increases direct spending also increases the deficit, a sequestration offsets the increase by reducing funding from entitlements not otherwise exempted by law.

A deficit that exceeds the maximum amount fixed by the 1990 act by more than a specified margin triggers across-the-board spending reductions. In general, sequesters must cut each program, project, or activity within a budget account by the same percentage; however, the president is permitted to exempt military personnel accounts if Congress is notified to that effect by August 10 of each year.

An end-of-session sequestration is one that occurs within fifteen calendar days after Congress adjourns. A within-session sequestration refers to one or more additional sequesters that can occur during the following session to eliminate any breach in the discretionary spending limits of the current fiscal year enacted before July 1.

During the course of a session, OMB and the Congressional Budget Office are required to issue several sequestration preview reports. In addition, OMB must provide Congress with cost estimates of budgetary legislation within five days of enactment.

(*See* Appropriation Account, Balanced Budget and
Emergency Deficit Control Reaffirmation Act of 1987,
Breach, Budget Enforcement Act of 1990, Budgetary
Resources, Cap, Congressional Budget Office, Deficit,
Direct Spending, Discretionary Appropriations, Entitlement Program, Fiscal Year, Gramm-Rudman-Hollings Act of 1985, Maximum Deficit Amounts, Obligation, Session. *See also* Budget and Accounting Act
of 1921, Look-Back, Pay-As-You-Go, Program, Project,
or Activity.)

Sergeant at Arms The officer in each house responsible for
maintaining order, security, and decorum in its wing
of the Capitol, including the chamber and its galleries.
In the House of Representatives, the mace is the
symbol of this office. The Senate sergeant at arms also
performs the duties of doorkeeper. Although elected
by their respective houses, both sergeants at arms are
invariably the candidates of the majority party. (*See*
Decorum, Mace, Order. *See also* Doorkeeper of the
House, Officers of Congress.)

Session (1) The annual series of meetings of a Congress.
Under the Constitution, Congress must assemble at
least once a year at noon on January 3 unless it
appoints a different day by law.

(2) The meetings of Congress or of one house
convened by the president under his constitutional
authority, called a special session.

(3) A house is said to be in session during the
period of a day when it is meeting. (*See* Congress. *See
also* Adjournment by July 31, Meeting Hour.)

Seven-Day Rule (1) In both houses, if a chairman fails to
call a special meeting of a committee to be held within
seven calendar days after three committee members
have requested it, a majority of the committee can call
such a meeting. (*See* Special Committee Meeting.)

(2) In both houses, a committee's report on a measure it has approved must be filed with the parent house within seven calendar days after a majority of the committee's members has signed a request for that purpose and submitted it to the committee's clerk. Before this rule was adopted in 1970, committee chairmen sometimes refused to file reports on measures they disliked. (*See* Committee Report on a Measure, Filed.)

(3) In the House, if a member who has reported a special rule from the Rules Committee does not call it up within the next seven legislative days, any member of the committee can call it up as a question of privilege one day after that member announces the intention to do so. (*See* Legislative Day, Questions of Privilege, Rule.)

(4) If the House has adopted a special rule making it in order to consider a measure and if no motion to consider it has been offered within seven days, the Speaker may recognize any authorized member of the committee that reported it to offer that motion. Usually, the chairman of a committee reports a measure and is entitled to recognition for calling it up. This rule was intended to permit the committee to circumvent a recalcitrant chairman, but it has been superfluous since 1983 when the House gave the Speaker discretionary authority to resolve the House into Committee of the Whole at any time after a rule has been adopted making it in order to consider a measure in that committee. (*See* Recognition, Report, Rule.)

(5) A motion to discharge a committee must remain on the discharge calendar at least seven days before it may be called up for consideration. (*See* Discharge a Committee.)

Severability (*or* Separability) Clause Language stating that if any particular provisions of a measure are declared invalid by the courts, the remaining provisions shall remain in effect. In rare instances (the Gramm-Rudman-Hollings Act is an example), a law has specified that an alternative provision shall become effective in the event that a particular provision is declared invalid. (*See* Gramm-Rudman-Hollings Act of 1985.)

Short Quorum In House parlance, a quorum call in Committee of the Whole that its chairman suspends when the presence of a minimum quorum (100 members) has been recorded. It is a device that saves the time of the committee and of the remaining members who need not answer the call. Although the rule gives the chairman discretion in invoking a short quorum, it must be announced in advance at the time the absence of a quorum is discovered. Short quorums are sometimes called notice quorums because of the prior notice requirement. (*See* Absence of a Quorum, Committee of the Whole, Quorum. *See also* Point of No Quorum.)

Short Title (*See* Title.)

Simple Resolution (*See* Resolution.)

Sine Die Without fixing a day for a future meeting. An adjournment sine die signifies the end of an annual or special session of Congress. (*See* Adjournment Sine Die, Session, Special Session.)

Sit (1) A house or a committee is said to sit when it is meeting. The rules of both houses forbid their committees to sit during certain proceedings of their parent bodies unless they receive special leave. (*See* Leave to Sit. *See also* Business Meeting, Hearing, House Sitting as the House.)

(2) To hold a committee or subcommittee assignment. A senator, for example, must sit on two committees. (*See* Committee Assignments, Subcommittee Assignments.)

Slip Law The first official publication of a measure that has become law. It is published separately in unbound, single-sheet form or pamphlet form. A slip law usually is available two or three days after the date of the law's enactment. (*See also* Act, Law, *Statutes at Large, U.S. Code.*)

Speak Out of Order To speak on a subject not relevant or germane to the matter under consideration when germane debate is required. To speak out of order requires unanimous consent. A member who speaks out of order without unanimous consent may be asked to sit down and be silent. Requests to speak out of order are more frequent in the House than in the Senate because all House debate must be germane, whereas the Senate's germaneness rules apply in only a few situations. (*See* Germane, Out of Order, Unanimous Consent. *See* also Cloture, Pastore Rule.)

Speaker The presiding officer of the House of Representatives and the leader of its majority party. The Speaker is selected by the majority party and formally elected by the House at the beginning of each Congress. Although the Constitution does not require the Speaker to be a member of the House, in fact, all Speakers have been members. The Speaker and his surrogates are addressed as "Mr. [or Madam] Speaker."

As presiding officer, the Speaker maintains order in the House, manages the flow of legislation to the floor, and has numerous administrative responsibilities, including general control of the House side of the Capitol. He refers measures to committees and, on multiple referrals, may require committees to report by a deadline and may discharge them if they fail to meet the deadline.

In many situations the Speaker has the power of discretionary recognition, and he uses that power to determine which measures may come up under suspension of the rules. He also appoints the members of select, special, ad hoc, and conference committees and the chairmen of Committees of the Whole. Moreover, under a House rule adopted in 1993, he may remove members of select and conference committees "at any time after an original appointment" and also appoint additional members to such committees.

As party leader, the Speaker chairs the party's Committee on Committees, plans the party's legislative strategy, and negotiates committee party ratios with the minority leader. In addition, the Speaker is second to the vice president in the line of succession to the presidency. (*See* Ad Hoc Select Committee, Bills and Resolutions Referred, Committee of the Whole, Committee on Committees, Committee Ratios, Conference Committee, Discretionary Recognition, House of Representatives, Multiple and Sequential Referrals, Order, Party Caucus, Select *or* Special Committee, Suspension of the Rules (House). *See also* Recess, Steering and Policy Committee.)

Speaker Pro Tempore A member of the House who is designated as the temporary presiding officer by the Speaker or elected by the House to that position during the Speaker's absence.

Usually, the Speaker appoints a Speaker pro tempore for a period of no longer than three days. If the Speaker is ill, he can make the appointment for up to ten days with the approval of the House. If the Speaker is unable to appear and does not make an appointment, the House elects a pro tempore to act during the Speaker's absence. An elected Speaker pro tempore takes over a wider range of the Speaker's duties, powers, and functions than does one designated or appointed. (*See* Speaker.)

Speakers List (*See* List of Speakers.)

Speaker's Table The Speaker is required to dispose of certain communications received by the House of

Representatives from the executive branch and from the Senate, and these communications are said to be on his table. He refers most of them to the appropriate committees. Two types of communications, however, may be disposed of as the House determines: House bills with Senate amendments that do not require consideration in Committee of the Whole, and Senate bills that are substantially the same as House bills favorably reported by a House committee. Other amendments between the houses usually rest on the Speaker's table until they are brought up for debate and disposition. (*See* Amendments Between the Houses, Committee of the Whole. *See also* Order of Business (House).)

Speaker's Vote The Speaker is not required to vote, and his name is not called on a roll-call vote unless he so requests. Usually, the Speaker votes either to create a tie vote, and thereby defeat a proposal, or to break a tie in favor of a proposal. Occasionally, the Speaker also votes to emphasize the importance of a matter or his special interest in it. (*See* Roll Call, Tie Vote.)

Special Appropriation Bill An appropriation measure other than a general appropriation bill and therefore not subject to the rules of the authorization-appropriation process. Both houses apply the term to measures providing appropriations for a single agency or purpose, but the House classifies a continuing resolution as special whereas the Senate regards it as a general measure. (*See* Authorization-Appropriation Process, Continuing Resolution, General Appropriation Bill.)

Special Committee (*See* Select *or* Special Committee.)

Special Committee Meeting A meeting convened at the request of a committee's members. In both houses, a majority of a committee's members can force the convening of such a meeting if its chairman refuses a request to call one.

The procedure requires at least three members to file a written request with the committee, specifying the business that the special meeting will consider. If, within three calendar days, the chairman does not call a meeting for that purpose to be held within seven calendar days, a majority of the committee's members can file a written notice specifying the date and hour the meeting will be held and the business it will consider. If the chairman does not attend that meeting, the next ranking majority member present at the meeting presides. (*See also* Business Meeting, Regular Meeting Day.)

Special Leave to Sit (*See* Leave to Sit.)

Special Order A temporary regulation or directive. In the House, it is often a rule (also called a special rule) reported by the Rules Committee that provides methods for the consideration of a measure or, rarely, a class of measures. Special orders are adopted by majority vote, unanimous consent, or occasionally by suspension of the rules.

A Senate rule requires a two-thirds vote to adopt special orders fixing a day and time for the consideration of legislative proposals, but in practice the Senate uses unanimous consent agreements for those purposes. (*See* Rule, Suspension of the Rules (House), Suspension of the Rules (Senate), Unanimous Consent, Unanimous Consent Agreement. *See also* Order, Order of Business (House), Order of Business (Senate), Special Order Speech, Standing Order.)

Special Order of Business In the House of Representatives, business that supplants the daily order of business, or that may do so, on specified days. It includes: (1) the consent calendar on the first and third Mondays of each month; (2) the discharge calendar and District of Columbia measures on the second and fourth Mondays of each month; (3) the private calendar on the first

Tuesday, and sometimes also on the third Tuesday, of each month; (4) motions to suspend the rules on any Monday or Tuesday; and (5) Calendar Wednesday on any Wednesday. (*See* Business, Calendar Wednesday, Consent Calendar, Discharge Calendar, District Day, Private Calendar, Suspension of the Rules (House). *See also* Order of Business (House).)

Special Order of Business Resolution A simple resolution reported by the House Rules Committee that provides for consideration of a measure; commonly called a rule or special rule. (*See* Order of Business (House), Rule.)

Special Order Speech A type of special order that, by unanimous consent, permits a member to address his house on any subject when it is not considering business. Unanimous consent is required because under the rules of both houses, members may be recognized to give speeches on the floor only during debate on a matter that has been brought up for consideration.

The House limits each special order speech to one hour and permits them after the program of the day has been completed. In 1984, the Speaker announced that he would alternate between majority and minority members in recognizing for special orders, first for speeches of five minutes or less and then for speeches of five minutes to one hour.

Under a somewhat analogous practice in the Senate, senators are often recognized by unanimous consent, after the leaders have used their special time at the beginning of a daily session, to deliver speeches, usually limited to five minutes on any subject. (*See* Business, Debate, Leader (*or* Leadership) Time, Questions of Privilege, Unanimous Consent. *See also* Hour Rule, Morning Hour.)

Special Pair A term sometimes used for a specific pair. (*See* Pairing, Specific Pair.)

Special Rule Another term for a simple resolution, reported by the House Rules Committee, usually making it in order for the House to consider a measure and mandating the methods for considering it. (*See* Rule.)

Special Session A session of Congress convened by the president, under his constitutional authority, after Congress has adjourned sine die at the end of a regular session. (*See* Adjournment Sine Die, Session.)

Specific Pair A pairing of two absent members on opposite sides of a question. In the House text of the *Congressional Record*, their names and positions on the question appear after the vote: "Mr. Smith for, Mr. Jones against." In the Senate text, they customarily appear before the vote in the form of an announcement by the party whips. Also called a special pair or, sometimes in the Senate, a dead pair. (*See* Dead Pair, Pairing.)

Spending Authority The technical term for backdoor spending. The Congressional Budget Act of 1974 defines it as borrowing authority, contract authority, and entitlement authority for which appropriation acts do not provide budget authority in advance. Under the Budget Act, legislation that provides new spending authority may not be considered unless it provides that the authority shall be effective only to the extent or in such amounts as provided in an appropriation act. (*See* Appropriation, Backdoor Spending Authority, Borrowing Authority, Budget Authority, Congressional Budget and Impoundment Control Act of 1974, Contract Authority, Entitlement Program.)

Split Referral A measure divided into two or more parts; each part is referred to a different committee. (*See* Division of Bills for Referral. *See also* Multiple and Sequential Referrals.)

Sponsor The principal proponent and introducer of a measure or an amendment. (*See* Bills and Resolutions Introduced.)

Stacked Votes Senate jargon for sequential roll-call votes held at a convenient time for senators, usually on a series of amendments to a measure that were debated at an earlier time. Unlike cluster voting in the House, the stacking of votes in the Senate requires unanimous consent and the presiding officer may not reduce the fifteen-minute guaranteed time for each vote. (*See* Amendment, Cluster Voting, Roll Call, Time Limits for Voting, Unanimous Consent.)

Staff Director The most frequently used title for the head of staff of a committee or subcommittee. On some committees, that person is called chief of staff, clerk, chief clerk, chief counsel, general counsel, or executive director. The head of a committee's minority staff is usually called minority staff director. (*See also* Investigative Staff, Minority Staff, Permanent Staff.)

Stage of Disagreement During the process of amendments between the houses, the stage reached when one house formally disagrees with an amendment proposed by the other house or insists on its own position. Ordinarily, a measure may not go to conference until this stage is reached.

The stage of disagreement also reverses the precedence of certain motions. Before disagreement, procedural priority is given to motions that perfect the text, such as motions to disagree to an amendment of the other house or to amend it further. After disagreement, priority goes to motions that bring the houses into agreement expeditiously, such as motions to recede from disagreement and concur in an amendment of the other house. Consideration of Senate amendments in the House is privileged after disagreement but not before that stage. (*See* Amendments Between the

Houses, Concur, Disagree, Perfect a Measure or Amendment, Precedence of Motions (House), Precedence of Motions (Senate), Privileged Business, Recede.)

Standing Committee A permanent committee established by a House or Senate standing rule or standing order. The rule also describes the subject areas on which the committee may report bills and resolutions and conduct oversight. Most introduced measures must be referred to one or more standing committees according to their jurisdictions. Of the four general types of congressional committees (standing, select and special, joint, and Committee of the Whole), standing committees are the most numerous.

Many standing committees have been in existence for many years. House Ways and Means dates back to 1802, and Senate Foreign Relations, Finance, and Judiciary to 1816. The Legislative Reorganization Act of 1946 substantially consolidated the standing committee structure in both houses; it was further modified in the House in 1974 and in the Senate in 1977. (*See* Bills and Resolutions Referred, Committee, Committee Jurisdiction, Committee Report on a Measure, Oversight, Standing Order, Standing Rules. *See also* Joint Committee, Legislative Committee, Select *or* Special Committee.)

Standing Joint Committee (*See* Joint Committee.)

Standing Order A continuing regulation or directive that has the force and effect of a rule, but is not incorporated into the standing rules. The Senate's numerous standing orders, like its standing rules, continue from Congress to Congress unless changed or the order states otherwise. The House uses relatively few standing orders, and those it adopts expire at the end of a session of Congress.

Some of the Senate's standing orders establish more or less permanent entities, such as the Select

Ethics Committee, the Senate Commission on Art and Antiquities, the Office of Deputy President Pro Tempore, and the Select Intelligence Committee. These and other standing orders appear in the *Senate Manual* under the heading "Nonstatutory Standing Orders Not Embraced in the Rules." (*See* Congress, Deputy President Pro Tempore, *Senate Manual,* Session, Standing Rules. *See also* Continuing Body, Order, Special Order.)

Standing Rules The rules of the Senate that continue from one Congress to the next and that appear in the *Senate Manual* under the title "Standing Rules of the Senate"; and the rules of the House of Representatives that it adopts at the beginning of each new Congress, and that appear in the House Manual under "Rules of the House of Representatives, with Notes and Annotations."

The houses are also governed by their precedents, standing orders, constitutional rules, statutory rules, and, in the case of the House, by many provisions of *Jefferson's Manual.* In addition, the Senate has rules for impeachment trials and its Rules and Administration Committee has promulgated several rules for the regulation of the Senate wing of the Capitol. (*See* Constitutional Rules, House Manual, Impeachment, Rule, *Senate Manual,* Standing Order, Statutory Rules. *See* also Continuing Body, Rule Citations, Special Order.)

Standing Vote An alternative and informal term for a division vote, during which members in favor of a proposal and then members opposed stand and are counted by the chair. (*See* Division Vote.)

Star Print A reprint of a bill, resolution, amendment, or committee report correcting technical or substantive errors in a previous printing; so called because of the small black star that appears on the front page or cover.

Stare Decisis Literally, let the decision stand. A principle holding that a court decision should not be overturned when similar cases subsequently arise unless for compelling reasons. On the same principle, the presiding officers of each house of Congress are expected to uphold previous decisions interpreting their respective rules, but each house can overturn the chair's ruling by a successful vote on an appeal. (*See* Appeal, Precedent.)

State of the Union Message A presidential message to Congress under the constitutional directive that he shall "from time to time give to the Congress Information of the State of the Union, and recommend to their Consideration such Measures as he shall judge necessary and expedient." Customarily, the president sends an annual State of the Union Message to Congress, usually late in January.

In 1913, President Woodrow Wilson revived the early tradition, abandoned in 1801, of delivering his messages in person before a joint session of Congress. Every president except Herbert Hoover has continued that custom. (*See* Joint Session, Message.)

Statement of the Managers (*See* Explanatory Statement.)

Statutes at Large A chronological arrangement of the laws enacted in each session of Congress. Though indexed, the laws are not arranged by subject matter nor is there an indication of how they affect or change previously enacted laws. The volumes are numbered by Congress, and the laws are cited by their volume and page number. The Gramm-Rudman-Hollings Act, for example, appears as 99 Stat. 1037. (*See also* Act, Law, Slip Law, *U.S. Code.*)

Statutory Rules Procedural rules mandated by law for one or both houses. Though embodied in law, they are enacted under the constitutional rulemaking power of Congress; consequently, each house may at any time change a statutory rule insofar as the rule applies to that house. The manual of each house usually includes the texts of its applicable statutory rules.

The Legislative Reorganization Acts of 1946 and 1970 contained numerous statutory rules, many of them subsequently incorporated into the standing rules of the two houses. Virtually all the rules of the congressional budget process are statutory, as are the numerous legislative veto rules. The House re-adopts these "applicable provisions of law" at the beginning of each Congress; the Senate does not need to do so since its rules continue from one Congress to the next. (*See* Budget Process, Congress, House Manual, Legislative Veto, Rule, Rulemaking Power, *Senate Manual*, Standing Rules. *See also* Continuing Body, Procedures.)

Steering and Policy Committee (House) A committee of the House Democratic Caucus that advises the party leaders on legislative strategy and scheduling for floor consideration and also serves as the party's Committee on Committees. When Democrats are the majority party, the committee is chaired by the Speaker. Its members include the majority leader, whip, chief deputy whip, caucus chairman and vice chairman, chairman of the Democratic Congressional Campaign Committee, twelve members elected by regions, up to nine members appointed by the Speaker, and the chairmen of the committees on Appropriations, Budget, Rules, and Ways and Means.

The Republicans in both houses and the Democrats in the Senate have policy committees to develop party positions and make recommendations to their party colleagues. (*See* Committee on Committees, Majority Leader, Policy Committees, Speaker, Whip. *See also* Committee Assignments, Party Caucus.)

Steering Committee (Senate) The committee of the Democratic Party Conference in the Senate that recommends committee assignments for party members. Its recommendations are subject to confirmation by the conference and adoption by the Senate. The Democratic Steering and Policy Committee performs the same function in the House of Representatives. (*See* Committee Assignments, Conference, Steering and Policy Committee (House).)

Straw Vote Prohibition Under a House precedent, a member who has the floor during debate may not conduct a "straw vote" or otherwise ask for a show of support for a proposition. Only the chair may put a question to a vote. (*See* Debate, Floor.)

Strike from the *Record* Expunge objectionable remarks from the *Congressional Record*, after a member's words have been taken down on a point of order. (*See* Expunging from the *Record*, Point of Order, Taking Down the Words.)

Strike Out A motion to eliminate a part of the text of a measure, an amendment, or a treaty. A simple motion to strike out may not be amended, but while it is pending, the text it seeks to strike out may be amended. (*See* Amendments, Voting Order on Amendments.)

Strike Out and Insert An amendment that replaces all or a part of the text of a measure or of another amendment. (*See* Amendment, Amendment in the Nature of a Substitute, Bigger Bite Amendment, Substitute.)

Strike Out the Enacting (or Resolving) Clause A House motion whose adoption kills a bill or joint resolution. Such a motion is not directly permitted in Committee of the Whole, but the committee can agree to a motion that it rise and report the measure to the House with the recommendation that the clause be stricken. Members frequently offer the motion merely to obtain time for debate in Committee of the Whole rather than for its ostensible purpose. In House usage, it is called a preferential motion because it takes precedence over all other motions during the amendment stage. When offered, it rarely prevails.

In Committee of the Whole, debate on the motion to report a recommendation to strike the enacting clause is under the five-minute rule, but no pro forma amendments are allowed. Only one such motion may be offered on any legislative day unless the measure under consideration has been materially changed since the last such motion was offered. (*See* Committee of the Whole, Enacting Clause, Five-Minute Rule, Legislative Day, Pro Forma Amendment, Reading for Amendment, Resolving Clause.)

Strike the Last Word A pro forma amendment that is not intended to make any actual change in the measure or amendment to which it is offered, but merely entitles a member to five minutes of debate. (*See* Pro Forma Amendment. *See also* Committee of the Whole, Five-Minute Rule, House as in Committee of the Whole.)

Subcommittee A panel of committee members assigned a portion of the committee's jurisdiction or other functions. On legislative committees, subcommittees hold hearings, mark up legislation, and report measures to their full committee for further action; they cannot report directly to the chamber. A subcommittee's party composition usually reflects the ratio on its parent committee.

The Senate's rules indirectly limit the number of a committee's subcommittees to the number of its majority party members. A House rule requires every committee with more than twenty members (except the Budget Committee) to establish at least four subcommittees. House Democratic Caucus rules direct its members on a committee, when they are in the majority, to establish the number, jurisdictions, and sizes of its subcommittees. Committees are also required to limit the number of subcommittees on most standing committees to six and on others to five. (*See* Committee, Committee Jurisdiction, Committee Ratios,

Markup, Party Caucus, Report. *See also* Subcommittee Assignments.)

Subcommittee Assignments The subcommittees on which a member serves. Each committee determines its subcommittee assignments, subject to the rules of its house or party organizations. For certain committees, the rules limit the number of subcommittee assignments and subcommittee chairmanships a member can hold. These rules also attempt to ensure an equitable allocation of assignments to each member.

By standing rule, a senator may sit on no more than three subcommittees on each of his class A committee assignments and on no more than two subcommittees on a class B committee. In the House, the rules of the Democratic Caucus limit each Democrat to a total of five subcommittee assignments on his standing committees.

A Senate standing order forbids a senator's assignment to a second subcommittee on any committee until all committee members have chosen one assignment in the order of their seniority, and the same standing order applies to third subcommittee assignments. Under the rules of the House Democratic Caucus, the Democratic members of each committee bid for subcommittee assignments in the order of their committee seniority; after each bid, the entire Democratic membership of the committee votes on whether to approve it. As in the Senate, no member may bid for a second subcommittee until all other members of the committee have received one assignment, and the same applies to additional assignments.

No senator may chair more than one subcommittee on each of his committees. With certain exceptions, a chairman of a class A committee can chair a subcommittee on only one of his class A assignments; he cannot chair more than one subcommittee on each of his class B committees. A chairman of a class B committee may not chair any of its subcommittees and may not chair more than one subcommittee on each of his class A committees.

In the House, Democratic members on each committee bid for, and are elected to, subcommittee chairmanships in the same way that they obtain subcommittee assignments. However, the Democratic Caucus selects all subcommittee chairmen on the Appropriations and Ways and Means committees. Caucus rules also prohibit most full committee chairmen from chairing more than one subcommittee with legislative jurisdiction. (*See* Class A Committees, Class B Committees, Committee Assignments, Party Caucus, Rule, Seniority, Standing Order, Subcommittee. *See also* Ex Officio.)

Subdivisions The Congressional Budget Act of 1974 requires that committees that are allocated budget authority and outlay amounts from a budget resolution must subdivide them by programs or subcommittees. The Appropriations committees must subdivide among their subcommittees. Other committees may subdivide by program or subcommittee, but under the Gramm-Rudman-Hollings Act they are not required to do so until after the fiscal year 1995 budget cycle. (*See* Budget Allocation, Budget Authority, Budget Resolution, Congressional Budget and Impoundment Control Act of 1974, Fiscal Year, Outlays.)

Subjects on the Table Business in the Senate, usually bills and resolutions, placed at the table of the chamber by unanimous consent and held there. A measure given this status is said to lie on the table and can be called up by a motion to proceed to its consideration, even though it has not been referred to a committee. (*See* Business.)

Subpoena Power The authority granted to committees by the rules of their respective houses to issue legal orders requiring individuals to appear and testify, or to produce documents pertinent to the committee's functions, or both. Persons who do not comply with subpoenas can be cited for contempt of Congress and prosecuted.

The Senate rule specifies no particular procedure for issuing subpoenas. The House rule requires a majority vote by a committee or subcommittee, provided that a quorum is present, but a committee may delegate the power to its chairman. Subpoenas can be signed by the chairman or any other member designated by the committee. (*See* Quorum. *See also* Congressional Response to Subpoenas, Contempt of Congress, Executive Privilege, Investigative Power.)

Subsidy Generally, a payment or benefit made by the federal government for which no current repayment is required. Subsidy payments may be designed to support the conduct of an economic enterprise or activity, such as ship operations, or to support certain market prices, as in the case of farm subsidies. Subsidies can also take the form of loans, goods, or services to the public at prices lower than market value, such as interest subsidies. Tax expenditures are indirect subsidies. (*See* Direct Loan, Tax Expenditure.)

Substantive Law Public law other than appropriations law; sometimes called basic law or, in some contexts, existing law. It often refers to law that authorizes an agency or program. (*See* Appropriation, Authorization, Changing Existing Law, Public Law.)

Substitute An amendment that proposes to replace the entire text of another amendment or of a measure. It is always in the form of an amendment to strike out and insert, but the text that it inserts may be entirely different from the text it strikes out, identical to that text except for a few words or numbers, or different to some extent between these extremes.

In the Senate, a substitute for a pending amendment (except an amendment in the nature of a substitute) usually is of the second degree. The House treats a substitute as a first degree amendment and therefore amendable to another degree. (*See* Amendment, Amendment in the Nature of a Substitute, Degrees of Amendment, Strike Out and Insert. *See also* Bigger Bite Amendment, Perfecting Amendment, Voting Order on Amendments.)

Suggest the Absence of a Quorum The phrase senators usually use to force a quorum call. Except under cloture, the Senate's presiding officer has no authority to count to determine whether a quorum is present; he must immediately direct the clerk to call the roll when a senator makes the suggestion.

Quorums are rarely present in the Senate during debate, but suggestions that a quorum is absent are frequently made not to establish a quorum but for the purpose of what some have called "constructive delay." Since the suggestion immediately suspends floor action while the roll is called, the pause gives senators time for informal discussions and negotiations or for an absent senator to arrive and offer an amendment or deliver a speech on whatever business may be pending. Aware of these purposes, the clerk calls the roll very slowly to avoid inadvertent disclosure of a quorum's absence, which would require senators to make an unnecessary trip to the floor. Once the call's purpose has been achieved, a senator asks unanimous consent that the call be dispensed with, a request invariably granted, and the Senate resumes its proceedings.

These so-called "dead quorums" are possible because Senate precedents impose no time limit on a quorum call. When a senator actually wants a quorum to be present, he warns the Senate that he wants a "live quorum." (*See* Absence of a Quorum, Call of the Roll, Counting a Quorum, Live Quorum, Pending Business, Precedent, Quorum, Quorum Call, Unanimous Consent.)

Sunset Legislation A term sometimes applied to laws authorizing the existence of agencies or programs that expire annually or at the end of some other specified period of time. One of the purposes of setting specific expiration dates for agencies and programs is to encourage the committees with jurisdiction over them to determine whether they should be continued or terminated. If the latter, it is said that the sun has set on them. (*See* Authorization, Committee Jurisdiction. *See also* Annual Authorization, Multiyear Authorization, Permanent Authorization.)

Sunshine Rules Rules requiring open committee hearings and business meetings, including markup sessions, in both houses, and also open conference committee meetings. However, all may be closed under certain circumstances and using certain procedures required by the rules. (*See* Business Meeting, Closed Hearing, Conference Committee, Markup, Open Hearing.)

Super Majority A term sometimes used for a vote on a matter that requires approval by more than a simple majority of those members present and voting; also referred to as extraordinary majority. (*See also* Absolute Majority, Calendar Wednesday, Cloture, Constitutional Votes, Private Calendar, Rule, Suspension of the Rules (House), Suspension of the Rules (Senate).)

Supplemental Appropriation Bill A measure providing appropriations for use in the current fiscal year, in addition to those already provided in annual general appropriation bills. Supplemental appropriations are often for unforeseen emergencies requiring urgent expenditures that cannot be postponed until enactment of the next regular annual appropriations act.

The funds may be in addition to those provided in previously enacted appropriation legislation, or to fund programs or activities authorized after enactment of the regular appropriation bills, or even for unauthorized programs. Supplemental appropriations enacted before July 1 trigger a sequestration fifteen days after enactment if they exceed the spending caps fixed by the Budget Enforcement Act of 1990 on discretionary spending categories. The sequestration involves automatic spending cuts to offset the excess budget authority over the cap. (*See* Cap, Discretionary Appropriations, General Appropriation Bill, Sequestration. *See also* Authorization-Appropriation Process.)

Supplemental, Minority, and Additional Views Statements in a committee report on a measure that present dissenting or other comments of committee members. Both houses require their committees to give members at least three calendar days to submit such views if the members give notice they wish to do so at the time the committee approves the measure. The submitted statements must be included in the report, and it must be indicated on the cover of the report that they are included. (*See* Committee Report on a Measure.)

Support Agency (*See* Congressional Support Agencies.)

Surplus The amount by which the government's budget receipts exceed its outlays for a given fiscal year. (*See* Budget Receipts, Fiscal Year, Outlays. *See also* Balanced Budget, Deficit.)

Suspension of the Rules (House) An expeditious procedure for passing relatively noncontroversial or emergency measures by a two-thirds vote of those members voting, a quorum being present. Debate on a motion to suspend the rules and pass a measure is limited to forty minutes; the time is evenly divided between proponents and opponents. Members may not offer amendments from the floor, but the motion itself can include amendments. The two-thirds vote simultaneously suspends the rules and passes the measure. If the motion is not supported by the required two-thirds vote, the House has not rejected the measure involved; it has only refused to suspend the rules in order to pass it. Therefore, the measure may be considered at another time under some other procedure.

Suspension motions are in order every Monday and Tuesday and during the last six days of a session (or during additional days toward the end of an annual session, if authorized by a rule from the Rules Committee), but the Speaker, exercising his power of discretionary recognition, determines which measures may be brought up under suspension.

The motion sets aside all rules that conflict with its purpose; consequently, points of order against any of the measure's provisions are not allowed. Its effect is so sweeping that it has been used to pass bills still pending in committee and even bills not yet formally introduced. To save time, the Speaker may postpone the votes on a series of suspension motions until later in the day or until some time within the next two legislative days. He may also reduce the voting time on each postponed vote, except the first, to five minutes.

The rules of the House Democratic Caucus direct a Democratic Speaker not to recognize suspension motions for measures that exceed $100 million in any fiscal year unless authorized by the party's Steering and Policy Committee. The rules also require the Speaker to give all House members at least three working days' advance notice about the measures he has scheduled for suspension. There is no suspension calendar, but members sometimes use that term when referring to the Speaker's list of measures. (*See* Conference Report, Floor Amendment, Legislative Day, Motion, Point of Order, Quorum, Recognition, Rule, Session, Steering and Policy Committee. *See also* Cluster Voting, Electronic Voting, Forty-Minute Debate, Special Order of Business.)

Suspension of the Rules (Senate) A procedure to set aside one or more of the Senate's rules; it is used infrequently, and then most often to suspend the rule banning legislative amendments to appropriation bills. A senator may move to suspend the rules at any time after giving one day's written notice, specifying the rule to be suspended and the purpose for suspending it. The motion is debated under the general rules of the Senate and requires a two-thirds majority vote. (*See* Motion, Rule. *See also* Legislation on an Appropriation Bill, Unlimited Debate.)

Sustained The presiding officer's affirmative ruling on a point of order. When the presiding officer makes an adverse ruling, the point of order is said to be overruled. (*See* Point of Order.)

T

Table (*See* Party Tables, Speaker's Table.)

Table a Bill, Amendment, or Motion (*See* Lay on the Table.)

Taking Down the Words Requiring that a member's remarks be read to the chamber so that the presiding officer may determine whether they are offensive or violate the rules of that house. When any member makes a point of order against such remarks and asks that the words be "taken down," the alleged violator must immediately sit down and await the chair's decision. If the words are ruled out of order, a motion may be offered to strike them from the debate to be published in the *Congressional Record.*

In the House, the member may not speak again on the same day without the chamber's permission, but he may withdraw or modify his remarks by unanimous consent. In the Senate, the member may not speak again until another matter is taken up unless the Senate agrees to a motion that he be allowed to proceed in order. On rare occasions, the House has censured a member for objectionable remarks.

Prohibited remarks are variously characterized as improper, disorderly, objectionable, offensive, intemperate, or unparliamentary. (*See* Censure, *Congressional Record*, Out of Order, Point of Order, Unanimous Consent, Unparliamentary. *See also* Comity, Decorum, Strike from the *Record*.)

Task Force A title sometimes given to a panel of members assigned to a special project, study, or investigation. The House Budget Committee uses task forces in place of subcommittees. Ordinarily, these groups do not have authority to report measures to their respective houses.

Party leaders sometimes appoint task forces to recommend policies or legislation to their caucuses, to resolve disputes between two or more committees that have jurisdiction over the same measure, or to mobilize support for a measure. In 1992, the House established a temporary bipartisan task force of members of the House Administration Committee to investigate misconduct in the House post office. (*See* Caucus, Committee Jurisdiction, Conference, Multiple and Sequential Referrals.)

Tax Expenditure Loosely, a tax exemption or advantage, sometimes called an incentive or loophole; technically, a loss of governmental tax revenue attributable to some provision of federal tax laws that allows a special exclusion, exemption, or deduction from gross income or that provides a special credit, preferential tax rate, or deferral of tax liability. The tax exemption or advantage is usually intended to assist a certain group or to encourage a certain activity, such as the purchase of homes.

In their impact on the federal budget, tax expenditures are, in effect, subsidies provided through the tax system. Instead of making direct payments to beneficiaries, the government permits certain taxpayers to pay lower taxes than they otherwise would have to pay. (*See* Subsidy.)

Tax Expenditure Statement A statement on the effect a measure will have on the level of tax expenditures. The statement is required to appear in the committee report on that measure. (*See* Committee Report on a Measure, Tax Expenditure.)

Tax Expenditures Budget An enumeration of tax expenditures and their levels by major functional categories of the federal budget. A tax expenditures budget is required to appear in the Budget Committee's report accompanying a concurrent resolution on the budget. (*See* Budget Resolution, Function *or* Functional Category, Report, Tax Expenditure.)

Technology Assessment (*See* Office of Technology Assessment.)

Televised Proceedings Television and radio coverage of the floor proceedings of the House of Representatives have been available since 1979 and of the Senate since 1986. They are broadcast over a coaxial cable system to all congressional offices and to some congressional agencies on channels reserved for that purpose. Coverage is also available free of charge to commercial and public television and radio broadcasters. The Cable-Satellite Public Affairs Network (C-SPAN) carries gavel-to-gavel coverage of both houses.

Each house employs personnel to operate all the equipment necessary for the coverage. In the House, the Speaker promulgates regulations for the coverage; the Rules and Administration Committee performs that function in the Senate. Both houses prohibit use of the coverage for any political purpose. The rules of the House also prohibit commercial sponsorship of the broadcasts except as part of bona fide news programs or public affairs documentary programs. (*See* C-SPAN.)

Teller An antiquated term for a member or clerk who counts members in certain voting or quorum-call situations. (*See* Quorum Call, Teller Vote.)

Teller Vote A voting procedure, formerly used in the House, in which members cast their votes by passing through the center aisle to be counted, but not recorded by name, by a member from each party appointed by the chair. Members voting "aye" were counted first, followed by those members voting "no," after which the counting members reported their totals to the chair. The House deleted the procedure from its rules in 1993, but during floor discussion of the deletion a leading member stated that a teller vote would still be available in the event of a breakdown of the electronic voting system.

Under the deleted rule, the chair could order tellers if he was in doubt of the results after a division vote, but he was required to order them upon a demand supported by one-fifth of a quorum—twenty members in Committee of the Whole, usually forty-four in the House. (*See* Committee of the Whole, Division Vote, Electronic Voting, Quorum, Teller. *See also* Recorded Vote by Clerks.)

Teller Vote by Clerks (*See* Recorded Vote by Clerks.)

Temporary Staff A term sometimes applied to committee staff authorized by annual or biennial resolutions rather than by rule or law. They are also called investigative staff. (*See* Investigative Staff. *See also* Minority Staff, Permanent Staff.)

Ten-Minute Debate (1) In Committee of the Whole, the five-minute rule actually permits ten minutes of debate on an amendment: five minutes for its proposer and five minutes for an opponent. Moreover, debate may be extended by pro forma amendments and by unanimous consent requests. (*See* Committee of the Whole, Five-Minute Rule, Pro Forma Amendment, Unanimous Consent Request.)

(2) Debate on a printed amendment considered in Committee of the Whole, after a motion to end debate has been agreed to, is strictly limited to ten minutes: five minutes for and five minutes against. (*See* Committee of the Whole, Printed Amendment. *See* also Debate-Ending Motion.)

(3) In the House, after the previous question has been ordered, a motion to recommit with instructions is nevertheless debatable for ten minutes: five minutes by the mover of the motion and five minutes by an opponent. However, debate is extended to one hour upon the demand of the majority floor manager, with the time equally divided between him and the mover of the motion. (*See* Floor Manager, Move, Previous Question, Recommit with Instructions.)

(4) In the House, ten minutes of debate, equally divided between proponents and opponents, is allowed on a motion to dispense with Calendar Wednesday and on a motion to dispense with the call of the private calendar on the first Tuesday of a month. (*See* Calendar Wednesday, Private Calendar.)

Terms of Office (*See* Congressional Terms of Office.)

Third Degree Amendment An amendment to a second degree amendment. Both houses prohibit such amendments. (*See* Degrees of Amendment.)

Third Reading A required reading to a chamber of a bill or joint resolution by title only before the vote on passage. The original purpose of a third reading was to give members the opportunity to hear the full text of the measure, as it may have amended, before voting on it. In the modern practice, it has merely become a pro forma step. (*See* Readings of Bills and Resolutions.)

Three-Day Rule (1) In the House, a committee report on a measure must be available for at least three calendar days before the measure may be considered. (*See* Committee Report on a Measure.)

(2) In the House, a conference report must be printed in the *Congressional Record* at least three calendar days before it may be considered. (*See* Conference Report, *Congressional Record*.)

(3) In both houses, a committee member is entitled to three calendar days in which to submit separate views on a measure for inclusion in the committee report. (*See* Committee Report on a Measure, Supplemental, Minority, and Additional Views.)

(4) In the House, the printed hearings on a general appropriation bill must be available for at least three calendar days before the bill may be considered. (*See* General Appropriation Bill, Hearing.)

(5) In the House, measures on the consent calendar may not be called unless they have been on the calendar at least three legislative days. (*See* Consent Calendar, Legislative Day.)

(6) In both houses, a majority of a committee's members may call a special meeting of the committee if its chairman fails to do so within three calendar days after three or more of the members formally request such a meeting. (*See* Special Committee Meeting.)

Tie Vote When the votes for and against a proposition are equal, it loses. The president of the Senate may cast a vote only to break a tie. Because the Speaker is invariably a member of the House, he is entitled to vote but usually does not. He may choose to do so to break, or create, a tie vote.

When a super majority vote is required—for example, the two-thirds vote on a proposed constitutional amendment—a tie vote cannot occur; either the necessary number of members vote in favor, or the proposition loses. (*See* Super Majority.)

Time Agreement *or* Time Limitation Agreement (*See* Unanimous Consent Agreement.)

Time Limits for Voting In the House, members have a minimum of fifteen minutes to vote on recorded votes, but on clustered votes the Speaker may reduce the minimum to five minutes on the second and subsequent votes in the series.

The Speaker may also reduce the minimum to five minutes for a recorded vote on (1) a special rule after there has been a recorded vote on the previous question on the rule; (2) an amendment reported by a Committee of the Whole after a recorded vote has been ordered on another amendment from that committee; and (3) on the passage or adoption of a bill, resolution, or conference report, as the case may be, after a roll-call vote has been ordered on a motion to recommit the matter at issue.

At the beginning of recent Congresses, the Senate has adopted an order giving senators a maximum of fifteen minutes to vote when the yeas and nays are taken, but the time may be shortened by unanimous consent or lengthened by the majority and minority leaders. (*See* Cluster Voting, Committee of the Whole, Conference Report, Congress, Previous Question, Recommit, Recorded Vote, Roll Call, Rule, Unanimous Consent, Yeas and Nays.)

Time Limits on Debate A parliamentary device that expedites the consideration of measures, motions, and other business and restricts opportunities for dilatory tactics. Virtually all debate in the House of Representatives is subject to a time limit.

The Senate's rules impose time limits in few situations, most notably under cloture, but the chamber often accepts voluntary time limits under unanimous consent agreements. Some statutory rules require time limits when one or either house considers certain specific measures. (*See* Cloture, Statutory Rules, Unanimous Consent Agreement. *See also* Five-Minute Rule, Hour Rule, Nondebatable Motions, Ten-Minute Debate, Twenty-Minute Debate, Two-Hour Debate.)

Timeliness A principle of parliamentary procedure that certain actions may be taken by a member only at a specified stage of the proceedings, after which the member loses the right to take such an action. The principle applies to actions such as the offering of motions and amendments and the making, or reserving, of points of order and objections.

In some situations, House practices are more restrictive than those of the Senate. For example, a point of order against an amendment usually must be made before debate on it begins in the House, but may come at any stage before disposition of the amendment in the Senate. (*See* Amendment, Motion, Point of Order. *See also* Objection, Reserving a Point of Order, Reserving the Right to Object.)

Title (1) A major subdivision of a bill or act, designated by a roman numeral and usually containing legislative provisions on the same general subject. Titles are sometimes divided into subtitles as well as sections. (*See also* Reading for Amendment, Section.)

(2) The official name of a bill or act, also called a caption or long title. Appearing above the enacting clause, the title is usually a concise statement of the measure's subjects and purposes. Example: "A Bill To improve the operation of the legislative branch of the Federal Government, and for other purposes." (*See* Enacting Clause.)

(3) Some bills also have short titles that appear in the sentence immediately following the enacting clause. In the bill mentioned above, the sentence declares that the act may be cited as the "Legislative Reorganization Act of 1970." A measure sometimes provides short titles for major subdivisions that deal with unrelated or distantly related subjects. The Congressional Budget and Impoundment Control Act of 1974, for example, cites titles I through IX as the Congressional Budget Act of 1974 and title X as the Impoundment Control Act of 1974. (*See* Congressional Budget and Impoundment Control Act of 1974, Enacting Clause.)

(4) Popular titles are the unofficial names given to some bills or acts by common usage. For example, the Balanced Budget and Emergency Deficit Control Act of 1985 (short title) is almost invariably referred to as Gramm-Rudman (popular title). In other cases, significant legislation is popularly referred to by its title number (see definition (1) above). For example, the federal legislation that requires equality of funding for women's and men's sports in educational institutions that receive federal funds is popularly called Title IX.

Track System An occasional Senate practice that expedites legislation by dividing a day's session into two or more specific time periods, commonly called tracks, each reserved for consideration of a different measure. For example, by unanimous consent, over several days (or weeks if necessary), measure A might be considered from 10 a.m. to 1 p.m., measure B from 1 p.m. to 4 p.m., measure C from 4 p.m. to 7 p.m., and so forth. When the Senate finishes with a measure, it may start another one on that track.

Under this system, a filibuster against a particular measure can be confined to one track while the Senate continues work on several other measures. Majority

Leader Mike Mansfield (D-Mont.) instituted the practice in the early 1970s, but it has been used infrequently in recent years. (*See* Filibuster, Unanimous Consent.)

Transfer Payment A federal government payment to which individuals or organizations are entitled under law and for which no goods or services are required in return. Payments include welfare and Social Security benefits, unemployment insurance, government pensions, and veterans' benefits. Some of these payments are indexed to the rate of inflation or some part of that rate; that is, the payments are automatically increased at that rate according to a formula established by law. These are called cost-of-living adjustments or COLAs. (*See* Entitlement Program. *See also* Trust Funds.)

Treaty A formal document containing an agreement between two or more sovereign nations. The Constitution authorizes the president to make treaties, but he must submit them to the Senate for its approval by a two-thirds vote of the senators present. Under the Senate's rules, that vote actually occurs on a resolution of ratification.

Treaties are first considered by the Senate's Foreign Relations Committee, and then, if reported, referred to the executive calendar. Except by unanimous consent, a treaty must remain on the calendar at least one day before the full Senate may consider it. Like legislative proposals, treaties are read three times, debated, and may be amended, but they are considered in executive session rather than legislative session.

The Senate's decisions on a treaty are then put into a resolution of ratification that the Senate takes up after a one-day layover. At this stage, amendments to the treaty are no longer in order, but senators may offer amendments to the resolution in the form of reservations, declarations, statements, or understandings. If agreed to, the resolution is then sent to the president for ratification unless the Senate's action requires him to renegotiate it.

Unlike legislative measures, a treaty not yet approved does not die at the end of a Congress; it may be considered in future Congresses unless the president withdraws it or the Senate votes to return it to him.

Although the Constitution does not give the House a direct role in approving treaties, that body has sometimes insisted that a revenue treaty is an invasion of its prerogatives. In any case, the House may significantly affect the application of a treaty by its equal role in enacting legislation to implement the treaty. (*See* Congress, *Executive Calendar*, Executive Session, Legislative Session, Readings of Bills and Resolutions, Report, Reservation, Revenue Legislation, Unanimous Consent. *See also* Advice and Consent.)

Trust Funds Special accounts in the Treasury that receive earmarked taxes or other kinds of revenue collections, such as user fees, and from which payments are made for special purposes or to recipients who meet the requirements of the trust funds as established by law. Of the more than 150 federal government trust funds, several finance major entitlement programs, such as Social Security, Medicare, and retired federal employees' pensions. Others fund infrastructure construction and improvements, such as highways and airports.

Technically, the monies credited to these accounts are restricted by law to their designated programs or uses and are not available for the general purposes of government. Nevertheless, the Treasury borrows from the trust funds for that purpose and the borrowings become part of the public debt. (*See* Earmark, Entitlement Program, Public Debt, User Fee. *See also* Backdoor Spending Authority, Revolving Fund.)

Twenty-Day Rule A House rule that permits the chamber to discharge or instruct its conferees by majority vote if they have not reported a conference report within twenty calendar days of their appointment. (*See* Discharge of Conferees, Instruct Conferees.)

Twenty-Minute Debate In the House, twenty minutes of debate, equally divided between proponents and opponents, is permitted on a discharge motion. (*See* Discharge a Committee.)

Two-Day Rule A Senate rule that prohibits floor consideration of a measure until the printed committee report on it has been available to senators for at least two calendar days. The rule may be waived by joint agreement of the majority and minority leaders. Although Senate committees are not required to provide such reports, they usually do. (*See* Committee Report on a Measure.)

Two-Hour Debate In the House, general debate on a measure called up on Calendar Wednesday is limited to two hours and is equally divided between proponents and opponents of the measure. (*See* Calendar Wednesday.)

Two-Page Rule A regulation by the Joint Committee on Printing that requires a member to submit a cost estimate from the public printer when that member requests permission to insert extraneous material in excess of two printed pages into the *Congressional Record*. (*See Congressional Record*, Extensions of Remarks, Leave to Print, Revise and Extend One's Remarks.)

Two-Speech Rule A Senate rule that limits senators to two speeches on any question on a single legislative day, unless the Senate grants leave for additional speeches. Because the limitation applies to each question, a senator may speak twice on a measure, twice on each amendment to it, and twice on any debatable motion, and may do the same on the next and subsequent legislative days if the measure is still pending. In practice, the Senate rarely enforces the rule. (*See* Legislative Day, Question.)

Two-Thirds Vote (*See* Calendar Wednesday, Cloture, Constitutional Votes, Private Calendar, Rule, Suspension of the Rules (House), Suspension of the Rules (Senate).)

U

Unanimous Consent Without an objection by any member. A unanimous consent request asks permission, explicitly or implicitly, to set aside one or more rules. Both houses and their committees frequently use such requests to expedite their proceedings. The Senate, in particular, relies heavily on the device because it has few other procedural methods for moving business promptly. Although members rarely object to routine unanimous consent requests, they have the right to do so and, thereby, force full compliance with the rules.

Because the Speaker is a member of the House, he too may object to a unanimous consent request, but he usually exercises his right by refusing to entertain it. He invariably refuses to entertain unanimous consent requests to bring measures up for floor consideration unless assured that they have been cleared with the floor and committee leaders of both political parties. When he permits a member to offer a request, he usually asks, "Is there objection to the request?" He often invokes unanimous consent on his own initiative, declaring, for example, "Without objection, the bill is passed and a motion to recommit is laid on the table," but any member may object to such summary action. Unanimous consent requests in the House came into use about 1832.

The Senate's presiding officer *must* entertain unanimous consent requests, but in noncontroversial situations he will say, "Without objection, it is so ordered." (*See* Lay on the Table, Objection, Recommit, Rule. *See also* Consent Calendar, En Bloc, House as in Committee of the Whole, One-Minute Speeches, Pass Over Without Prejudice, Private Calendar, Reserving the Right to Object, Revise and Extend One's Remarks, Speak Out of Order, Special Order Speech.)

Unanimous Consent Agreement A special order approved without objection, usually to permit floor consideration of a measure under restrictive procedures; it is sometimes called a time agreement or a time limitation agreement. A unanimous consent agreement is a device to expedite legislation, frequently used in the Senate, but rarely employed in the House. Most often it is the Senate's majority leader who verbally proposes such an agreement on the floor. Once approved, it may be altered only by unanimous consent.

In its most complete form, a Senate agreement bypasses the requirement for a motion to bring a measure to the floor; imposes time limits for debate on the measure, amendments, debatable motions, points of order, and appeals; and requires that all or most amendments be germane. Many agreements specify that only certain named senators may offer amendments, and sometimes they specify the subjects of amendments that may be offered. Debate time assigned solely to the measure or to debate on final passage, rather than to amendments and other actions, is usually called "bill time" and is controlled by, and equally divided between, the majority and minority floor managers. On an amendment, the sponsor and an opponent divide and control debate time.

Unanimous consent agreements on major legislation are customarily printed and sent to all senators in advance of floor debate; all agreements are published on the first or second page of the Senate calendar. It is not unusual for the Senate to enter into a time agreement after it has begun consideration of a measure.

In many respects, unanimous consent agreements in the Senate resemble and perform the same functions as House special rules. However, the House approves special rules by majority vote, whereas a single objection blocks a Senate agreement. Consequently, protracted negotiations among party leaders and key senators, on or off the floor, are often necessary and are not always successful. (*See* Appeal, Floor, Germane, Motion, Objection, Point of Order, Rule, Senate Calendar, Special Order, Unanimous Consent. *See also* Consider, Reserving the Right to Object, Unlimited Debate, Yielding Time.)

Unanimous Consent Request A member's request to set aside one or more rules for some purpose. (*See* One-Minute Speeches, Special Order Speech, Unanimous Consent, Unanimous Consent Agreement.)

Unauthorized Appropriation An appropriation for a purpose not authorized in law or one that exceeds the amount authorized in law. The rules of both houses prohibit unauthorized appropriations in general appropriation bills, but permit some exceptions.

In a technical sense, in both houses an unauthorized appropriation also violates the rules that ban legislation on a general appropriation bill, because it proposes to enact a provision of law that does not yet exist. (*See* Authorization, Authorization-Appropriation Process, General Appropriation Bill, Legislation on an Appropriation Bill.)

Uncontrollable Expenditures A frequently used term for federal expenditures that are mandatory under existing law and therefore cannot be controlled by the president or Congress without a change in the existing law.

Technically, such expenditures are referred to as "relatively uncontrollable under current law." Uncontrollable expenditures include spending required under entitlement programs and also fixed costs, such as interest on the public debt and outlays to pay for prior-year obligations.

In recent years, uncontrollables have accounted for approximately three-quarters of federal spending in each fiscal year. (*See* Entitlement Program, Expenditures, Fiscal Year, Obligation, Outlays, Public Debt. *See also* Controllable Expenditures, Direct Spending.)

Unexpended Balance The amount of budget authority that has not been spent. The obligated portion of the balance remains available until it is spend or rescinded by law. The unobligated portion of the balance remains available for spending or obligation only until the end of the period for which it was made available. The rules of both houses forbid the reappropriation of unobligated unexpended balances. Under the Gramm-Rudman-Hollings Act, sequestration applies to both obligated balances and unobligated unexpended balances. (*See* Budget Authority, Gramm-Rudman-Hollings Act of 1985, Obligation, Reappropriation, Sequestration. *See also* Unobligated Balance.)

Unfinished Business A measure under consideration that is still pending when a house adjourns or recesses its daily session. If displaced by other business, unfinished business remains pending until the chamber acts on it in some fashion.

At the Senate's next meeting after an adjournment, unfinished business automatically comes up for continued consideration after the morning hour.

At the next meeting of the House after an adjournment, it is resumed after business on the Speaker's table is disposed of, but it is temporarily displaced by business that is in order on special days, such as the call of the consent or private calendars. After a recess, unfinished business is the first order of business in both houses. (*See* Adjourn, Consent Calendar, Morning Hour, Pending Business, Private Calendar, Recess, Speaker's Table, Special Order of Business. *See also* Business.)

Union Calendar A calendar of the House of Representatives for bills and resolutions favorably reported by committees that raise revenue or directly or indirectly appropriate money or property. In addition to appropriation bills, measures that authorize expenditures are also placed on this calendar. The calendar's full title is the Calendar of the Committee of the Whole House on the State of the Union. A measure on it must first be considered in Committee of the Whole before the House may act on them. Measures appear on the calendar in the order in which they were reported. (*See* Appropriation, Authorization, Calendar, Committee of the Whole, Report, Revenue Legislation. *See also* Adverse Report.)

Unlimited Debate The absence of time limits on the length of speeches or on the duration of debate on most measures and motions—a distinctive feature of Senate procedure. The standing rules of the Senate impose time limits only under cloture, during a call of the calendar in the morning hour, and during an impeachment trial. In all other situations, any debatable matter in the Senate is almost endlessly debatable unless it is tabled and thereby killed.

These conditions permit individual senators to delay Senate action at great length and give a determined minority of forty-one senators—the number that can prevent cloture—the absolute power to prevent any affirmative action. Consequently, the Senate conducts its business at a reasonable pace only through the restraint of its members and their toleration of unanimous consent requests that place time limits on debate. To protect certain important measures from the vagaries of voluntary restraint and toleration, many statutes, such as the Congressional Budget Act of 1974, impose fast-track, restrictive procedures on the Senate. (*See* Call of the Calendar, Cloture, Fast-Track Procedures, Impeachment, Lay on the Table, Morning Hour, Statutory Rules, Unanimous Consent. *See also* Filibuster, Hold, Nondebatable Motions, Unanimous Consent Agreement.)

Unobligated Balance The portion of budget authority not yet committed as payment for specific products or services. In one-year accounts, the unobligated balance expires at the end of the fiscal year for which it was made available. In multiyear accounts, it remains available for obligation for the specified number of years.

Unobligated balances in no-year accounts are carried forward indefinitely until either the purposes for which they were provided have been accomplished, disbursements have not been made against the appropriation for two full consecutive years, or they are rescinded by law. The Gramm-Rudman-Hollings Act permits sequestration of both obligated and unobligated balances. (*See* Budget Authority, Fiscal Year, Gramm-Rudman-Hollings Act of 1985, Multiyear Appropriation, No-Year Appropriation, Obligation, One-Year Appropriation, Rescind, Sequestration. *See also* Unexpended Balance.)

Unparliamentary Behavior contrary to the practices of parliamentary bodies, including words or remarks that violate the rules and customs of decorum or comity. (*See* Comity, Decorum, Parliamentary Law. *See also* Taking Down the Words.)

Unprinted Amendment A Senate amendment not printed in the *Congressional Record* prior to its offering. Unprinted amendments are numbered sequentially in the order of their submission through a Congress. (*See*

Amendment, Congress, *Congressional Record. See also* Printed Amendment.)

Upper Body A common reference to the Senate, but not used by members of the House. (*See* Body. *See also* Lower Body.)

Urgent Supplemental Appropriation Bill A title sometimes given to a supplemental appropriation bill for political public relations purposes. Such a title has no legal, parliamentary, or procedural significance. (*See* Supplemental Appropriation Bill.)

U.S. Code Popular title for the *United States Code: Containing the General and Permanent Laws of the United States in Force on. . . .* It is a consolidation and partial codification of the general and permanent laws of the United States arranged by subject under fifty titles. The first six titles deal with general or political subjects, the other forty-four with subjects ranging from agriculture to war, alphabetically arranged. A supplement is published after each session of Congress, and the entire *Code* is revised every six years.

The preface to the June 1989 edition of the *Code* declares: "Because many of the general and permanent laws that are required to be incorporated in the Code are inconsistent, redundant, and obsolete, the Office of the Law Revision Counsel of the House . . . has been engaged in a continuing, comprehensive project authorized by law to revise and codify, for enactment into positive law, each title of the Code. When this project is completed all the titles of the Code will be legal evidence of the general and permanent laws and recourse to the numerous volumes of the U.S. Statutes at Large for this purpose will no longer be necessary. [As of 1989, 22 titles had been] revised, codified, and enacted into positive law and the text thereof is legal evidence of the laws therein contained. The matter contained in the other titles of the Code is prima facie evidence of the laws." (*See* Law, Law Revision Counsel, *Statutes at Large. See* also Slip Law.)

User Fee A fee charged to users of goods or services provided by the federal government. When Congress levies or authorizes such fees, it determines whether the revenues should go into the general collections of the Treasury or be available for expenditure by the agency that provides the goods or services. (*See also* Offsetting Receipts.)

V

Vacate Proceedings To nullify a chamber's previous action, such as the passage of a measure, adoption of an amendment or conference report, or an order for the yeas and nays; also referred to as vitiating an action. Requests to vacate proceedings require unanimous consent and are usually made to correct some inadvertent error in the proceedings. (*See* Amendment, Conference Report, Unanimous Consent, Yeas and Nays.)

Vehicle Another term for a legislative measure, in the sense that it is the means for conveying legislation through the legislative process. (*See* Legislative Measure.)

Veto The president's disapproval of a legislative measure passed by Congress. He returns the measure to the house in which it originated without his signature but with a veto message stating his objections to it.

When Congress is in session, the president must veto a bill within ten days, excluding Sundays, after he has received it; otherwise it becomes law without his signature. The ten-day clock begins to run at midnight following his receipt of the bill. (*See also* Committee Veto, Item Veto, Override a Veto, Pocket Veto.)

Vice Chairman By House rule, the title of the ranking majority member, after the chairman, of a standing committee or subcommittee. The rule requires the vice chairman to preside in the absence of the chairman. In the Senate, the title is given only to the ranking minority member of the Indian Affairs Committee and the select committees on Ethics and Intelligence. On permanent joint committees, when a senator is chairman, the ranking majority member from the House is called the vice chairman, and vice versa. (*See* Joint Committee, Select *or* Special Committee, Standing Committee. *See also* Rank *or* Ranking.)

Vice President (*See* President of the Senate. *See also* Casting Vote, Constitutional Votes.)

Views and Estimates Report A report commenting or making recommendations on budgetary matters for the upcoming fiscal year that each House and Senate committee with legislative jurisdiction must submit to the Budget committee in its house. The Budget Enforcement Act of 1990 requires the submission of the reports within six weeks after the president transmits his annual budget to Congress to give the Budget committees time to review the comments and suggestions before preparing and reporting the annual budget resolution. (*See* Budget, Budget Process, Budget Resolution, Committee Jurisdiction, Fiscal Year.)

Vitiate an Action (*See* Vacate Proceedings.)

Viva Voce Vote Literally, a vote with living voice; hence, a voice vote. (*See* Voice Vote.)

Voice Vote A method of voting in which members who favor a question answer "aye" in chorus, after which those opposed answer "no" in chorus, and the chair decides which position prevails.

The chair always puts a question to a voice vote first, unless preempted by a demand for another type vote, he puts the question to a division vote.

The term is also used to indicate affirmative action on a question by unanimous consent or without objection. (*See* Division Vote, Put the Question, Question, Unanimous Consent, Without Objection.)

Voting Members vote in three ways on the floor: (1) by shouting "aye " or "no" on voice votes; (2) by standing for or against on division votes; and (3) on recorded votes (including the yeas and nays), by answering "aye" or "no" when their names are called or, in the House, by recording their votes through the electronic voting system.

House rules set a minimum time for recorded votes; the Senate usually limits the time for a yea-and-nay vote to fifteen minutes. Ordinarily, members may not vote or change their votes after the chair announces the result. (*See* Division Vote, Electronic Voting, Recorded Vote, Voice Vote, Yeas and Nays. *See also* Automatic Roll Call, Casting Vote, Cloture, Cluster Voting, Constitutional Votes, Ghost Voting, Majority Vote, Proxy Voting, Randolph Rule, Recapitulation of a Vote, Reconsider a Vote, Recorded Vote by Clerks, Roll Call, Speaker's Vote, Teller Vote, Tie Vote.)

Voting Order on Amendments The order of precedence or priority in which pending amendments are put to a vote: First, perfecting amendments to a first degree amendment; second, perfecting amendments to a substitute amendment (but these are not permitted in the Senate); third, the substitute amendment, as amended if amended; and finally, the first degree amendment, as amended if amended.

When a motion to strike out is pending, votes are permitted on amendments to the text it proposes to strike before the motion to strike is put to a vote. Similarly, when an amendment in the nature of a substitute is pending, amendments to the text of the measure are voted on first, then amendments to the amendment in the nature of a substitute, and finally to the substitute, as amended if amended. (*See* Amendment in the Nature of a Substitute, Degrees of Amendment, Perfecting Amendment, Strike Out, Substitute.)

W

Waiver A temporary setting aside of one or more rules by prohibiting points of order that might be raised to enforce them against a measure. The House uses special rules from the Rules Committee for this purpose. These rules may contain specific waivers, most frequently to protect unauthorized appropriations and legislative provisions in appropriation bills, or a blanket waiver that protects a measure or an amendment from all possible points of order.

In addition, the House procedure for suspending the rules and passing a measure implicitly imposes a blanket waiver because it suspends all rules, including statutory rules, that might conflict with the measure's passage. The Senate sometimes accomplishes the same purpose through unanimous consent agreements and by suspension of the rules. In addition, the Congressional Budget Act of 1974 permits nondebatable motions to waive some of its provisions. (*See* Budget Process, Point of Order, Rule, Statutory Rules, Suspension of the Rules (House), Unanimous Consent Agreement, Unauthorized Appropriation. *See also* Authorization-Appropriation Process.)

Waiver Rule A special rule from the House Rules Committee that waives points of order against a measure or an amendment, or both. (*See* Point of Order, Rule.)

War Powers Act of 1973 An act that requires the president "in every possible instance" to consult Congress before he commits U.S. forces to ongoing or imminent hostilities. If he commits them to a combat situation without congressional consultation, he must notify Congress within forty-eight hours. Unless Congress declares war or otherwise authorizes the operation to continue, the forces must be withdrawn within sixty or ninety days, depending on certain conditions.

The act also provides for a congressional concurrent resolution directing the president to withdraw the troops; however, in light of the Supreme Court's 1983 decision declaring legislative vetoes unconstitutional, the resolution probably would have no legal effect. (*See* Concurrent Resolution, Legislative Veto.)

Well The sunken, level, open space between members' seats and the podium at the front of each chamber. House members usually address their chamber from their party's lectern in the well on its side of the aisle. Senators usually speak at their assigned desks. (*See also* Aisle, Desk, Floor.)

Whereas Clause (*See* Preamble.)

Whip The majority or minority party member in each house who acts as assistant leader, helps plan and marshal support for party strategies, encourages party discipline, and advises his leader on how his colleagues intend to vote on the floor. In the Senate, the Republican whip's official title is assistant leader.

Whips are elected by their party caucuses. They are assisted by other party members variously called deputy whips, assistant whips, regional whips, and at-large whips. By far the largest whip organization—94 members in the 102d Congress—supports the House Democratic whip. (*See* Party Caucus, Zone Whip.)

Whip Notices Weekly communications, prepared by each party's whip in the House, advising their party's members about the following week's floor program. (*See* Whip.)

Withdrawal of Motions Except in Committee of the Whole, a member may withdraw his amendment or other motion so long as the chamber has not yet acted on it. Actions that prevent withdrawal include ordering the yeas and nays on the motion (in the Senate), amending it, or, of course, a vote agreeing to it. Withdrawal in Committee of the Whole requires unanimous consent. (*See* Amendment, Committee of the Whole, Motion, Unanimous Consent, Yeas and Nays.)

Without Objection To permit an action to take place in violation of a rule, or without following the full requirements of the rules, when no member objects. It is used in lieu of a vote to act on noncontroversial motions, amendments, and measures on the floor or in committee. (*See also* Point of Order, Unanimous Consent.)

Words Taken Down (*See* Taking Down the Words.)

Y

Yeas and Nays A vote in which members usually respond "aye" or "no" (despite the official title of the vote) on a question when their names are called in alphabetical order. The Constitution requires the yeas and nays when a demand for it is supported by one-fifth of the members present, and it also requires an automatic yea-and-nay-vote on overriding a veto.

Senate precedents require the support of at least one-fifth of a quorum, a minimum of 11 members with the present membership of 100. In recent years, the Senate has customarily limited the time for such a vote to fifteen minutes, but the party leaders may extend it at their discretion. Unlike the House, the Senate permits debate on a question to continue after the yeas and nays are ordered on that question, and a senator may demand the yeas and nays at any time while the question is pending.

In the House, the Speaker counts all members present to determine whether one-fifth of them support the demand for the yeas and nays; his count may not be appealed. Rather than by a call of names, the House usually takes the yeas and nays through its electronic voting system unless the Speaker orders otherwise (usually because the system is not working). When the House is sitting as the House, a member may demand the yeas and nays only when a vote is about to occur or before it is announced. Although the yeas and nays are not permitted in Committee of the Whole, members can demand its functional equivalent: a recorded vote. (*See* Appeal, Committee of the Whole, Electronic Voting, Override a Veto, Precedent, Question, Quorum, Recorded Vote. *See also* Automatic Roll Call.)

Yield Back the Balance of One's Time A member who controls a specific amount of time for debate is not required to use all of it, and he may give up any remaining portion of it by informing the chair that he yields back the balance of his time. (*See also* Reserve the Balance of One's Time, Yield the Floor, Yielding, Yielding Time.)

Yield the Floor To give up possession of the floor voluntarily. Senators often say, "Mr. President, I yield the floor," when they have completed their remarks. The expression is not used in the House. (*See* Floor, Hold (*or* Have) the Floor. *See also* Lose the Floor, Recognition, Yield Back the Balance of One's Time, Yielding, Yielding Time.)

Yielding A voluntary action by a member holding the floor that permits another member to speak. The member seeking permission usually asks: "Will the gentleman [senator] yield?" A member may refuse to yield or, after yielding to a colleague, may cut him off at any time.

In both houses, a member who yields for a motion, including an amendment, loses the floor. To avoid that possibility, members often announce that they are yielding for debate only. Under Senate precedents, senators may yield only for questions, but violations of those precedents are often tolerated. House members may yield for statements as well as questions. (*See* Hold (*or* Have) the Floor, Lose the Floor. *See also* Colloquy, Yield Back the Balance of One's Time, Yield the Floor, Yielding Time.)

Yielding Time When a member controls a specific amount of time for debate, another member may speak only if the controlling member yields some or all of his time for that purpose. He may yield for a specified amount of time or for an indeterminate time: "I yield to Mr. Smith such time as he may consume."

Because debate under a time limit is usually divided equally between proponents and opponents, the controlling member usually yields only to his supporters. Customarily, the controlling member first yields some specific amount of time to himself for an opening statement. When a senator who has not been yielded time begins to speak, the presiding officer interrupts and asks: "Who yields time?" (*See* Equally Divided, Time Limits on Debate. *See also* General Debate, Unanimous Consent Agreement, Yield Back the Balance of One's Time, Yield the Floor, Yielding.)

Z

Zone Whip A member responsible for whip duties concerning his or her party colleagues from specific geographical areas. Zone whips are particularly necessary in the 435-member House of Representatives, but Senate Democrats also use them. (*See* Whip.)

Walter Kravitz, who compiled the *American Congressional Dictionary* for Congressional Quarterly, is a teacher, lecturer, and private consultant on congressional organization and procedures. Previously, Kravitz was the senior expert on Congress at the Congressional Research Service. During his twenty-two years at CRS, Kravitz assisted House and Senate committees in developing proposals on virtually every facet of congressional organization, operations, administration, rules, and procedural systems. He assisted in the development of the Legislative Reorganization Act of 1970 and was the first executive director of the House Budget Committee.

Congressional Quarterly, an editorial research service and publishing company, serves clients in the fields of news, education, business, and government. It combines the specific coverage of Congress, government, and politics contained in the *Congressional Quarterly Weekly Report* with the more general subject range of an affiliated publication, *CQ Researcher*.

Congressional Quarterly also publishes a variety of books, including college political science textbooks under the CQ Press imprint and public affairs paperbacks on developing issues and events. CQ also publishes information directories and reference books, including *The Legislative Drafter's Desk Reference, Guide to Congress, Politics in America*, and CQ's ready reference encyclopedias: *Congress A to Z, Presidency A to Z*, and *Supreme Court A to Z*. The *CQ Almanac*, a compendium of legislation for one session of Congress, is published each year. *Congress and the Nation*, a record of government for a presidential term, is published every four years.